Enhancing Staff and Educational Development

Staff and educational development, the systematic support for improving education and learning, has in recent years grown in scale and moved to centre stage within further and higher education around the world. This growth is in the booming membership of professional development bodies.

This title complements the editors' introductory volume *A Guide to Staff and Educational Development* (RoutledgeFalmer), by providing more detailed attention to some of the more fundamental issues and practices in staff and educational development. It analyses the context in which development functions, the roles undertaken by practitioners and ways in which staff and educational development can be promoted and managed at senior and institutional as well as individual levels.

Written in an engaging, accessible and scholarly style, it is rooted in practice, with a wealth of case study material and practical advice. The book covers a wide range of topics including: how professionals learn and develop; institutional policy and strategy; leading an educational development unit; and career pathways for developers.

Enhancing Staff and Educational Development describes the insights and innovations of both seasoned and new developers. It will be a compelling, stimulating, and rewarding read for anyone dedicated to the improvement of teaching and learning.

David Baume is an international consultant in higher education and a respected worker, author and editor in the field. He was previously Director of Teaching Development in the Centre for Higher Education Practice at the Open University, UK. He is a SEDA Fellowship holder.

Peter Kahn is Teaching Development Officer at the University of Manchester, UK. He has led the SEDA summer school for new staff and Educational Developers and holds a SEDA fellowship.

The Staff and Educational Development Series
Series Editor: James Wisdom

SEDA is the Staff and Education Development Association. It supports and encourages developments in teaching and learning in higher education through a variety of methods: publications, conferences, networking, journals, regional meetings and research – and through various SEDA Accreditation Schemes.

SEDA
Selly Wick House
59–61 Selly Wick Road
Selly Park
Birmingham B29 7JE
Tel: 0121-415 6801
Fax: 0121-415 6802
E-mail: office@seda.ac.uk
Website: www.seda.ac.uk

Enhancing
Staff & Educational
Development

Edited by David Baume and Peter Kahn

RoutledgeFalmer
Taylor & Francis Group

LONDON AND NEW YORK

11 New Fetter Lane, London EC4P 4EE
Simultaneously published in the USA and Canada
by RoutledgeFalmer
29 West 35th Street, New York, NY 10001

RoutledgeFalmer is an imprint of the Taylor & Francis Group

© 2004 David Baume, Peter Kahn and Individual Contributors

ISBN 0-415-33504-3 (HB)
ISBN 0-415-33505-1 (PB)

British Library Cataloguing in Publication Data
A catalogue record for this book is available from the British Library

Library of Congress Cataloging in Publication Data

Enhancing staff and educational development / [edited by] David Baume and Peter Kahn.
    p. cm. – (SEDA series)
Companion volume to: A guide to staff & educational development.
Includes bibliographical references and index.
    ISBN 0–415–33504–3 (hard) – ISBN 0–415–33505–1 (pbk.)
    1. College teachers—In-service training—Great Britain. 2. Career development—Great Britain. I. Kahn, Peter (Peter E.) II. Baume, David, 1943– III. Guide to staff & educational development. IV. Series.
LB1738.E54 2004
378.1'2'00715—dc22

                            2003023704

Typeset in Baskerville by Keystroke, Jacaranda Lodge, Wolverhampton
Printed and bound in Great Britain by TJ International Ltd, Padstow, Cornwall

David Baume is very grateful to his friends and colleagues in the staff and educational development community across the world for their support and encouragement over the years and on into the future.

Peter Kahn would like to thank both his colleagues in the Teaching and Learning Support Unit at the University of Manchester and those more widely in the sector for their support.

We both further appreciate the commitment of all those involved bringing this book to publication, especially the staff at the publishers and those who have contributed chapters.

Contents

Notes on the editors and contributors

EDITORS

David Baume is a higher education consultant. Current and recent consultancy work includes student progress files; course design; assessment strategies; project and programme evaluation; University teaching awards; University leadership development; case studies on learning and teaching innovations; staff development for part-time teachers; staff development for enquiry-based learning; and developing and implementing frameworks and processes for supporting tutor development and accreditation. Current research and publication is about the assessment of portfolios produced on a course in teaching in higher education, and about personal development planning and progress files. He is also an external examiner for postgraduate certificates in teaching and learning in higher education.

Previously he was a Director of the Centre for Higher Education Practice at the Open University. There, he led production of courses on teaching in higher education. He was also a founding member of the National Co-ordination Team for the HEFCE Teaching Quality Enhancement Fund. David taught in higher education for twenty years before becoming a staff and educational developer. He was founding chair of SEDA from 1990 to 1995 and a founding editor of the International Journal for Academic Development. He is a member of the Council and the Accreditation Committee of the ILTHE. He holds a Masters in Higher Education and Fellowship of SEDA. ADBaume@aol.com

Peter Kahn is Teaching Development Officer in the Teaching and Learning Support Unit at the University of Manchester. The role involves taking a particular concern for promoting professional development related to teaching and the support of learning. In this capacity he also acts as Project Manager for a regional programme of staff development that aims to build capacity for learning based around processes of enquiry. This current position follows his earlier experience in mathematics. Following a PhD in the mathematical modelling of brain function at Imperial College London, he was awarded the Society for Research into Higher Education 'Younger Academic Research Award' for 1995–6, while based at the Institute of Education, London.

Peter subsequently worked as a Lecturer in Mathematics at Liverpool Hope University College, where he developed wider interests in educational development. He has recently published two books on learning and teaching in mathematics.

He holds a Fellowship from the Staff and Educational Development Association (SEDA) and a Masters Degree in Education from the University of Liverpool. He is active within the SEDA on the committee that oversees the SEDA Fellowship Schemes, and is involved in delivering the annual SEDA Summer School for New Educational Developers.

THE CONTRIBUTORS

Dr Paul Ashwin is Research Fellow at the Institute for the Advancement of University Learning, University of Oxford. He has experience of research and educational development in further and higher education and has published widely on peer learning. He is currently undertaking research into students' and teachers' perceptions of the Oxford Tutorial and students' perceptions of the learning environment at the University of Oxford.

Dr Angela Brew is Associate Professor in the Institute for Teaching and Learning at the University of Sydney. She has worked and published in academic development for over 25 years and has researched in teaching and learning in higher education and related fields in the UK and Australia. Recent publications include *The Nature of Research: Inquiry in Academic Contexts,* published by RoutledgeFalmer in August 2001. From 1999–2003 she was President of the Higher Education Research and Development Society of Australasia (HERDSA). Angela is co-editor of the *International Journal for Academic Development.*

Ali Cooper is Teaching and Learning Developments Coordinator at the Centre for the Enhancement of Learning and Teaching at Lancaster University, where she has been programme Director for the Certificate of Learning and Teaching in HE since 1999. She led a similar programme at Liverpool John Moores University from 1996–9, having been a senior lecturer in Education there for six years. She spent eleven years as a secondary English and Drama teacher. Her research interests are in HE teacher development and education.

Professor George Gordon is the founding Director and Professor of Academic Practice at the University of Strathclyde. He has undertaken many research, evaluation and development projects in the UK and overseas. Recent examples include work for HEFCE, JISC, DfES, TSN, HESDA, The British Council, the University of Hong Kong and Dublin Institute of Technology. He is Honorary Treasurer of the Society for Research into Higher Education.

Professor Fred Percival is currently Director of Educational Development at Napier University, Edinburgh. He has been actively involved in staff and educational development in HE for over 25 years in three UK universities. His interests include learning and teaching strategies, excellence in teaching, interactive learning and teaching methodologies (including simulation and gaming) and the pedagogy of e-learning. He has written or edited over 10 books and authored over 50 papers and articles on a range of educational topics.

Rhona Sharpe is a staff and educational developer in the Oxford Centre for Staff and Learning Development based at Oxford Brookes University, where she has particular responsibility to promote the effective use of learning technologies. Previously she worked at the Open University managing distance and online tutors, and before that at the University of Plymouth running programmes for new lecturers and graduate teaching assistants. Rhona has been chair of the SEDA Fellowships committee and SEDA's Accreditation Co-ordinator. She is Associate Editor of the International Journal for Academic Development.

Holly Smith is a lecturer in the Department of Education and Professional Development at University College London. She is programme leader of the Certificate in Learning and Teaching in Higher Education and taught on similar professional development programmes at Liverpool John Moores University and the Open University. Previously a lecturer in Psychology, she has been Editor of the Psychology of Education Review. Her current research interests include research methods and teacher development in higher education.

Sue Thompson is Head of the Learning Development Unit at Liverpool John Moores University where the focus of her work is on promoting and supporting developments that will enhance the quality of student learning. She has a long standing interest in teacher accreditation, having developed and managed the university's Postgraduate Certificate in Learning and Teaching in Higher Education. Prior to that she worked in initial teacher training and in secondary schools. Her main professional interests are in supporting the continuing professional development of staff.

Keith Trigwell is Reader in Higher Education and Principal Research Fellow at the Institute for the Advancement of University Learning at the University of Oxford, and Fellow of Kellogg College. He has worked in academic development for over 20 years. His research interests include students' approaches to learning and teachers' approaches to teaching, and at the University of Oxford he is working with Paul Ashwin on research on students' experience of their learning context.

Professor Gill Tucker is currently Vice-Principal at Napier University, Edinburgh. Originally trained as a pianist at the Royal Academy of Music, Gill was appointed Dean of Learning and Teaching at Oxford Brookes University in 1966, where she headed the Oxford Centre for Staff and Learning Development. Gill has acted as a consultant on the UK's e-University project and has chaired SEDA's Advisory Group. She has given keynotes and conference papers and has published on Higher Education policy and practice.

Graham Webb is Professor and Director of the Centre for Higher Education Quality, which leads and supports quality assurance and improvement in teaching, research and support services at Monash, Australia's largest University. His 30 years of experience include working for Universities in Ireland, Jamaica, New Zealand and Australia. He has written or edited nine books and numerous chapters and papers concerning the theory and practice of educational, staff and organizational development.

Foreword

This book is a companion volume to *A Guide to Staff and Educational Development* published in 2003. That two books were commissioned together on this topic is testament to the fast-growing importance of this work. Higher education is now recognized as being of fundamental importance for the life chances of individuals and for the dynamism and wellbeing of society. The content and the process of higher education therefore must respond to the growing demands put upon it to meet the needs of a diverse and growing student body alongside the regional and national needs of business and the community. Universities and colleges as a result are experiencing rapid changes, changes that require a consciously strategic approach to the development of courses and educational processes and to the deployment of an increasingly skilled and specialized workforce. Staff and educational developers have therefore found themselves on the front line in responding to the needs of modern-day higher education.

While developing higher education in this changing environment is a challenge, it also offers a welcome support to those people who champion the scholarship of learning and who identify themselves with staff and educational development. They have increasingly found ways to share their experiences with each other and across the sector. The community of practice to which they belong is now large, diverse and robust. The Staff and Educational Development Association, with its long history of work in this field, has more recently found itself with growing support among other agencies sharing similar aims. The recent Government White Paper in England gave a huge boost to this area by mandating professional qualifications for teaching; funding new Centres for Teaching Excellence; expanding the National Teaching Fellowship Scheme; and supporting the incorporation of an Academy for the enhancement of learning and teaching to bring together the work of the Institute for Learning and Teaching in Higher Education, the Learning and Teaching Support Network and the Higher Education Staff Development Agency. The support for this ambitious programme of work will require many new partnerships; among academics, learning support staff, technologists and information specialists, and students, educational researchers, universities and other employers, and staff and educational developers.

The scholarship underpinning such practices as flexible course design and professional teaching has a long history, but its importance has only recently been acknowledged. This book illustrates the growing wealth of knowledge and experience on which we can build. It champions reflective insights through case examples, and analyses policy and strategy as well as more practical approaches. It provides an excellent foundation for and account of the enhancement of staff and educational development.

Dr Liz Beaty, Director (Learning and Teaching),
Higher Education Funding Council for England

Introduction – An overview of enhancing staff and educational development

David Baume and Peter Kahn

STAFF AND EDUCATIONAL DEVELOPMENT?

We introduced the field of staff and educational development in the Introduction to the companion volume to this (Kahn and Baume 2003: 1–8). Staff and educational development have changed only marginally in the few months between the completion of that and this book. So; pausing only to quote with approval Lorraine Stefani's description of staff and educational development, often in this book simply called development, as 'systematic and scholarly support for improving both educational processes and the practices and capabilities of educators' (Stefani 2003); we refer you to pp 1–3 and 7–8 of that Introduction for a more extended consideration of the field, and move on to introducing the structure and contents and styles of this book.

STRUCTURE AND STYLE

The book is constructed in three thematic sections with a conclusion.

The first section, comprising Chapters 1 and 2, looks outwards. It is primarily concerned with the contexts in which development functions. Chapter 1 locates staff and education development in the broader national contexts of government policies and strategies in which Universities, and therefore necessarily development, function. Chapter 2 considers the institutional context, and explores how development and senior management can work together closely and productively.

The second section, comprising Chapters 3–5, looks inwards. It considers three major roles that developers undertake. Chapter 3 explores some of the complexities that lie behind the title 'Head of Educational

Development Unit'. Chapter 4 does much the same for 'Programme Leader', specifically for the design and operation of programmes on learning and teaching in higher education. Chapter 5 explores a widely practised but rarely discussed development method – writing – and shows some of the ways in which we can use writing for development and some of the complex issues involved in using it effectively.

The third section, the largest, looks inwards still further. It has two sub-themes – our practices and ourselves. Chapter 6 asks how we can identify the effects, the impact, of our work as developers while Chapter 7 analyses ways in which we can investigate our practices as developers. Chapter 8 considers careers and career development for developers while Chapter 9 looks at development from both inside and outside and draws lessons for the practice of development and for careers beyond development.

The conclusion, inspired by what goes before it, explores and looks to the future of staff and educational development.

You will find a variety of voices and styles in this book. Good development successfully combines the academic, the professional and the personal. So does good writing about development. This combination can be achieved in many ways, and has we believe been achieved in different ways by different chapter authors here.

You find a greater still variety of voices. Several of the chapters contain other voices, from sentences to short case studies, the voices of other developers. Individual stories and accounts by individual developers add to the explorations of theory, ideas and explanations by chapter authors. In style as in content, the chapter authors adopt a pluralist approach.

You will also see the authors moving between practice and theory, interrogating each with the other, seeking to advance both practice and understanding.

SECTION 1 – THE CONTEXTS IN WHICH DEVELOPMENT FUNCTIONS

In Chapter 1, 'Locating academic development: identifying and working with national contexts, policies and strategies', George Gordon, Director of the Centre for Academic Practice at the University of Strathclyde, analyses how staff and educational development units can work with national policy agendas to advance academic practice within the institution. Outside the institution, a growing number of national policies and initiatives clamour for the developer's attention, offering the chance to bid for funds and the need to negotiate plans for projects of a form that will benefit institutional as well national priorities. The complexity of all this is acknowledged. For example 'the institution' is of course a mixture of different and not always fully co-operating constituencies. Further, as well as meeting the needs of 'the institution', educational development is also expected to serve at least two other constituencies – a growing range of individual staff with some responsibility for supporting learning, and the disciplines represented within the institution. George Gordon's thorough exploration of the developers' extra- and intra-institutional environments will be valuable to those negotiating the jungles of opportunity and challenge that national agendas present to the developer.

To quote from the authors' introduction to the chapter, Chapter 2 'This chapter considers the relationships between policy, resourcing, implementation and practice for staff and educational development. It considers these relationships from the respective standpoints of a university senior manager and a head of educational development.' After a quick review of the literature on the scope, functions and nature of staff and educational development, the authors; Fred Percival, Director of Educational Development, and Gill Tucker, Vice Principal, both of Napier University, Edinburgh; explore the academic development implications of nine key institutional issues. These include implementing an institution's strategy for learning, teaching and assessment; using external agendas as leverage for change; formal development programmes for new and experienced teachers; meeting the challenges of mass higher education, greater social inclusion and a more differentiated student body; providing incentives through rewarding learning, teaching and academic development; enhancing learning, teaching and assessment through learning technology and flexible learning delivery; developing scholarship and research in learning and teaching to underpin development and change; and supporting academic development and keeping abreast of the external agendas and good practice elsewhere through networking and environmental scanning. This chapter doesn't simply advocate collaboration between development and senior management; it shows such co-operation in action.

SECTION 2 – THREE MAJOR ROLES THAT DEVELOPERS UNDERTAKE

After exploring what it is that 'staff and educational development units do that needs to be led and managed', Sue Thompson, Head of the Learning Development Unit at Liverpool John Moores University, in Chapter 3 reports and considers the results of her survey of heads of educational development. The survey question was 'What is the biggest leadership challenge you have faced as head of an educational development unit?' This generated a wonderfully diverse set of responses, ranging from 'Getting [educational development] onto the [institution's] agenda' through many issues in working effectively in the institution and managing the unit and the team to knowing whether you are making difference. As well as unpicking under 13 headings the answers to her survey question, Sue also provides both short accounts and longer case studies from unit and centre heads in both research- and teaching-led institutions which illuminate the more general comments and show in action some of the principles that Sue elucidates. Sue ends with the very thoughtful views of her own staff on 'what would you hope or expect a leader/manager of an educational development unit to do as part of their role'. Interestingly and appropriately, more than three times as many of these answers from her staff relate to the leader's work outside than inside the unit.

One role for most educational development units is running a post-graduate certificate in learning and teaching in higher education, almost always in the UK professionally accredited by the Institute for Learning and Teaching in Higher Education or the Staff and Educational Development Association (and sometimes both) as well as leading to a university award. Ali Cooper leads such a course in the Higher Education Development Centre at Lancaster University. In Chapter 4 Ali shows the very complex University environment in which such a course must run and the many pressures to which such a course is subjected. These pressures are both external – the sometimes competing national agendas which influence the University's work – and also internal as these agendas are interpreted within the University by different departments, groups and individuals. Ali proposes a model that shows how factors from the institution, department and individual teacher's context and factors within the programme itself 'are ever-present as dynamic tensions and dilemmas'. Ali considers many other difficult and important issues, including relations between experiential learning and a taught course in learning and teaching in higher education; the place of the teacher's discipline in such a course; individual versus group learning; and the ever present and problematic relations between teaching and research.

If we look at how we spend our time as developers we may soon realize that, yes, we do a lot of writing. In Chapter 5 Angela Brew of the Institute for Teaching and Learning at the University of Sydney goes beyond consideration of conventional academic writing, the book chapters and research papers that we write (or hope to write), and asks 'What skills do we need as developers in order to make the best use of [writing]? What may we lose by spending time on writing? How we can use writing to enhance our work as developers?' Angela identifies four types of audience for our writing for development. Individual academics and groups of academics; University managers and academic and other committees; committees to consider applications of some kind, for example for teaching awards; and the wider academic and staff development community. Within each section Angela identifies sub-categories of writing for development, provides examples of such writing and considers some issues surfaced by each type of writing. Angela concludes that 'We might move . . . to a focus on writing as a developmental process in and for itself. I hope so, because writing has the power to challenge and change both the writer and the reader, and surely that is what we are about as academic and educational developers?'

SECTION 3 – OUR PRACTICES AND OURSELVES AS DEVELOPERS

As developers we work in these many and complex contexts and use these various development methods – but how do we know we are having any effect, let alone the effects we seek? In Chapter 6 Holly Smith from the Department of Education and Professional Development at University College London considers mainly how to gauge the impact of accredited programmes in teaching in higher education, but offers an approach which, as Holly says, 'can also be adapted and applied to shorter, less formal staff development activities'. Holly tackles three big questions about measuring impact. First, what is being evaluated? Using a HESDA project on the evaluation of accredited HE teaching programmes, Holly suggests how we could start to determine the effects of such a programme on the organization, the department, the experience of the students taught by participants, the careers of participants and the individual participant. Holly also acknowledges the many different intentions of those designing and running such programmes. Second, Holly proposes some epistemological questions that we should address in attempting to measure impact, and shows the effects that our answers will have on our choice of evaluation goals, our methods and claims for our data. Holly follows with a wide set of data collection methods, and concludes with a case study which illuminates many of the issues considered earlier in the chapter.

Paul Ashwin and Keith Trigwell from the Institute for the Advancement of University Learning at the University of Oxford in Chapter 7 argue 'that investigation of practice (but not necessarily research) is an essential component of professional activity. [They] identify three qualitatively different aims of investigation of practice: investigations that develop personal knowledge, those that develop local knowledge and those that develop public knowledge.' The authors identify what is common and different in these three types of investigation, suggesting that the different audiences for each have clear implications for the ways the investigation is undertaken, verified and recorded. But all such investigations should be undertaken in a reflective and scholarly way. The authors also analyse the concept of the scholarship of professional practice. *Before* the work is done, there is need for the developer to be aware of their conceptions of educational development, of their knowledge of development and of processes. *During* the investigation, capabilities are required in development, investigation, reflection, communication and learning. *After* the work, outcome elements include enhanced development practice, satisfaction with the practice, documentation of various forms, the learning of the developer; and, perhaps, a publication. But if the work is to be shared with peers or the wider community then this needs to be planned from the start of the work. Three case studies show these principles in action.

How do we developers support the professional development of teachers? In Chapter 8 Rhona Sharpe from the Oxford Centre for Staff and Learning Development at Oxford Brookes University approaches this question by considering teaching in the first instance as just another profession, and by reviewing a wide literature on how professionals learn and develop to see how this literature illuminates our work as developers. Rhona's approach is both multidisciplinary, using ideas from disciplines including sociology, psychology, anthropology and management, and multi-professional, drawing on ideas about the development of professionals in many fields. Rhona organizes the chapter 'around the *what, how, where* and *when* of professional learning'. Considering the *what*, Rhona explores how professionals variously learn and then integrate the knowledge, the values and the competences that together form the bases of professionalism. As in each succeeding subsection, Rhona draws implications for our work as developers. Under the *how* of professional learning, Rhona draws on ideas of adult learning, reflection and learning from experience. *Where* professionals learn might at first seem relatively unproblematic, but Rhona uses ideas of situated learning and communities of practice to explore how teachers learn in informal as well as formal, disciplinary as well as multidisciplinary, settings. Rhona's consideration of *when* professionals learn explores various accounts of the stages in the development of a teacher, shows the sometimes conflicting relations between what teachers believe about learning and what they practise, and draws implications for both initial and continuing professional development. Rhona concludes with four recurrent powerful ideas, and a reasoned plea for making professional development a more collaborative business.

There is a growing literature on how people become developers and what educational development units do, but little if anything until now about careers within development. In Chapter 9 Peter Kahn uses case studies to show five very different ways of being and changing as a developer. Charles Juwah from the Robert Gordon University Aberdeen explores the transitions he made from a scientist and further education lecturer to running a course in teaching in higher education. Paul O'Neill leads the undergraduate medical education programme at the University of Manchester and talks about the career transition he made to take this role. He notes that, although 'greater credit is still given for primary research, so promotion in many cases is difficult, . . . [f]ortunately this is changing with the increased number of opportunities to take on educational development roles.' Gwen Van der Velden, who heads the Unit for the Enhancement of Learning and Teaching at the University of Kent at Canterbury, describes her development of two crucial qualities; a strategic sense and confidence. James Wisdom gives an unflinching and balanced account of the life of a higher education consultant, stressing the personal qualities as well as the capabilities that this life needs. Richard Blackwell, a Senior Adviser with the Learning and Teaching Support Network (LTSN) Generic Centre, reviews the transitions, the life and role, the pleasure and the demands of his work. Peter concludes the chapter by suggesting that the development community still needs to do much more to support the career development of developers.

I (DB) had originally planned to write what became the current Chapter 11, to be called something like 'Beyond development', to consider what developers who had moved on to higher, or just to other, things had taken from their work as developers. Graham Webb in his conclusion to the chapter gives his account of the genesis of the current chapter. I here add my (complementary) account. I was failing to make enough progress on the interviews that were to underpin 'Beyond development'. Graham's reluctance to write the chapter I had initially suggested to him; on theories of knowledge relating to staff and educational development; offered a way to meet both of our needs. For Graham, a chapter he wanted to write. For me, a chapter that I wanted for the book but was failing to write. Land's 'developers as vigilant opportunists' made manifest! Graham has in fact gone well beyond the (revised) brief for this chapter. Looking back on development from the inside, Graham draws conclusions about the nature of development, conclusions which are powerful and not always comfortable for us. Moving outside the world of development, Graham gives a management-eye view of development, reminding us clearly and forcibly what a small part of the world-view of senior management our world of development may sometimes comprise. Graham concludes by identifying two qualities that above all characterize developers, qualities that developers will find valuable in all manner of future lives. These qualities are particular forms of emotional and cognitive understanding. And, perhaps as a nod to the chapter I had originally asked him to write, Graham explores how some ideas about the nature and the making of knowledge and meaning can inform our current and our future practice of development, whether or not 'developer' is part of our title.

The conclusion, on how we may enhance staff and educational development, can speak for itself.

REFERENCES

Kahn, P. and Baume, D. (Eds) (2003). *A Guide to Staff and Educational Development*. The Staff and Educational Development Series. London, Kogan Page.

Stefani, L. (2003). What is staff and educational development? *A Guide to Staff and Educational Development*. P. Kahn and D. Baume (Eds). London, Kogan Page: 9–23.

1

Locating educational development: identifying and working with national contexts, policies and strategies

George Gordon

INTRODUCTION

In Chapter 10 of *A Guide to Staff and Educational Development* (2003), the companion volume to this book, Diana Eastcott and Neill Thew illustrate from their personal experiences how staff and educational developers, or as they are sometimes called academic developers – hereafter often called, for brevity, developers – have worked creatively with national agendas.

This chapter explores the framing, designing and provision of staff and educational development from the perspective of national contexts, policies and strategies. Later in the chapter reference is made to the knotty issue of how these are translated into meanings which resonate within institutions and departments/subject groupings and with individual practitioners.

BACKGROUND

Staff and educational development have a substantial and complex history. At the local level the level of institutions, there is considerable variation in detail, e.g. remit, staffing, location, resourcing, management and priorities. Such variety would imply that local policies, strategies and issues are dominant, determining arrangements and dictating outcomes. In large measure that deduction is valid, although often there has been filtering through the complex, often unrecorded, lenses of localized and cosmopolitan traditions of expectations and practice. Additionally, developments have always been open to external influences. Indeed, notwithstanding the resistance within the academy to externally-driven agendas, these have figured prominently in the historical evolution of staff and educational development.

For example, provision at the University of Strathclyde dates from studies in the 1960s and early 1970s into the preparation of new lecturers for their roles as university teachers. That led to the appointment of a single individual, Dr Alex Main, who held the post of Adviser in Educational Methods. Supported actively by the Principal and Vice-Chancellor, he drove forward a series of developments over a decade and a half. A different phase at Strathclyde commenced in 1987 with the creation of the Centre for Academic Practice, with myself as founding Director.

Another illustration of complex influences can be found in the USA, where student, faculty and public concern about the preparation of graduate teaching assistants has resulted in the widespread development of dedicated programmes of preparation and indeed, a number of specialist centres. Whilst some argue that the position of teaching can be understated in research universities, those are the institutions which tend to make the greatest use of postgraduate tutors, otherwise known as graduate teaching assistants (GTAs), to release faculty from some teaching to enable them to dedicate more time to research, and they feature prominently in the provision of GTAs.

Handling procedures for the evaluation of student feedback provides another illustration of what might be described as a climatically determined role for development. Not all centres have the role, and many which have it often find that it is something of a mixed blessing, but until recent developments in managed learning environments, the development centre was often viewed both as the source of relevant expertise on student evaluation and the logical base for the operation of the procedures.

FRAMING THE DISCUSSION

Much could be written on the way in which the national context can, does and should help to shape local provision. It is important, however, first of all to highlight a number of key issues that help to frame this discussion. In particular, we focus on six aspects.

First, within institutions, staff and educational development are generally expected to serve the needs and priorities of three constituencies, namely: the institution, disciplines/subjects, and individuals. The latter will always include staff, invariably academic staff, increasingly research, academic-related and analogous, and occasionally other groups or grades of staff, depending upon the locus and remit of the particular provision. Sometimes direct involvement with students is excluded from the remit, although even in such situations they can be accessed via departments, e.g. through curriculum design or assessment projects. Whilst it is difficult to cite substantive statistical evidence, the trend has been towards greater involvement in aspects of the learning experience of students. The reasons for this will be discussed later in this chapter, particularly under 'Widening participation and massification'.

Second, and directly related to the foregoing, development is generally classed as an academic service. Serving the needs of others is a motivating and honourable activity, and it has permeated much of the thinking and operational practice of development practitioners. A dilemma, or at least tensions, can occur when key members of the 'served' constituencies place particular, and restrictive, interpretations upon the nature of the academic service. In a nutshell, the debate frequently pivots around arguments by managers and/or other internal voices that developers should primarily, even exclusively, function as 'locals', focused upon serving internal needs. It would generally, if sometimes reluctantly, be acknowledged that developers must be given developmental opportunities and support. The principal bone of contention tends to surround the extent to which developers should become 'cosmopolitans', i.e. recognized national and international experts and practitioners and the proportion of their time which should properly be devoted to such activities. Suffice to say that there is no simple solution which will please all parties. The issue resurfaces in the section below on working with national contexts.

Third, as Land (2003) discovered in his research, staff and educational developers hold differing orientations to their work and role. Land identified 12 orientations, namely:

- managerial;
- political strategist;
- entrepreneurial;
- romantic;
- vigilant opportunist;
- researcher;
- professional competence;
- reflective practitioner;
- internal consultant;
- modeller-broker;
- interpretative–hermeneutic; and
- discipline-specific.

Each orientation favours a particular operational focus. Each also colours the preferred strategy and approach. Combinations of orientations can, and do, occur, especially amongst those inclined to strategic matters.

Some orientations represent a strong personal preference about the approach to the task, such as the orientation to work as an internal consultant or to promote the ethos and practice of the reflective practitioner. If you espouse that orientation, others certainly tend to expect it to be axiomatic that you model it in your practice. Of course, that is true of each orientation, but the crucial, and easily overlooked, factor is that what is being modelled differs, sometimes greatly. You may find it helpful to bear Land's orientations in mind as you read through the following discussion about national contexts, policies and strategies. Which of Land's orientations do you think will be most effective in working on which national agendas?

Fourth, the preceding points infer that staff and educational (academic) development is concerned with helping people, disciplines and institutions to reflect, evaluate and improve or as Gosling and D'Andrea (2002) have argued, to manage change: 'You can't be in the business of educational development without also being committed to bringing about change' (p. 1).

They sought to frame their research in terms of three strategies for change:

- power/coercive strategies;
- rational–contractual strategies; and
- normative–re-educative strategies.

They deduce that many developers favour normative-re-educative strategies which build upon a winning hearts and minds philosophy and endeavour to work within institutions on the basis of commitment and involvement, and seeking to utilize the interests and engagement of individuals. Much has been written on that vein of argument. It has the considerable merits of going with the grain of academia, although it often can be problematic to achieve up-scaling/wider dissemination and uptake.

Fifth, everyone involved in staff and educational (academic) development is committed to the work, convinced of its importance and can cite examples of successes and achievements. However, as in so many areas of educational practice, it can be quite difficult both to document improvements and, more particularly, to attribute these exclusively to specific interventions or actions.

Finally, in pursuing change, developers need to become adept at distinguishing trend from fad, substance from fashion – not easy tasks. Predicting which current enthusiasms are fads and which have a longer future in a medium with a life as long as a book is a sure way to being proven wrong, but I am reasonably confident that the professionalization of teaching in higher education, in some form or another, is here to stay, and that the use of technology to support learning will increase. It is hard to be as confident in predicting government policies and enthusiasms.

National contexts

In the opening chapter of the second edition of *Academic Tribes and Territories* (Becher and Trowler 2001), the authors highlight nine macro-sets of influences upon academic cultures, namely:

- the post-industrial environment;
- the globalized landscape;
- massification;
- the relationships between academia, government and industry;
- marketizing knowledge;
- economy, efficiency and effectiveness;
- patterns of growth and fragmentation;
- changing landscapes; and
- shifting academic territories.

Staff and educational developers need to be aware of paradigm shifts in disciplines and ongoing changes in the production of knowledge and sensitive to different academic discourses. That is assisted where there is an academically-based cluster of developers within an institution and/or strong collaborative links exist with faculties/schools and departments/ disciplines. That said, it is difficult to be knowledgeable of every nuance, especially in situations of rapid change or considerable internal academic turmoil. Yet such conditions often foster the greatest sensitivities, when developers can, unwittingly, be perceived by individual academics as favouring a viewpoint which they oppose.

Currently there is an extensive array of topics which could legitimately be covered in a discussion of national contexts, policies and strategies. For practical purposes the primary focus will be upon the situation in the UK, although many of the initiatives and issues affect other systems of higher education. The ten topics which I have chosen for more detailed discussion in this chapter are:

- the changing scene in relation to quality assurance, assessment and audit;
- widening participation;
- massification;
- the influence of the Learning and Teaching Support Network (LTSN) and the Institute for Learning and Teaching in Higher Education (ILTHE);

- enhancement initiatives promoted by the funding bodies;
- research policies;
- borderless education and e-learning;
- the increasing emphasis upon the learning experience of students;
- student employability; and
- specific legislation.

Before turning to that imposing list, five further points should be borne in mind.

First, there can be, and have been, significant differences, even divergences, between the responses to various aspects of the changing scene by institutional managers, individual academics and developers.

Second, considerable variation exists within the system, largely based upon institutional mission and tradition.

Third, developers can, and do, access external support, as well as building internal bridges and partnerships. Some sources of external support are well-established such as the Staff and Educational Development Association (SEDA), others are newer, e.g. LTSN, ILTHE and the Association for Learning Technology (ALT).

Fourth, as the range of influences and the sources of support increase, there is the consequential dangers of 'noise' or overlap, which busy academics can readily criticize. Whilst the World Wide Web appears to offer a solution, 'it is only a click away', that can often prove untrue and frustrating and lead to tensions and criticisms.

Fifth, in the climate where some academics fear that external agendas are impinging too closely upon their academic identities, developers need to pay a great deal of attention to the way they phrase arguments for change. Perhaps the appropriate prayer for developers is: '*Please don't let them shoot the messenger*'. However, that highlights crucial questions, such as whether, when and how to act as the messenger?

TEN AREAS OF NATIONAL CONTEXTS/POLICIES/STRATEGIES

With these points in mind, the remainder of this chapter explores the ten areas of national contexts/policies/strategies identified above. Most are UK wide, but some apply primarily or solely to institutions covered by a specific Funding Council. The order of treatment is a personal preference rather than a strictly chronological one, although there is a broad pattern of deviation and scale of impact upon developers. Throughout the ten areas runs the thread of potential as against actual impact. A degree of post-hoc rationalization and coherence could be introduced by marshalling everything within the Learning and Teaching Strategy or

Enhancement Strategy which institutions are required to submit to their respective Funding Council. However to do so would in my view conceal traditions which exist in institutions and the tensions or messiness (Newton 2002) which are strong features of practice on the ground.

Quality assurance and audit

Reference is made in the *Interim Report* of the Teaching Quality Enhancement Committee (2002) to the fact that many participants in the focus groups drawn from across the academic community commented that the work of Quality Assurance Agency for Higher Education (QAA), and its predecessors, whilst not universally welcomed, had led to the enhancement of practice within institutions. Those views echo the research by Brennan (1997, 2000) that learning from assessment (and audit) had occurred.

Elsewhere I have observed that:

> At the level of the department or course team, effective learning and enhancement involves welding together individual commitment, professionalism, expertise and creativity in a coherent and explicit manner, which can be communicated effectively to students (actual and prospective), assessors, external assessors, internal reviewers and other interested parties.
>
> (Gordon 2002: 215)

Viewed from the bridge (the perspective of senior management), the challenges may be to improve institutional performance, as measured by the external report, and/or improve practices and enhance the student experience and/or purposefully contribute to the institutional strategy and culture. Individual

> practitioners are influenced by other factors such as their professional desire to do a good job, concerns about the view which students and peers hold of them, personal intellectual curiosity to learn new things and explore new ideas and practices.
>
> (Gordon 2002: 215)

To date institutions have responded in a variety of ways to external quality assurance, assessment and audit. Some have created dedicated units which provide briefings, guide preparation and even train staff.

In some instances developers contribute to, or undertake, some or all of these activities. More generally, they have worked formatively with disciplines/subjects, normally some 2 to 3 years in advance of the external assessment/review. In some institutions there has been a careful separation of roles, with staff and educational (academic) development contributing formative, reflective and evaluative functions and another central source undertaking briefings, co-ordination and the many detailed preparations.

Many assessment, subject review and audit reports have made favourable references to the contributions of development centres and units. There have been frequent exhortations to make better use of these resources and to disseminate good practice more widely within the institution. Those responsible for overseeing these processes nationally have expressed frustration that the explicit learning from audit/assessment/subject review appears to be less than they would expect or wish, i.e. that follow-up is largely responsive rather than proactive. If that view holds some validity, it may represent a lacuna, probably often undetected internally, in the priorities of institutional managers, heads of academic departments and heads of development.

But what of the future? These external processes are currently being substantially revised. Changes in Scotland are being viewed with particular interest, both by Vice-Chancellors and staff and educational (academic) developers. The Scottish Higher Education Funding Council (SHEFC) commissioned QAA to design and implement an enhancement-led institutional review (ELIR) process to work in tandem with the Council's policies and strategies on quality enhancement. The new procedures became operational in 2003/4. Briefly the ELIR will involve:

- An annual discussion between each institution and QAA. In the year preceding ELIR that will address the preliminary agenda for the Review.
- A reflective analysis (on a four year cycle) covering internal monitoring, the student experience, the quality enhancement strategy, case studies of effective management of enhancement, illustrations of processes and the use of reference points, and dissemination of good practice.
- The visit associated with ELIR which will normally involve a two-day part which establishes an understanding of QA and QE at the institution and some verification through audit trials, followed by a 3–5 day visit that explores institutional learning, the operation of enhancement strategies and use of reference points.

The published Report will lead to a judgement on the ability of Internal Review Systems to monitor and maintain quality and standards. The remainder of the Report will address various dimensions of effectiveness and of the quality and accuracy of public information. It is intended that part of the process will focus upon specified enhancement themes, and views were sought on two potential generic themes to be used in 2003/4. The options offered were: assessment, employability, and meeting student needs. Assessment and responding to student needs were chosen. SHEFC has involved practitioners in the articulation of the processes and the arrangements. The programme was launched in September 2003 with a one-day conference in Dundee. Presently focus groups are being held with academic and administrative staff and with students respectively. A series of workshops is also planned. The developmental thrust should be very attractive to developers and hopefully of considerable utility for their work, especially if they can find a viable means of enacting the roles of guide, shaper and facilitator.

Whatever detailed processes and procedures are enacted, many items from earlier practices will be carried forward, e.g. subject benchmark statements, the QAA Code of Practice, specified learning outcomes and programme specifications.

At least one further component of the planned changes will significantly influence academic practice and the work of developers. That dimension could be framed narrowly in terms of the expectation that greater attention is paid to a richer array of sources of student feedback, but it might be wiser to set it more broadly within the ministerial requirement that the revised processes feature a strengthened student voice. Of course, views are likely to differ on: what that should involve?; how should it be translated into action?; and, where should the locus of action and support be?

Both generally and specifically, developers need to consider the nature of their potential contribution and involvement in this changing scene. They may be encouraged to be proactive by the perception that there has been a climatic shift towards a more facilitative, enabling and enhancement-oriented thrust in the purposes, processes and procedures of quality audit.

Widening participation and massification

There is a temptation, even a tendency, to conflate massification with widening participation. Yet the statistics indicate that they are separate, although related, topics. Massification is taken to mean the growth of the number of students in the system to the level at which aggregate rates of participation are sufficiently high to merit the term, mass participation.

Certainly in the UK that expansion has largely happened in the relatively recent past (the last 15 years). It has also been associated with a massive decline in the unit of resource, in part because Treasury economists assumed that economies of scale would apply and quite a lot of growth could occur at marginal, or less than full, cost. The issue here is not whether or not those economic arguments are valid or wise, but the correlates that have become associated with massification in the UK, e.g. deteriorating staff-student ratios, larger groups, pressures on faculty, and escalating workloads.

Peter Scott (2002) has commented that it has been one of the remarkable achievements of UK higher education that massification has taken place without radical change to academic practices and values. That interpretation is validated by Henkel's research (2000) which found that there had been evolution rather than revolution in academic identities, notwithstanding the substantial changes which had affected the system, institutions and individuals.

Some senior managers in the focus groups held as part of the research on behalf of the Teaching Quality Enhancement Committee (2002, 2003) suggested that further accommodation to the pressures of massification will be difficult. Put simply they thought that it was increasingly becoming difficult to maintain existing practices and traditions, and that more radical changes were likely to affect at least some areas and activities. To date, the evidence is mostly of shifts in the balance of activities and approaches and/or supplementation rather than radical reformulation, redesign or restructuring. Working within an evolutionary setting is a commonplace experience for developers. When more radical scenarios come into play, issues of provenance, commitment, ownership and expertise, come to the fore. Yet one of the paradoxical facets of academic life is that 'radical' developments often occur within institutions, but at a very localized level. It is when efforts are made to foster or lever wider adoption of the innovation that the issue becomes more challenging, even problematic. Using the champions of the innovation can be a powerful tool, especially when they are widely respected within the institutional peer community or indeed within the peer community of the discipline.

Widening participation refers to increasing the participation from under-represented groups such as students from particular socio-economic backgrounds, ethnic groups or other sectors of society which are perceived as being disadvantaged by the prevailing pattern of participation. Widening participation is also increasingly linked in public policy to the issues of student retention and achievement.

Common areas of activity for developers include: the provision of study skills support; work on curriculum development; work on approaches to teaching and learning and on methods of assessment. In addition to the vast array of excellent practical work which has been undertaken, some also work at a strategic level within their institution, contributing to policy formulation and, indeed, drafting sections of the institutional teaching and learning, or quality enhancement, strategy. Increasingly colleagues find benefit in connecting strategy with their operational practice and priorities. The transparency of the linkages is helpful, as are the issues of authority and involvement, provided the strategy was the outcome of widespread involvement and consultation. Where a more top-down approach is favoured, developers can be confronted with mixed emotions from academic staff as they question or even criticize elements of the strategy.

The influence of LTSN and ILTHE

For developers within the UK, both the LTSN and the ILTHE offer opportunities and challenges. The principal opportunities in each case are a means of engaging with all three of the primary audiences for development identified near the start of this chapter. These audiences are the institution, the disciplines/subjects, and individual academics. The engagement takes different but cognate forms. With LTSN and its 24 Subject Centres the engagement happens through the primary focus of interest of individual academics, which is of course their discipline. With ILTHE, the engagement happens through the wish of individual academics to be recognized for the capabilities of teaching their subject and the wish of institutions to show a successful commitment to improve the quality of teaching. The likely successor body to these organizations, the emergent Higher Education Academy, will similarly offer scope to engage with individual academics, hopefully focusing at least in part on the teaching of individual disciplines.

Some institutions have created explicit internal structures that link LTSN champions for each discipline into co-ordinating networks across the institution. Such arrangements offer developers potentially powerful avenues for dialogue and collaboration.

In addition to the rapidly expanding output from the LTSN Subject Centres, the LTSN Generic Centre is engaging with the development community on a wide range of themes and activities and is generating valuable resources such as those on assessment and on the scholarship of teaching. The Generic Centre has defined its remit broadly, embracing many aspects of academic practice. That enables the Centre to address topical issues which are of concern within the sector, albeit that concern is not always sector-led.

In summer 2003 the ILTHE had some 15,000 members – a remarkable achievement in a short period of time. It has offered four useful sets of opportunities to staff and educational development.

First, most institutions now have ILTHE accreditation for their formal provision for the initial development of staff involved in teaching and supporting learning. Second, as has happened with the LTSN, it has become an additional means of catalysing communities of practice. Third, it has allowed experienced staff membership on the basis of clear criteria. Fourth, the criteria for membership have been enhanced and will be supplemented shortly by a formal structure for continuing professional development.

It has not been axiomatic that developers have been closely involved in LTSN or ILTHE related initiative within their institutions, although that has frequently happened.

A number of approaches to initial provision have been accredited. Two illustrations of approach are:

- A modular postgraduate programme, such as the PG Certificate at Strathclyde University. Here participants must undertake a double module on learning, teaching and assessment and a module on personal and professional development planning. The remaining module is selected from a list of options.
- A portfolio approach, where the instructional components inform and support the required sections of the 'portfolio'. In some institutions these elements remain distinct but linked, in others the portfolio is intended to be focused upon a specific aspect or theme.

Enhancement initiatives of the Funding Councils

Over the last decade the range of initiatives has been extensive. Here attention will be limited to two illustrations, the phases of the Fund for the Development of Teaching and Learning (FDTL) funded by the Higher Education Funding Council for England (HEFCE) and some of the SHEFC sponsored e-learning initiatives. An important thrust of the FDTL initiative is the dissemination of good practice initially identified in QAA reports. Since many of the projects are discipline-based, it is not unreasonable to presume that engagement of the community of that discipline is the key to wider dissemination. However there is also the expectation that wider dissemination will spread across disciplinary boundaries.

Arguably developers have an important role to play in that form of facilitation or brokerage. Some institutions elected to use their staff and educational development centre as a managerial base for their FDTL bids and projects. Others used individuals as advisers. A different opportunity flowed from the engagement of developers as educational consultants to specific FDTL projects, in a manner akin to such individuals being Associates of LTSN. Those inputs have aided FDTL projects (and LTSN). There is a return to the centre and institutions of the contributor, although it can be diffused, deferred, tacit or concealed.

Following upon the investment in the Metropolitan Areas Network for Scottish higher education, SHEFC has sought to promote use of the network for teaching and learning. These projects fostered collaboration between institutions and more specifically groups of developers. They created products, built networks, disseminated findings and catalysed interactions. As with FDTL these projects sat within the broad enhancement strategy of the Funding Council, which attaches considerable importance to external support as a source of stimulus and assistance, whilst emphasising that the locus firmly rests within institutions.

Some institutions have established new units or centres dedicated to educational technology or supporting the implementation of online learning. As with earlier initiatives such as Enterprise in Higher Education this can be an important source of refreshment, addition and extension. Equally, it can create tensions, especially when resources are under pressure. Developing inter-centre synergy can be complicated by traditions, differing pools of expertise and even favoured approach.

Research policies

Research-intensive universities tend to talk of their focus upon research led teaching. More widely Henkel's (2000) research demonstrated the intricate inter-relationship between research and teaching to the academic identity of practitioners. Thus research cannot be a 'foreign country' for developers.

It is not appropriate to analyse here the merits or intricacies of the Research Assessment Exercise (RAE). However reference should be made to some aspects. First, there is the view that the growing emphasis upon the performance in the RAE has reduced the priority attached to enhancing teaching and learning. Put simply, the argument is that the ambitious, even prudent, academic should maximize the allocation of their discretionary time to their research rather than to enhancing their teaching. Moreover the knock-on effects of performance in the RAE are sharpening and extending. Now there is the possibility it will be used to benchmark eligibility for financial support from the Funding Councils for postgraduate provision.

A different dimension of the importance of research for developers stems from the centrality of research in academic identities. Where that is the case, divorcing the dialogue from research can introduce an unhelpful barrier. Equally making the connection poses a challenge which is often bridged by using the experiences of the participants.

Whilst there is a substantial body of research and scholarship on teaching and learning, it is well recorded that it is difficult to persuade academic staff to engage with it. In part that reflects the disciplinary origins and discourses of much of the research e.g. sociology or psychology, but it is unlikely that all of the resistance can be accounted for by these factors. Yet there is a growing fashion in public policy for evidence-based policy and a specific determination in the Economic and Social Research Council (ESRC) Teaching and Learning Research Programme (TLRP) to promote evidence-based professional practice in education. It will be interesting to see how academics and developers react to, and make use of, the outputs of the TLRP studies.

There are some encouraging signs. Colleagues are reporting much greater levels of engagement with the research literature as a major positive outcome of their ILTHE accredited initial development programmes for teaching staff and those who support learning. We should not be surprised by that situation, because research is characterized by immersion and sustained interest and personal application.

Borderless education and e-learning

A recent survey (Observatory on Borderless Higher Education 2002) of Commonwealth Universities reported enthusiasm for online learning but little evidence of widespread integration into the curriculum. Institutions believed that many staff did not have the necessary skills. Many of the staff may also prefer to use a mixed approach and there is some evidence emerging which suggests students also favour that strategy.

In addition to the issue of competency in technical skills, there may also be issues of new pedagogical approaches and skills, such as e-moderation. Gibbons *et al.* (1994) describe a shift in research and the production of knowledge from Mode 1 (which, briefly, characterizes knowledge as being produced through research and then as a separate act disseminated and made available for practice) into Mode 2 (research, dissemination and implementation being either the same or at any rate very closely inter-twined acts). Some would argue that online learning and widespread use of the world-wide web show Mode 2 knowledge production in action for teaching and learning. If that analogy holds some validity, then it could mean that e-learning will profoundly change the nature of educational development.

The student learning experience

This is well-trodden and familiar territory for staff and educational developers, involving topics such as active learning and student evaluation and feedback. Numerous successful active learning strategies have been developed and used in institutions – sometimes virtually independent of inputs from educational developers but often with their active involvement.

As concerns mount about students' retention and motivation, academic staff seek strategies which will achieve engagement and commitment.

Employability

Some national contexts are enduring or recurrent. Employability is an example. It has been actively on the external policy agenda for over a decade. That could be interpreted as indicating that earlier strategies had not become embedded within the system. Equally it could simply reflect the importance and complexity of the issue.

Many approaches to defining and then developing employability have been used. The prevailing consensus favours a curricular solution to the topic of key skills. That is logical, since the curriculum is the basic component of the formal education of students. However research consistently demonstrates that other influences have a powerful effect on student learning, notably peer communities and extra-curricular activities. Moreover both of these can involve crucial inter-personal dimensions which employers recurrently cite as key qualities which they seek when recruiting.

Developers frequently work on key skills development. Many contribute directly into specific academic programmes, in addition to working with departments on relevant aspects of curriculum development.

I shall use our experience at Strathclyde as an illustration. We contribute directly to programmes across the five faculties, particularly on topics such as presentation skills. We have worked at length and in depth with departments which have decided to embed key skills development explicitly within the curriculum and approached the Centre for Academic Practice for assistance. Recently my colleague Rowena Murray has developed, in conjunction with Learning Services, a suite of online resources for postgraduate students on topics such as presentation skills, poster presentations and thesis writing.

In this field developers often work in close collaboration with colleagues in the Careers Service. Alternatively, the two services may agree a division of labour and specializations. Communicating such agreements widely is important.

Specific legislation

Increasingly legislation forms a major dimension of the national context. The Disability Discrimination Act is a powerful example. It has resulted in a wide range of activities and responses including:

- the production of materials (see, for example, *Staff Development*, Disability Rights Commission, October 2002);
- funded projects;
- the QAA Code of Practice; and
- numerous initiatives within institutions.

The SHEFC funded the Creating an Accessible Curriculum project which was led by Anne Simpson, Special Needs Adviser at the University of Strathclyde. The first phase piloted work in specific academic departments in five HEIs in West Scotland. One output was an audit tool which departments could use to determine the accessibility of the curriculum. The second phase extended the work to all Scottish HEIs and strengthened the connection between institutional strategies on disability and action plans.

   The importance of the topic has resulted in many institutions supplementing their expertise in this field. That enhanced provision often means that associated training is vested with those staff. Nonetheless, the legislation presents significant challenges for developers. Foremost are the issues of mainstreaming the activities and of seeking to ensure that all activities, initiatives and events take an inclusive approach.

CONCLUDING REMARKS

Rather than summarize the foregoing material, I want to focus briefly upon emerging contexts. First, there is the growing diversity of context between the Funding Councils. An obvious illustration surrounds the new procedures of the QAA. In Scotland these will entail enhancement-led institutional review, which is quite different from an ethos of checking on standards. Second, there are the potential outcomes over time of the implication of the core plus approach to funding by HEFCE. Third, there are the implications of what Americans have described as the changing of the guard – the pending retirement of a significant cohort of senior academics. Finally, there are the complex changes associated with the cumulative impact of trends and episodic turbulence.

   Spotting many of these sources of change is not unduly difficult, although it is demanding to specify timescales and the scale and nature of impact. The strategic challenge for staff and educational developers is deciding when, and how, to put such matters on to the development agenda. Yet in the climate of operational plans and priorities such thinking is needed for forward-looking strategies and matching 3 to 5 year plans.

REFERENCES

Becher, T. and Trowler, P. R. (2001) *Academic Tribes and Territories* Second Edition, SRHE/OUP, Buckingham

Brennan, J., Frederiks, F. and Shah, T. (1997) *Improving the Quality of Education: The Impact of Quality Assessment on Institutions* Report to HEFCE, Quality Support Centre

Brennan, J. and Shah, T. (2000) *Managing Quality in Higher Education* SRHE/ OUP, Buckingham

Disability Rights Commission (2002) *Staff Development: Good Practice Guide* Disability Rights Commission EDU 13, Stratford upon Avon

Eastcott, D. and Thew, N. (2003) Working creatively with national agendas, in P. Kahn and D. Baume (Eds) *A Guide to Staff and Educational Development* Kogan Page, London pp 159–70

Gibbons, M., Nowotny, H., Limoges, C., Trow, M., Schwartzman, S. and Scott, P. (1994) *The New Production of Knowledge: The Dynamics of Science and Research in Contemporary Societies* Sage, London

Gordon, G. (2002) Learning from quality assessment, in S. Ketteridge, S. Marshall and H. Fry (Eds) *The Effective Academic* Kogan Page, London, pp 201–17

Gosling, D. and D'Andrea, V. (2002) How educational development/learning and teaching centres help education institutions manage change *Educational Developments* 3(2), pp 1–3

Henkel, M. (2000) *Academic Identities and Policy Change in Higher Education* Jessica Kingsley, London

Land, R. (2001) Agency, context and change in academic development *International Journal for Academic Development* 6(1), pp 4–20

Land, R. (2003) Orientations to academic development, in H. Eggins and R. Macdonald (Eds) *The Scholarship of Academic Development* SRHE/Open University Press, Buckingham, pp 34–46

Newton, J. (2002) *From Policy to Reality: Enhancing Quality is a Messy Business.* LTSN Generic Centre website

Observatory on Borderless Higher Education (2002) Online Learning in Commonwealth Universities. Selected data from the 2002 Observatory Survey – Part 1

Scott, P. (2002) Partnerships for progression: evolution or transformation? *Educational Developments* 3(3), pp 1–3

Teaching Quality Enhancement Committee (2002) Interim Report, HEFCE website

Teaching Quality Enhancement Committee (2003) Final Report on the Future Needs and Support for Quality Enhancement of Learning and Teaching in Higher Education. HEFCE/UUK/SCOP

2

Developing institutional policy and strategy for academic development: how can senior management and educational development units work productively together?

Fred Percival and Gill Tucker

INTRODUCTION

Higher education institutions (HEIs) are engaging with an ever more diverse and complex body of learners. Each individual learner has their own background, motivations, constraints and preferred learning style. One size will not fit all, and so portfolios of programmes and of delivery methods must be evolved and applied. 'Mass customization' is essential.

An HEI must progress on many fronts at once. For example it must widen access, promote lifelong learning, improve the student experience and enhance the quality of provision. This means that institutions must continually develop and shape both policy and strategy in order, in some cases, to survive, let alone to thrive. HEIs must be clear about the educational development and staff development implications of strategic change, and they must develop operational tactics to implement strategy.

This chapter considers the relationships between policy, resourcing, implementation and practice for staff and educational development. It considers these relationships from the respective standpoints of a university senior manager and a head of educational development. After noting the main challenges and potential for educational development in helping the institution to achieve its many goals, the chapter identifies a range of interrelated themes, topics and examples, and identifies how synergies can be sought and conflicts avoided or resolved. The chapter introduces each of a range of themes and topics through a short simulated dialogue between a university senior manager and its head of educational development. Each dialogue is followed by an exploration of the issue, showing how senior manager and head of development can work productively together.

THE SCOPE AND CHALLENGES OF EDUCATIONAL DEVELOPMENT

Before exploring the interface between educational developers and senior management in facilitating and driving change, it is useful to remind ourselves briefly of the scope of educational development. Lorraine Stefani (2003) has defined educational development as 'the systematic and scholarly support for improving both educational processes and the practice of educators'. Additionally, David Gosling (2001) in surveying the range of activities that educational development units undertake, and from searching the literature, concluded that the six key goals of educational development are:

(a) improvement of teaching and assessment practices, curriculum design, and learning support – including the place of information technology in learning and teaching;
(b) professional development of all staff with responsibility (directly or indirectly) for supporting student learning;
(c) organizational and policy development to promote the academic goals of the institution;
(d) learning development of students – supporting and improving effective student learning;
(e) promotion of informed debate about learning, teaching, assessment, curricular design and the goals of higher education;
(f) promotion of the scholarship of teaching and learning, and research into higher education goals and practices.

Scott (1995) has further identified that, in an HE sector with diverse institutional types, educational development serves different functions and has different reporting lines and different relationships with other functional units within the HEI. Land (2001) has researched and reflected on different approaches to educational development. He concludes that these different approaches are influenced significantly by institutional culture, which includes key factors such as the type of institution, preferred management style of institutional leaders, the declared mission of the institution, history of the institution, sources of income, staff and student profiles, and institutional structures.

Meanwhile, Philip Candy (1996) has ventured a seven-part model for academic development. One element of this model was that academic development must be 'anticipatory' – educational development must not simply react to changes already experienced, but must constantly scan the horizon and seek to prepare people for likely futures before these arrive. This highlights a need for educational development to balance the attainment of the best of scholarly values and practices on the one hand with the inexorable and irresistible demands for change and innovation on the other.

The need for educational development to be centrally involved in quality enhancement of teaching and student learning has also been highlighted (Jackson 2002). Drivers of quality enhancement in institutions include the need for public accountability; the competitiveness of an inter-institutional market; league tables and other responses to key performance indicators; and what might be termed academic self-governance through accrediting and professional bodies. How educational developers can most effectively influence continuous improvement has become a key strategic focus for many institutions.

WORKING TOGETHER: EDUCATIONAL DEVELOPMENT AND SENIOR MANAGEMENT

All of the above indicates that educational development operates within a broad range of structures and hierarchies, and within a rich diversity of institutional cultures and missions. Nevertheless there is considerable commonality within educational development, and particularly in the purposes of educational development. This broad commonality of purpose lets us consider how a range of policy goals and strategic developments might be effectively progressed by productive and symbiotic working relationships between the educational development function and senior management within an HEI. Whether or not there is a direct line management relationship, good and open lines of communication between senior management and educational development are essential.

We assume in the rest of the chapter that the HEI has developed, or is in the process of developing, an institutional strategy for learning, teaching and assessment as a key document in setting institutional directions, goals and targets for learning and teaching development. This strategy can usefully be seen as the 'DNA' of the development process, determining the broad direction and some details of development and implementation but subject to local and environmental factors which determine other details.

We explore the academic development implications of:

1   implementing an institution's strategy for learning, teaching and assessment, and embedding a culture of continuous quality enhancement;

2   using external agendas as leverage for change, development and enhancement;
3   improving practice through formalized teaching development programmes and models of continuing professional development;
4   meeting the challenges of mass higher education, greater social inclusion and students with differing learning needs, styles and motivations;
5   providing incentives to staff through human resources and promotion policies which reward learning, teaching and academic development;
6   enhancing the effectiveness and efficiency of learning, teaching and assessment through learning technology and other forms of flexible learning delivery;
7   developing scholarship and research in learning and teaching to underpin development and change;
8   effectively using good generalists and expert specialists to support academic development; and
9   keeping abreast of the external agenda (including national and international developments) and good practice elsewhere through networking and environmental scanning.

All of these topics can be legitimately mapped on to the aspects of the educational development role previously identified by Gosling (2001), Candy (1996) and Jackson (2002). Collectively these comprise a huge agenda for educational development which can only be met with the full and active support of senior management.

TOPIC 1 – IMPLEMENTING AN INSTITUTION'S STRATEGY FOR LEARNING, TEACHING AND ASSESSMENT AND EMBEDDING A CULTURE OF CONTINUOUS QUALITY ENHANCEMENT

SENIOR MANAGER: Well, the Learning, Teaching and Assessment Strategy was approved by Academic Board last week – a positive discussion too, I thought.
EDUCATIONAL DEVELOPER: Yes – I think that was at least in part due to the engagement and involvement of staff, both academic and support, during the development of the strategy.
SENIOR MANAGER: Now all we need to do is implement it! There are a lot of good sentiments in there, but how do we make it happen? It's really important we get this right!
EDUCATIONAL DEVELOPER: I know – and we need to work across the institution to help faculties, departments and staff relate to the strategy and 'own' it – while being able to monitor how well we are doing in achieving our targets.

The academic strategy should be the main driver of any institutional plan. A key component of this is the design and delivery of programmes and courses and the support of the learner: a student centred agenda, focused on their needs. Such mass customization is best developed through a learning, teaching and assessment strategy. This strategy should be consistent with other strategies for research, estates, human resource, C&IT, . . . This HEI-wide collection of strategies should collectively support the implementation of the learning and teaching strategy.

HEFCE (1999) provided guidance to institutions explaining why learning and teaching strategies might be needed today, accepting that HEIs have managed without them in the past. Reasons to have such a strategy include:

- The changing context of higher education in terms of resource deployment and participation profiles. Learning and teaching strategies are often designed to support larger scale change than individuals can bring about on their own.
- The infrastructures which evolve to support traditional patterns of learning and teaching may be less appropriate to some more flexible types of delivery, and may obstruct change.
- Some new forms of teaching often involve new teaching and support roles, and these in turn may require new categories of staff on new conditions of service – there are clear necessary links here with human resource strategy.
- Strategic plans and projects may be needed to embed innovations in the mainstream.

The senior manager is likely to see the Learning, Teaching and Assessment (LTA) strategy as a component of and a vital element for the delivery of the academic strategy. The academic strategy is the overarching framework within which the LTA strategy sits. The academic strategy will comprise a vision, objectives and targets (qualitative and quantitative) for the institution. It will be the responsibility of the senior manager to ensure that the vision and targets are clear. Elements of the academic strategy might comprise:

- the size and shape of the institution;
- the balance between teaching and research;
- the learning environment;
- the educational philosophy;
- mode of delivery, method of delivery, learning support and guidance; and
- the quality key performance indicators.

The LTA strategy should be inextricably linked to these higher level goals. It is often left to educational development to ensure that the LTA strategy directly contributes to the overall academic strategy. It is here that the working relationship between senior management and educational development might most productively flourish. This good working relationship will involve, among other things:

- providing a clear and coherent rationale and framework for the LTA strategy;
- concentrating on organizational development rather than classroom tactics;
- being proactive and selective in activities;
- operationalizing goals and setting targets;
- becoming involved in monitoring and evaluating of the strategy;
- re-organization and rationalization of support functions; and
- considering of resourcing and staffing implications.

(Gibbs 2000)

These activities will increasingly involve educational development units in a range of strategic policy and operational decisions and activities within which they have, traditionally, not been centrally involved. Learning and teaching strategies place educational development in the role of a key institutional change-agent. To capitalize on this opportunity, educational development will increasingly need to become less involved in responding to the idiosyncratic interest of teaching enthusiasts, rather to develop a more planned and strategic focus (Gibbs 2000).

The support, encouragement, and (sometimes) coaching of senior management is critical to maximize the effectiveness of this evolving role for educational development. When this relationship works well, the LTA strategy will be linked to and coherent with the institutions' financial and infrastructure planning, including its other major strategies as referred to above. In some institutions the educational development function has, in the past, been marginalized. This cannot continue if the full potential of educational developers is to be recognized and exploited within an institution. In working with senior management to achieve core strategic goals, educational developers will have to discard some of their pet activities and projects. Senior management and educational development need to develop constructive and open channels of communication, to develop mutual respect, and to share goals, targets and operational tactics. For some, both senior managers and developers, this may be a longer journey than for others!

TOPIC 2 – USING EXTERNAL AGENDAS FOR CHANGE, DEVELOPMENT AND ENHANCEMENT

SENIOR MANAGER: The Quality Assurance Agency will be due to visit us in 2 years for an institutional quality audit. I hope we can use the event to further embed our approach to quality enhancement.

EDUCATIONAL DEVELOPER: Absolutely! But we need to start working now to help develop a process which will be ongoing – and not stop after the event.

SENIOR MANAGER: It's obviously important to get good results and a clean 'bill of health' from the QAA – but we won't gain any benefit if we just 'play the game'.

EDUCATIONAL DEVELOPER: Agreed – and just playing the game is too dangerous as well!

External influencers on the sector such as funding councils, national quality agencies and professional bodies can often provide much-needed leverage to encourage change and development within a given timescale. They can also provide a legitimate way for both senior management and educational developers to work with academic departments and faculties. National priorities; for example for widening access and participation or the embedding within curricula of employability skills; provide senior management with added weight to justify and encourage institution-wide activity to respond and react to these national priorities. In turn, management-backed pressure and encouragement to implement national priorities provide educational development with a legitimized role in supporting departments and faculties to respond effectively and to implement appropriate learning and teaching practices and processes. Similarly, planned external visitations such as an institutional audit within the UK can provide a longer-term basis on which to evolve and embed improved academic practice. Similarly, at a more local level, departmental quality reviews and programme validations and reviews provide a useful vehicle for educational development to work productively with departments.

Given such legitimate ways to engage with practice within the HEI, it is important that the educational development input is seen to make a real difference. It is preferable if some institutional and local (for example departmental) as well as national goals and objectives are also achieved or furthered en route. This is how the senior manager can most clearly come to see the value that educational development would bring to the institution. The educational developer will at the same time look for support and steerage from the senior manager.

Too often, academic staff see both external and internal policies (such as widening participation) and events (such as quality assurance visits) as inconveniences, interferences and hoops to jump through. But if the looked-for outcomes of these policies and events are properly aligned to local goals and objectives, they become opportunities to develop deeper and reflective analysis of processes and practices, to achieve real, lasting and valued results, rather than just playing game to get the best scores. Educational development can work with departments and faculties to embed locally appropriate and accepted approaches to improving the design and operation of courses, programmes and student support. Senior management and educational development should not under-estimate the potential of both external and internal policies and events as development opportunities and agents of change, as long as they are planned and implemented with some regard to local priorities.

TOPIC 3 – IMPROVING PRACTICE THROUGH FORMALIZED TEACHING DEVELOPMENT PROGRAMMES AND MODELS OF CONTINUING PROFESSIONAL DEVELOPMENT

EDUCATIONAL DEVELOPER: I've sent you up this year's staff develop-ment programme. This includes the Post-Graduate Certificate in Learning and Teaching, which as you know is now compulsory for new staff.

SENIOR MANAGER: Great – and does it include the dates for staff induction courses? – I always like to come along to meet the new staff.

EDUCATIONAL DEVELOPER: It does – and that induction programme now runs twice a year. The staff really appreciate your support. But we need you to be aware of the resource pressures these activities are causing, and their effects on other priorities.

Many HEIs, indeed within the UK almost all, now have in place accredited programmes for new teaching staff. These programmes often include an induction programme and a post-graduate level certificate in learning and teaching in higher education. Senior management have a vital role to play in reinforcing the importance of such programmes. They can:

- Ensure a clear link from the programme to probation, preferably with a requirement for successful completion of the course.
- Provide a link to promotion, the programme providing a first step qualification on a clearly defined career path for teachers in higher education (HE).

- Actively promote the programme and its importance and value, through visible support and presence as well as through papers and policy.

As educational developers become increasingly involved with organizational change and development, Gibbs (2000) has envisaged the day when such programmes 'may be re-conceptualised as tools for long term organisational development, growing the change agents of the future, rather than as staff development for individuals who know how to lecture'.

With the advent of learning and teaching strategies, the focus of educational staff development activity can become more refined and directed more strategically. Staff development can provide a range of support activities at university, faculty, departmental and even individual level. Increasingly there will be a need to support the continuing professional development (CPD) of teachers in higher education, not only through developmental programmes and workshops but also through the process of developing CPD portfolios.

All of the above activities require time and attention. Senior managers will need to have evidence from evaluation that staff development activities are meeting goals and providing value for money. And again there needs to be close liaison between educational development and senior management to ensure that the programme, and subsequent staff development, target key strategic priorities, such as e-learning or widening participation.

Discussions about resources for the programme need to be set within this framework, and implications captured and discussed during the institution's annual planning cycle. Priorities will need to be analysed, balanced and recognized. It needs to be explicit to both senior management and educational development what the implications are of re-focusing resources and activities on specific areas and activities such as the programme for new teaching staff. In the zero sum financial game that is budget setting and resource allocation in most HEIs, these goals and objectives will have to supersede other activities.

TOPIC 4 – MEETING THE CHALLENGES OF MASS HIGHER EDUCATION, GREATER SOCIAL INCLUSION AND STUDENTS WITH DIFFERING LEARNING NEEDS, STYLES AND MOTIVATIONS

SENIOR MANAGER: This year's University enrolment statistics are really buoyant. It's also clear that we have a broader diversity of students than ever before, in terms of ethnicity, age range and social background. And we have more international students and direct entrants from further education than ever before.

EDUCATIONAL DEVELOPER: Fantastic! But we really need to think through the implications. This diversity is great for meeting our financial targets, and it means we've well achieved some of our widening participation and other targets. But we now need to put in place appropriate support if these new students are to succeed.

SENIOR MANAGER: Agreed. As well as educational and business reasons we also have a moral obligation to these students to give them a good experience and maximize their chances of success.

In the UK, national demographics, which currently indicate a steadily falling pool of school leavers, and government policy, which emphasizes increased participation rates, wider access, greater social inclusion and lifelong learning have combined to encourage HEIs to broaden substantially their view of who are potential students. There are also educational and financial pressures to increase the numbers of international students, studying both within the institution and at a distance. The need to cater for this diverse population of students has become a major issue. HEIs need to consider the implications for socialization, acculturization, induction, study skills development, learning activities, assessment and curriculum design. Clearly there are both staff and student development issues here.

Senior management have an obvious role to play in determining the mission and academic strategy of the institution. These will have implications for the institution's shape, size and student profile. However, planning comprises more than determining and responding to student numbers. Management needs to work closely with educational development, student support services, administration and academic departments, not only to maximize student satisfaction and student retention, but also fully to capitalize on the educational opportunities and potential which diversity in the student population can provide. Increasing diversity in HE will have implications for almost every part of the institution – even the refectory.

A student might legitimately expect from an institution a wide and coherent range of services and support. Educational development is uniquely placed to make and shape this coherence of provision through the policy frameworks and strategies in support of diversity. Co-ordinated action on these complex issues, however, must be overseen or managed by a senior member of the institution. This overview may result in:

- a reshaping of the infrastructure to support students;
- reorganization and structural changes in supplying services; and

- a reshaping and development of the learning environment.

Change, however, must be the result of a recognition of student need. Again we are back to the central issue of mass customization for our increasingly consumer-led sector. Educational development and senior management have key roles in identifying and planning to meet these needs. Responses will be shaped by the senior manager, but linked and supported through educational development in cooperation with learner support services and academic staff.

TOPIC 5 – PROVIDING INCENTIVES TO STAFF THROUGH HUMAN RESOURCES AND PROMOTION POLICIES WHICH REWARD LEARNING, TEACHING AND ACADEMIC DEVELOPMENT

SENIOR MANAGER: I'm worried, after speaking to some staff today, that there's a strong perception that the only way to get promotion here is through research.

EDUCATIONAL DEVELOPER: It may be more perception than reality, but I know a lot of staff believe that. There are many models around now to reward staff for achievements in teaching – it's also quite timely with the development of our Human Resources Strategy. Let's have a chat about possibilities, including the costs and the benefits.

Many HEIs, often encouraged by funding council incentives, are now seeking to shift the balance of actual or perceived rewards between achievement in research and achievements in teaching. This involves senior management signalling and valuing the importance of excellence in teaching, and embedding this valuing of teaching within the institution's human resource strategy. Incentives such as promotion based largely (rather than exclusively) on teaching performance and the operation of a teaching excellence recognition and reward scheme (which may involve individual or group awards) are critical to the perceptions of staff of the importance among the institutions' priorities of teaching. The development and operation of such promotion or teaching awards schemes will involve educational development and senior management working closely together. It is important to develop, and very clearly apply, criteria that meet the needs of the institution and its students. Consideration must be given to the type of scheme to be operated, its cost and potential benefits.

Finally, although promotion or an award of itself provides rewards and incentives, there is more. Planning how excellent teachers can be used strategically will over time ensure that teaching performance is valued still more highly across the institution – excellent teachers can do more than either senior managers or educational developers to act as role models and motivate others.

There are many new and interesting teaching reward schemes being put in place in HEI's across the world. Ramsden *et al.* (1995) provide a comprehensive review of issues concerning recognition and reward of teaching based on the Australian experience, including the effectiveness of such schemes. Warren and Plumb (1999), following a survey of UK schemes, highlight the most common features of schemes and distinguish four types: 'traditional' award schemes, teaching fellowship schemes, educational grant schemes and promotion/bonus schemes. Gibbs and Habeshaw (2002) consider a range of approaches to the recognition and reward of teaching and provide a range of illustrative case studies. They also, usefully, consider issues raised by mechanisms to reward excellent teachers.

TOPIC 6 – ENHANCING THE EFFECTIVENESS AND EFFICIENCY OF LEARNING, TEACHING AND ASSESSMENT THROUGH LEARNING TECHNOLOGY AND OTHER FORMS OF FLEXIBLE LEARNING DELIVERY

SENIOR MANAGER: Do we know how many staff are using the university's Virtual Learning Environment (VLE), and how effective it is?

EDUCATIONAL DEVELOPER: A number of enthusiasts in each department have become 'early adopters', but I do have concerns about some of the educational effectiveness – and of course increasing the staff development effort around the VLE will cost.

SENIOR MANAGER: We introduced the VLE to increase flexibility for our full-time students, and to allow us to develop support for part-time and flexible learning students. We really have to think strategically about what we want to achieve with it.

EDUCATIONAL DEVELOPER: Well, we have a good steer within the Learning, Teaching and Assessment Strategy. But we do need to clarify targets and resources.

Most institutions make reference to the potential of more flexible forms of delivery, including online learning, within their strategies for learning, teaching and assessment. This is perhaps because, in the global market-place, institutions feel the need to respond to the perceived threat from the more exclusive world HE brands as well as the growing Corporate Universities. However, scaling up to mass markets through e-learning is only one reason for deploying learning technology. The technology plays an increasingly important role in the lives of students through providing a portal for their customized learning and learner support: a virtual or managed learning environment (VLE or MLE). Where this is taken on seriously and strategically, senior managers have a key role in leading, coordinating, supporting and appropriately resourcing or pump-priming this activity. Educational developers, on the other hand, need to be centrally involved in supporting the strategy through staff development. Developers also need to find ways to influence, and help to design in and embed, good practice in learner activity, learner support and assessment. Educational development must be actively encouraged and resourced by senior management if e-learning is to achieve its educational and efficiency potential.

Where there is a significant strategic drive and investment in, for example, online learning, and the determined development of an MLE, senior managers need to be centrally involved in developing vision, policy, managing a university-wide project plan. They also need to take a central role in coordinating the full range of institutional functions which will require to develop and implement successfully the MLE, e.g. educational development, computing services, library, registry, marketing, as well as academic input. Issues of organizational change to support online learning and MLE developments are often overlooked, as content-driven, supply-led e-initiatives founder in ever increasing numbers. If senior management and educational development can better share perspectives, information and expertise, and work together towards shared goals, the likelihood of success will be much greater.

TOPIC 7 – DEVELOPING SCHOLARSHIP AND RESEARCH IN LEARNING AND TEACHING TO UNDERPIN DEVELOPMENT AND CHANGE

SENIOR MANAGER: I notice that one of the objectives of our Strategy for Learning and Teaching is about developing a concept of scholarship within the teaching role. What will that involve?

EDUCATIONAL DEVELOPER: Well, it's part of the professionalization of teaching in higher education and the development of HE staff as reflective practitioners – as well as being recognized for their achievements in their subject, such staff are recognized for their abilities as research-informed teachers.

SENIOR MANAGER: I can see this happening in some areas – but it would mean a significant culture shift in others. How can we make progress?

EDUCATIONAL DEVELOPER: I guess it's partly to do with rewards, recognition and expectations – and the signals given within the institution.

There is a growing concept of teachers in higher education as reflective practitioners, who are not only subject experts within their discipline but whose approaches to learning, teaching and assessment are evidence-based and/or research informed. This involves developing a concept of scholarship of teaching which recognizes and rewards achievements in educational practice, the facilitation of learning, and research into learning and teaching practice. However, as has been pointed out by Beaty and Cousin (2002), 'practitioner research into university learning and teaching is relatively new'. It has not been helpful that the Research Assessment Exercise (RAE) in the UK has largely excluded the pedagogy of HE as a returnable unit of assessment. Thus, encouragement of the development of scholarship in learning and teaching and research into academic practice has been largely left to the enthusiasm of the individual. There has been little, if any policy and/or resource backing from institutions, despite the fact that this research and scholarship has significant positive impact on the quality of learning and teaching and on the individual academic's views of their role and practices.

If scholarship in teaching and practice-based research is to be successfully nurtured by educational development, senior management must overtly encourage this within the research and scholarship agenda of the institution.

This may involve rewards and encouragement being explicit, for example through support for membership of the Institute of Learning and Teaching in Higher Education (ILTHE) (in the UK) and involvement in the work of subject teaching networks; support for continuing professional development in teaching and learning; and enthusiasm for staff to publish in teaching-oriented journals. Activities such as these could be legitimized within an institution's appraisal scheme for academics, within promotion criteria or other aspects of the HR strategy. Also, as argued by Brew (2002), it is incumbent on educational development itself to be research-led and evidence-based!

TOPIC 8 – EFFECTIVELY USING GOOD GENERALISTS AND EXPERT SPECIALISTS TO SUPPORT ACADEMIC DEVELOPMENT

EDUCATIONAL DEVELOPER: There are a lot of really good people in this institution who are well respected in their own area, but could be used to better effect across the university, if we could loosen up some structures and boundaries – any thoughts?

SENIOR MANAGER: Some . . . we really need to think much smarter about how we can maximize our staff resources. We also need to get more from our IT and other specialists, and reduce 'tribalism'. Any suggestions how we can promote more project and team-working?

To be fully effective, educational development must work both closely and strategically at many local levels across the institution. This will become increasingly important as implementation of institutional learning and teaching strategies is devolved to departments and faculties (Gibbs 2000).

An effect of working at local level is that an (often) very small central educational development function can become very thinly spread. Strategic operational decisions need to be made in consultation with senior management as to where the resource is to be most productively focused. Often this may be influenced by the external agendas and internal priorities, as discussed in Topic 2 above.

Educational development can also provide mechanisms for sharing good practice across schools and faculties. These can include good practice showcase events, online good practice guides and the sponsorship of university-wide events and conferences focusing on sharing practice and experiences from within and outwith the institution. Where senior management and educational development have collaborated in implementing schemes to recognize and reward effective teaching, this can provide a network of role-models who can form the focus for development and sharing across the institution (Seden, 2002; Gibbs and Habeshaw, 2002). Napier University, for example, has appointed over 40 Teaching Fellows. They form a network of expertise with a legitimized development role which works closely with the central educational development function to support the implementation of the institution's strategy for learning, teaching and assessment. The Teaching Fellows scheme is highly valued in the institution, perhaps because it is supported through a financial increment; is warmly and publicly endorsed by senior management; and it is often a stepping stone to further promotion.

Some staff find it difficult to work in project teams, where loyalty and effort are geared towards project goals and outcomes, in contrast to the more familiar individual or departmental goals and ways of working. Senior management and developers can both help to develop a culture of cross-disciplinary project working. Educational development is usually skilled in working across an institution, and can facilitate project groups. Complementing this expertise in facilitation, senior management can act as a role-model for cross-disciplinary working by convening and driving some cross-institutional projects and priorities, such as user groups or resource-intensive strategic priorities such as online learning.

TOPIC 9 – KEEPING ABREAST OF THE EXTERNAL AGENDA (INCLUDING NATIONAL AND INTERNATIONAL DEVELOPMENTS) AND GOOD PRACTICE ELSEWHERE THROUGH NETWORKING AND ENVIRONMENTAL SCANNING

SENIOR MANAGER: I've just read your report on the recent Heads of Educational Development Group residential meeting – seems really interesting.

EDUCATIONAL DEVELOPER: Yes, it was – and good to meet up with my equivalents in other institutions again. It's great that there is so much sharing and collaboration. I often think there is too much insular debate in this University. I have a number of suggestions as to how we could encourage much more externalization of our academic practices.

Staff working in educational development are often very well networked. In the UK networks such as the Staff and Educational Development Association (SEDA) and the Heads of Educational Development Group (HEDG) provide national vehicles for sharing and debating ideas and forthcoming development. In Australia the Higher Education Research and Development Society for Australasia (HERDSA) acts as a similar network. Similarly, members of senior management have a range of professional networks, as well as links with government, government agencies and funding bodies, which inform and influence national policy and developments. Many of these development and management networks are supported by electronic discussion lists and useful websites.

Academic staff have their own, often discipline-based networks, as well as membership of organizations (in the UK) such as the Institute for Learning and Teaching in Higher Education (ILTHE) and involvement in subject-based learning and teaching networks such as provided in the Learning and Teaching Support Network (LTSN). These provide opportunities for external contact, sharing good practice and benchmarking.

It is important that institutional strategy, policy, debate and practice are all informed by analysis of international and national policy. Funding council reports, UK government White Papers and European declarations will each influence the sector, primarily through funding incentives and disincentives. Senior management and educational development can ensure that external policy, and more particularly its influence and impact on internal strategy, is well understood within the institution. At a more operational level, both senior management and educational development, together with departmental managers, can further help staff and departments to learn from experiences elsewhere. This learning can in turn inform internal benchmarking and quality enhancement activities. Examples could include a policy to increase the number of staff with external examinership appointments, or encouragement to participate in quality assurance activities and events, both at other institutions and nationally. In some institutions, senior management has organized a series of institutional raids where a group of staff, often led by a member of senior management, visit another institution or group of institutions to help inform strategic development and/or academic practice internally. Another model involves staff invited and funded to attend national events, or visit other institutions, on the condition that they fully disseminate their findings on return.

Together, senior management and educational development can help promote and facilitate a culture where external involvement and environmental scanning become integral to the work of staff across the institution.

CONCLUSION

In a higher education sector increasingly strategically driven and monitored by results against targets the agenda described in this chapter can only be achieved through a strong synergy between the senior management of an institution and its educational development function. They need to work closely together towards mass customization for a truly student-centred higher education practice.

The development and implementation of a progressive, developmental and change-oriented institutional agenda demands short, open and constructive lines of communication between all concerned; senior management, educational development, academics and support areas. It requires understanding and effective communication of the vision, objectives, imperatives, processes and implications of change. Senior management need to support change through appropriate resourcing, structural and practical work to promote cultural evolution and the embedding of appropriate change within the institution. The resource and structural implications of implementing and embedding change must be carefully analysed and identified. Agreements on these issues can usefully be formalized within an institution's annual planning processes.

The particular issues and strategic priorities for development will vary in importance and emphasis between HEIs. We have no doubt failed to mention what are key issues for some institutions. The personalities, politics and motivators of those centrally concerned in promoting change and development within institutions provide a complex set of factors which need to be understood, or at least accepted, for senior management and educational development to work constructively together. Accepting all these variables, however, little will happen without mutual respect; shared, even passionate commitment to goals; effective communication and dialogue; and a developed common ownership of directions, targets and operational processes. If these things are in place, then there is a solid basis for change and development across the institution.

REFERENCES

Beaty, L. and Cousin, G. (2002) Turning the light on ourselves: researching pedagogic practice and policy *Exchange* **3**, pp 23–4

Brew, A. (2002) Towards research-led educational development *Exchange* **3**, pp 25–6

Candy, P. C. (1966) Promoting lifelong learning: academic developers and the university as a learning organisation, *International Journal for Academic Development* **1**(1), pp 7–18

Gibbs, G. (2000) Learning and teaching strategies: the implications for educational development, *Educational Developments* **1**(1), pp 1–5 SEDA, Birmingham

Gibbs, G. and Habeshaw, T. (2002) *Recognising and Rewarding Excellent Teaching – A Guide to Good Practice* The Open University, Milton Keynes

Gosling, D. (2001) What educational development units do – five years on, *International Journal for Academic Development* **6**(1), pp 74–92

HEFCE (1999) *Institutional Learning and Teaching Strategies: A Guide to Good Practice*, Circular HEFCE 99/00, HEFCE, Bristol

Jackson, N. (2002) Principles to support the enhancement of teaching and student learning: implications for educational development, *Educational Developments* **3**(2), pp 1–6 SEDA, Birmingham

Land, R. (2001) Agency, context and change in higher education, *International Journal for Academic Development* **6**(1), pp 4–20

Ramsden, P., Margetson, D., Martin, E. and Clarke, S. (1995) *Recognising and Rewarding Good Teaching in Higher Education*, Australian Government Publishing Service, Canberra

Scott, P. (1995) *The Meaning of Mass Higher Education*, SRHE/Open University Press, Buckingham

Seden, R. (2002) Supporting excellence in teaching and learning through dispersed professional development, *Educational Developments* **3**(2), pp 5–7 SEDA, Birmingham

Stefani, L. (2003) What is educational and staff development in P. Kahn and D. Baume (eds) *A Guide to Staff and Educational Development* SEDA/Kogan Page, London

Warren, R. and Plumb, E. (1999) Survey of distinguished teacher award schemes in higher education, *Journal of Further and Higher Education* **23**(2), pp 245–55

3

Leading an educational development unit

Sue Thompson

INTRODUCTION

What is it that staff and educational development units do that needs to be led and managed? What are the leadership challenges for heads of staff and educational development units? How do effective leaders meet those challenges? These are the questions that this chapter seeks to address.

It is axiomatic, given the diversity of higher education institutions and the history of staff and educational development, that those with a leadership role in this area will be operating in a range of settings and that they will have a variety of functions and responsibilities. Further, not all those with a leadership role will be the head of an educational development unit, but may be leading initiatives and projects within or across institutions. Since the territory and the context are so varied, the purpose of this chapter will be, in the first major section, to illuminate some common leadership challenges and then to suggest strategies for tackling them. In doing this it will draw on a range of perspectives and case study examples from experienced staff and educational developers.

WHAT IS IT THAT STAFF AND EDUCATIONAL DEVELOPERS DO THAT NEEDS TO BE LED AND MANAGED?

A recent overview study of the current state of educational development in the UK summarized the central functions of educational development as being concerned with all, or a combination, of:

1 improvements of teaching and assessment practices, curriculum design and learner support – including the place of information technology in learning and teaching;

2   professional development of academic staff, or staff development;
3   organizational and policy development within the context of higher education;
4   learning development of students – supporting and improving effective student learning;
5   informed debate about learning, teaching, assessment curriculum design, and the goals of higher education; and
6   promotion of the scholarship of teaching and learning and research into higher education goals and practices

(Gosling 2001, p. 75)

All heads of educational development units who responded to the survey saw improving teaching and learning across the institution and providing staff development for learning and teaching as part of their remit. Almost all also thought that promoting innovation in learning, teaching and assessment was part of their role. The extent to which the remit of educational development units extended beyond provision of a service to being directly involved in influencing and developing policy varied. Increasingly educational development units see themselves as having an important role to play in promoting the scholarship of teaching and research into learning and teaching. Although not all educational development units will do all of these things, they can be said to reflect the range of functions of an EDU that need to be managed and led.

WHAT ARE THE LEADERSHIP CHALLENGES FOR STAFF AND EDUCATIONAL DEVELOPERS?

What is the biggest leadership challenge you have faced as head of an educational development unit? This question was put to heads of educational development units working in a range of contexts in an opportunistic sample via email exchange and telephone conversations. What follows is a paraphrased summary of their responses:

- getting it on the agenda was the hardest struggle;
- the time spent on internal politics, fighting to save the unit, or aspects of it, in terms of its location in the institution and its role in key policy developments;
- getting people to take teaching as seriously as research;
- establishing a clearly defined role for myself, understood by those in the unit and by the university at large;
- knowing how to act strategically in an organizational context;
- having a clear idea of what I wanted to achieve and setting priorities;

- knowing about the management of change and how to operate as a change agent;
- the importance of communication both within the team and across the university;
- developing skills in managing and leading a team;
- vulnerability of the unit, reliance on external funding and staff not being on permanent contracts;
- integrating academic and support staff within the unit;
- providing support and professional development for the team; and
- knowing whether you're making a difference – how do you measure impact?

Although this cannot be said to be a definitive or exhaustive list, it does highlight the range of challenges facing heads of staff and educational development units. It will also serve as a broad organizing framework for the rest of this chapter.

Getting it on the agenda

Comparative surveys of educational development in the UK (Gosling 1996, 2001) clearly show that educational development is now on the agenda in ways that it was not just a few years ago. There has been a considerable increase in the numbers of HEIs that have some kind of EDU and in the size and breadth of their institutional role. There is evidence that national policy is being strongly influenced by the ideas that have emerged from the educational development community and that there is a growing and maturing body of literature and research relating to pedagogy within higher education and a developing culture of educational development research (Gosling 2001). 'Getting it on the agenda' may be less of a challenge than it was, but there are continued challenges in keeping it on the agenda and, perhaps more particularly, in *mainstreaming* educational development.

The political challenge: being strategic

Historically the image of educational developers has been as warm, caring and infinitely supportive people, experts in what has been described, sometimes pejoratively, as the 'touchy feely' approach. Educational and staff developers are assumed to be skilled in the technical aspects of learning, teaching and assessment and in facilitating and providing staff development. For those in leadership roles the 'development' element has another dimension. It means knowing how to manage and provide leadership, and how to act strategically in an organizational context.

Arguably it has been the political element of their roles that educational developers were least well prepared for. In an article applying work on organizational change by management educators to higher education, Blackwell and Preece (2001) suggested that the failure to recognize and explicitly address the political element is a key weakness in the work of educational developers. They argue that the political dimension; what Buchanan and Badham (1999) describe as 'winning the turf game'; is a critical element in Higher Education. The challenge here for the leader of a development unit is to be politically effective without sacrificing their base of values. Baume's account of educational developers needing to be 'principled, proactive opportunists' (Baume 2003a: 160) addresses this point. Further, we need to know and understand our institutions well in order to function effectively within them.

The advent of the HEFCE Teaching Quality Enhancement funding in 2000 in support of institutional learning and teaching strategies presented educational developers with new opportunities and challenges. In an article which outlined the implications of learning and teaching strategies for educational development Gibbs (2000) described educational developers as being used to using tactics for helping individuals implement policy or improve practice, but less used to developing policy and devising mechanisms for implementing it. Although they may have superb interpersonal and training skills they have little in the way of organizational development experience. Gibbs argued that educational developers needed to become less focused on tactics and more strategic in the way they operate, aligning their help and efforts with institutional priorities rather than following their own interests or being merely reactive to requests from frequent or valued clients.

Competition with the research agenda

It is a dream; in some cases a goal; for many developers that teaching should have at least parity of esteem with research in the eyes of staff and the institution as a whole. Dearing reported 'our survey of academic staff indicates that only three per cent [of teaching staff] believe that the present system rewards excellence in teaching' (NCIHE 1997 Section 14.6). The figure Dearing reported would very likely by now be considerably higher, but we probably remain far short of parity of esteem. Gosling's (2001) survey of EDUs reported that the research culture, and the promotion and recognition that goes with success in publications, continues to militate against engagement with educational development for many staff. He concluded that competition with the research pressures created by the Research Assessment Exercise is as much an issue now as it was in 1995, the year of the original survey.

The recent White Paper on higher education (DfES 2003) devotes a chapter to delivering excellence in teaching and learning and sets out a clear agenda for valuing teaching and for rewarding and promoting good teachers. Putting promotions policies in place is one means of addressing the inequity between teaching and research. There is a role for educational developers here in working towards a closer integration between learning and teaching and human resource strategies. On their own, though, policies are not enough; much will depend on perceptions of how policy is implemented (or not) as a major determinant for staff in allocating their effort between research and teaching.

Educational development units should promote teaching and its improvement, but they do not need to do this in competition with research. There is evidence that a substantial number of EDUs see research as an important part of their work, and that even more see themselves as having a role in facilitating or promoting research into learning and teaching by others (Gosling 2001). Units may become more credible, more valued and hence more effective if they undertake research, and also if they support colleagues across the institution to seek funding for and undertake research, both in their own discipline and into teaching and learning.

Having a clearly defined and understood role

Research into the perceptions that educational developers have of their roles shows wide variations. These range from seeing support of the strategic objectives of the institution as their primary function to more neutral stances of supporting staff to cope with, or even subvert, senior management change initiatives (Badley and Land cited in Gosling 2001). Land's research on the ways that educational developers practise within specific organizational contexts and cultures identifies different orienta-tions that developers consider appropriate to the strategic terrain that they operate within. For example, a developer with a 'managerial' orientation will be most concerned with developing staff towards achievement of institutional goals and mission. Here the operational focus or level would be that of the institution. A 'vigilant opportunist' on the other hand will take advantage of developments and opportunities in a strategic way as they arise within the institution. In operating in this way their focus or level is that of the EDU. A 'reflective practitioner' will seek to foster a culture of self/peer evaluation and critical reflection amongst colleagues and will be most concerned with helping colleagues cope in uncertain and ambivalent environments. Here the operational focus is at the level of the individual practitioner. As Land says, in identifying twelve different orientations to educational development practice, educational developers can in some respects be described as a 'fragmented community of practice' (Land 2001).

Who are educational developers? What do they do and how should they do it? In a paper addressing questions of identity, ethics and organization for educational developers Andresen (1996) described an imaginary dinner party conversation where, as an educational developer, he attempts to describe his job to two other quests who work in public relations. Try it! How would you describe your role as an educational developer to someone else? How do you see your role as head of an educational development unit? How do others see your role?

> If only I had known that everyone in the university would have a different view of what my job entails. I realised that I couldn't hope to meet all their expectations.

> It is vital to have a clearly defined role, understood by those in the unit and by the university at large – otherwise people create it for you or at least assume you do things that you don't!

> There is a danger, as well as an attraction, in believing that you can help everyone. Be focussed!

Knowing how to manage change

The key leadership challenges here are two-fold. The first is knowing how to operate strategically in a climate of rapid and continual change. The second is the ability to work as an effective agent for change within the organizational culture. The work of educational developers is often, by its very nature, concerned with bringing about cultural change. It also involves working in areas where the territory may be contested. The educational developer is more likely to be familiar with the 'Long Marches' rather than the 'Bold Strokes' approach to change, although a bold stroke that captures and works well with a current institutional mood, enthusiasm, concern or priority can be very effective. The 'Long March' approach focuses on relatively small scale and operationally focused initiatives which are slow to implement and where the benefits are achieved in the long rather than the short term (Kanter *et al.* in Burnes 2000).

> You need to take the long view. The change process is almost imperceptible. You keep thinking that what you did last month/ year/three years ago had no impact at all, but maybe after that you'll see it take off, but you need to keep going back and stoking it in different ways so they don't notice you're nagging.

Buchanan and Boddy (1992) argue that the change agent has to engage in 'performing' and 'backstaging', that is, supporting the 'public performance' of rationally considered and logically phased and visibly participative change with 'backstage activity', in the recruitment and maintenance of support and in seeking and blocking resistance. Typical examples of 'backstaging' might be:

- How to get action from a senior manager who has given agreement, but who will not do anything practical, public or visible about it
- How to reconcile actual resource requirements with senior management expectations
- How to get the willing cooperation of other people, sections and functions during critical stages of implementation
- How to get those who are making unreasonable demands or requests to back-off tactfully
- How to avoid or to deal appropriately with other activities – whether urgent or trivial – that will delay progress by diverting staff energies and other resources in other directions

(Buchanan and Boddy 1992, p. 129)

Communication

Communication is important on several counts. It can be used for publicity, to keep people informed and 'on-side' and to support the work of groups and teams. Regular, not just one-off, effective and early communication is a means of avoiding the uncertainty that change can promote. It is also a means of getting people involved, of encouraging people to assist rather than resist change (Burnes 2000).

A very powerful communication tool is listening. 'Giving someone a good listening-to', as one developer described it, leaves the speaker feeling heard and understood and the developer with a lot of useful information and insight.

Communication is considered further below under 'Making it work'.

Keep those above you informed. I didn't as it felt creepy, but I realise that they need to know, even just a few bullet points each term with the promise of more information if they want it.

As a manager I've got a pretty good idea of what all my team are doing. . . . However, it's easy to forget that not everybody else you are working with has such a broad overview. . . . Even when working in such close proximity, team members can sometimes feel isolated.

Leading, managing and supporting a team

The leadership challenges of heads of educational development units are not just 'out there', across the university and beyond. They are also 'in here' in the responsibilities heads of EDUs have for leading and managing others. The research literature on management and leadership is vast and it is beyond the scope of this chapter to explore models of leadership. Ramsden defines leadership as 'a practical and everyday *process* of supporting, managing and developing and inspiring academic colleagues' (1998, p. 4). His target audience is primarily heads of academic departments but his work on leading in higher education is equally relevant to educational developers in leadership roles. Ramsden describes the leadership role as having multiple responsibilities. The issues a leader has to address are:

1 What do I want my work unit to achieve, and how can I enlist the support and resources I need to pursue these goals? This is the problem of *vision, strategy and planning*.
2 How do I provide the means for my staff team to achieve these objectives? This is the problem of *enabling academic people*.
3 How can I help my colleagues to develop their skills and align their personal goals with those of the work unit? How do I monitor their progress and assess their achievement? This is the problem of *recognising and developing performance*.
4 What do I need to do to survive and grow as an academic leader? How can I improve my own performance – and my university's performance? These are the closely related problems of *learning to lead* and *improving university leadership*.

(Ramsden 1998, p.132)

When I first became head of the unit I had confidence in myself as an educational developer based on my experience and track record. I didn't have a clue about managing a team or leading a unit. I've had to develop a whole new set of skills.

I think I had the idea that people in universities, and perhaps especially academics, don't like to be managed. That's not true. People want to be managed, and managed well.

The important thing for me is integrating the academic and support staff. Sometimes we educational developers speak as though it is self-evident what we do and what we are trying to achieve as we work. It is the leader's job to facilitate the understanding of each professional group by the other and to give value to both approaches.

I'm very aware that my team have their own professional development needs and there are challenges in identifying appropriate ways to meet these. Who develops the developers?

Measuring impact

The crunch question is, how do you know you're making a difference?

Historically educational development has seldom had to evaluate its impact in quantitative ways or think about setting measurable targets,

> [It] has been content to account for *inputs* (how many workshops run on putting a teaching portfolio together) rather than *outputs* (how many people submitted teaching portfolios as part of cases for promotion) let alone *outcomes* (has the culture changed so that teaching is valued to a greater extent?). We have a lot to learn about how to specify the outcomes of our efforts in useful and convincing ways, and how to measure the achievement of these outcomes.
>
> (Gibbs 2000, p. 4)

Evaluating the impact of an educational development unit presents particular challenges. Evaluating whether stated goals and objectives of the unit have been met is one thing. Knowing whether you have made a difference to the staff and student learning experience is more difficult to ascertain. The most comprehensive overview study to date of educational development units in the UK found that relatively few units were required to systematically evaluate their impact on the institution and that some new units had been created without any clear strategy for evaluation. The study concluded that there is a need for a more sophisticated approach to the evaluation of impact (Gosling 2001). The evaluation of staff and educational development is considered further in the chapter in this book on the impact of staff and educational development, and also in Baume (2003b 76–95).

MAKING IT WORK – STRATEGIES FOR EFFECTIVE LEADERSHIP

This section focuses on some practical strategies for addressing the leadership challenges that have been described by drawing on the views and suggestions of heads of educational development units working in a range of contexts. These practical hints and tips will also be supplemented by case study examples that focus in some more detail on a particular aspect of leading an educational development unit.

Be strategic

Being a head of an EDU is about *making things happen*. It's about influencing the structures, procedures and taken for granted assumptions of organizational life.

It is important to have clearly established strategic priorities and accompanying action plans. This enables you to make and report on progress and to evaluate.

As head of the unit I was responsible for co-ordinating the writing of our institutional learning and teaching strategy and for supporting its implementation across the university. This has been really important in giving the unit a more strategic role and profile within the university.

CASE STUDY 1: INTEGRATING POLICY AND PRACTICE: THE ROLE OF EDUCATIONAL DEVELOPMENT

The following case study focuses on the strategic role of an EDU in a university-wide management of change initiative. As head of the unit Professor Liz Beaty describes the key leadership challenges she faced and the strategies she used to address these challenges. Key aspects of leadership highlighted in this case study are the process of how people worked together and the importance of communication.

In 1997 I joined Coventry University as Head of Learning Development. My job involved leadership of a Task Force of seconded academics undertaking development projects in learning and teaching. My aim was to make more than the sum of the parts from these development projects. I wanted to develop the institution rather than simply provide a set of project outcomes. The opportunity was a valuable one. I had a strong champion in the PVC whose idea this had been. He wanted to create a critical mass of innovators to take Coventry University forward in relation to new technology in teaching. The secondments were half time for two years and so I had time to work with these staff to think about dissemination as well as production issues.

The leadership challenge was to create conditions where policy and practice were linked together. This involved three key objectives:

• developing qualities of change agency within the Task Force;

- creating systems for dialogue and discussion between different Schools and Departments across the University; and
- producing evidence based examples of innovation and action evaluation for a continuous development cycle.

We were fortunate in having two waves of change supporting our developments. The first was a strong push nationally for teaching quality to be taken seriously. With this background it was easier to gain resources for educational development and for creative staff to be interested in using their energies for this. The second was the inevitable imperative to experiment with new learning technology. This second trend allowed our softer focused developments in pedagogy to have a clearly articulated focus. We were all working to develop pedagogy but rather than being split into different subject groupings everyone was in one way or another focused on the need to harness the opportunities of new technology in their teaching.

My leadership was used in relation to the process of how we worked. I introduced action learning sets to encourage group based project planning and the inevitable sharing of ideas that this engenders. I also created a post of research assistant, providing the capacity for scholarship and evaluation for the Task Force projects through action research. We also met regularly in a larger group made up of Task Force, educational development specialists and representatives from service departments. This created a powerful group, cutting across departmental boundaries and hierarchies, and we used this to solve infrastructural problems in the way of change.

The key leadership qualities for educational and staff developers, based on my experience, are about communication. We need the techniques of action learning and action research to make institutional wide innovations embed widely but the key issue is creating a culture of inquiry, interest and innovation which transcends the boundaries created artificially by structural divisions. Being able to create opportunities for discussion and dialogue and creating a trusting backdrop where views are listened to is crucial to development. Just as individuals need to build confidence in order to learn and develop so too do institutions need to build confidence and mutual respect between different levels of the hierarchy. Educational development is fundamentally about the facilitation of discussion between policy and practice and across the institution.

Professor Liz Beaty, formerly Director of the Centre for Higher Education Development (CHED), Coventry University, currently Director of Learning and Teaching at the Higher Education Funding Council for England

Find champions/make alliances

My job was transformed when I got the support of a PVC who took teaching and learning seriously and understood what it is about.

It's important to have a senior champion in the university and to work constantly at keeping them informed, on-side and supportive.

Find your champions and get them working for you. Dig possible changers out of the woodwork and find what you can do for them.

Build strong alliances at all levels in the institution.

I think it's also important to build strategic alliances with other HEIs. It's important for a critical mass. We need to do more to exploit each other's skills and experience.

Be flexible – use a range of strategies

The goalposts changed as new PVCs were appointed and as the quality agenda changed. There was a need to respond swiftly.

Have a good flexible sense of direction but also be a strategic opportunist. Adopt several means of achieving your goals. Avoid getting trapped into a very restricted agenda (the fashion can pass, often with that senior manager).

Be credible

In terms of leading the unit, if I am successful I think a large part of that is through leading from the front, not expecting anyone to do things you don't do and to be good at it (Caesar's wife syndrome).

Be visible in terms of the strategy and provision. I make sure I open the induction programme for new staff and contribute to the management development sessions run by the unit.

I think I'm able to take a strategic role within the university on learning, teaching and assessment because of the credibility I have in turning things into practice.

Pay a lot of attention to credibility. Try to avoid being an internal critic, a whinger or a management groupie – they run the risk of alienating key constituencies.

Communicate

Communication is important as a leadership strategy for a range of reasons. It is a means of informing, of telling others about your work, but it is also about listening and hearing what people are saying. In the first extract Dr Helen King, an LTSN Subject Centre Manager, describes the communication strategy for her team and for a range of stakeholders. In the second extract Carole Baume, as national co-ordinator for FDTL projects describes the importance of good communications within a team that includes both educational developers and administrative and technical support staff.

Manage and support your team

I think it is vital to give others freedom and delegated authority but to be constantly interested in and supportive of what they do.

The most important thing I have learnt (and have to keep reminding myself to do) is about communication. I have responsibility for writing bi-annual reports to the funding councils so I need to be on top of all the information regarding our Subject Centre and wider HE issues. My team includes a UK-wide Steering Group and three Senior Advisers based in other institutions. We only meet up three times a year and communication by email, telephone conference and newsletters is vital to keep everyone up to speed in between times in order to make the most effective use of the limited time we have face-to-face. I also schedule time for regular meetings of the group based at the university. Although we work in adjacent offices and often informally compare notes or discuss issues, scheduled meetings are crucial for ensuring you know what they are doing and they know what you are doing. I've also started sending out monthly newsletters to our Steering Group and Senior Advisers to advise them on our recent and forthcoming activities from an 'internal' point of view. This hopefully will save time in meetings as we won't be spending hours getting everyone up to speed before we can start to discuss important issues. It's also important for the people I work with on a day-to-day basis, it's so easy to get so deeply into a piece of work you forget that no-one else has a clue what you are doing!

Dr Helen King, Centre Manager, Learning and Teaching Support Network Subject Centre for Geography, Earth and Environmental Sciences (LTSN-GEES)

My experience comes from leading a team where academic staff acted as national co-ordinators working with projects across the country, supported by a strong central administrative team. The co-ordinators were often out of the office, visiting projects and it was important that they found ways to share with the administrators some of the *feel* as well as the *facts* about the educational development work they did. Educational development is not a very well documented professional activity. Sometimes we educational developers speak as though it is self-evident what we do and what we are trying to achieve as we work. Equally, educational developers often do not fully understand the requirements of a good administrative system with its emphasis on collecting specified data and following specified procedures. Tension can ensure. It is the role of the leader of the unit to facilitate the understanding of each professional group by the other and to give value to both approaches. I think similar tensions can also be felt between learning technologists and non-technologists, between educational developers and the faculty staff with whom they are working. It's the head of the unit's job to prevent and resolve such tensions. How should they do this? Clear and agreed unit or project goals, methods and operating plans are important but they are not enough. It is also necessary for each professional group to understand, and if possible also to respect, the values base of the other group.

Carole Baume, National Co-ordination Team, Centre for Higher Education Practice, Open University

About eighteen months ago we achieved Investors in People accreditation as a team. Working towards IiP was useful in that it provided us with a development framework and it involved everyone.

Providing appropriate development opportunities for the team has been a real challenge. Our team administrator is now working to provide our VLE (Virtual Learning Environment) systems administration and resource support which I suppose is an example of 'on the job' development. Our Learning Technology Manager has started an MA in Research in Learning Technologies and the member of the team who has a particular responsibility for work based learning and professional development is undertaking an Open University PG Certificate in Life Long Learning. Another member of the team who has joined the team from an academic research background is enrolled for the university's Postgraduate Certificate in Learning & Teaching in Higher Education.

When it comes to managing, the leader needs to be an effective delegator. The leader of the unit needs to have a wide knowledge/understanding but must also be able to delegate or call on others within/outside the institution to help facilitate change.

Take a research focus to the work of the unit

CASE STUDY 2: PROMOTING EDUCATIONAL DEVELOPMENT IN A RESEARCH-LED ENVIRONMENT: STRIKING THE RIGHT BALANCE

Engaging research orientated academics in learning and teaching developments is a particular challenge for educational developers. Increasingly educational development units are taking a research focus to their own work. Gosling's survey of EDU's found that 66 per cent of respondents had undertaken research in learning and teaching as part of their work, with more planning to do so. Even if not pursing research themselves more EDU's see it as part of their role to facilitate or promote research into learning and teaching by others (Gosling 2001).

In this case study, Dr Paul Blackmore describes how the Centre for Academic Practice at the University of Warwick promotes educational development in a research-led environment. In this case study a key leadership quality highlighted is that of pragmatism, of striking the right balance between being research-orientated and also intensely practical.

The University of Warwick is a research-intensive institution, with all but one of its departments rated 5 or 5* at RAE 2001. For many staff, teaching is not the prime activity; they see themselves as undertaking teaching, research and administration/management, usually in closely inter-related ways.

The title of Centre for Academic Practice was chosen with care, displaying an intention to work with the grain of the institution, rather than in spite of it. The majority of CAP's activity is, nevertheless, in the support of teaching and learning development. In such a context, trying to develop teaching in isolation may be a mistaken strategy, since it ignores the motivating influence of research and the beneficial links between research and teaching that are there to be made. CAP therefore purposely makes and strengthens links.

A TLTP-funded project TELRI (Technology-Enhanced Learning in Research-Led Institutions), based in CAP, sought to find ways that higher level capabilities could be developed through the focused use of learning technologies. More recently, a research-based learning initiative has investigated real and potential links across the university and has developed a four-part model that emphasizes common processes, research cultures and research tools alongside the 'cutting edge' research into the curriculum link that is commonly recognized. An Undergraduate Research Scholarship Scheme (URSS) has been launched, enabling a number of undergraduate students to participate in live research projects, alongside academic staff.

One might expect an academic community to be rigorously critical when invited to review its practices. Many ideas on approaches to teaching make little headway in universities because they appear to be based on un-evidenced assertion. CAP seeks to be research-orientated, basing the advice it offers to staff on its own research and that of others. At the same time it has to be intensely practical: it is a difficult balance to strike.

Disciplinarity is an important force in all higher education institutions, and particularly so in research-led institutions. In addition, Warwick faculties are weak and departments strong, and there is little tradition of interdisciplinarity. Teaching development must therefore take account of disciplinary difference if it is to be acceptable. The mandatory award for probationary teachers has required significant extra resourcing to ensure that delivery and materials reflect disciplinary difference. In reality, the differences may not be as great as is often supposed, and many participants note the value of cross-university discussion, but paying close attention to disciplinarity is vital.

Academic staff may often be meticulous about their research methodology but less careful about their approaches to preparing for and evaluating teaching. Ideally, one might like to encourage staff to turn their research rigour on to their own practice. This is not straightforward, partly because of the immense variety in research methods employed across a university and because of the nature of teaching and learning, that often requires particular approaches. However, introductions to practitioner-based research frameworks and evaluation tools help academic staff to review and develop their practice. Particular attention has to be paid to differences in scientific and social–scientific research paradigms if outright rejection is not to occur on occasion.

Promotion procedures are of great importance. Educational development units are often surprisingly remote from this source of influence. Traditionally, promotion has been on the basis of research excellence, and intangible rewards, such as the esteem of colleagues, have reinforced this. At Warwick, there has been a recognition for some years that promotion for teaching excellence should be possible. However, few such promotions took place, mainly because applications looked insubstantial when set against research cases which marshalled objective evidence. CAP has been extensively involved in assisting the University to devise procedures by which teaching applications can be made and can be judged, and also in helping staff to assemble evidence in a convincing fashion. Once again, this offers a way of bringing evaluation practice to the notice of academic staff.

Finally, research-active staff are under particular pressures. It is helpful if academic development staff are themselves active researchers or, at least, scholars. They can thus understand academic roles and their perspectives, and can gain the credibility that comes with having a research profile.

The leadership qualities that appear to be required in this context are an ability to be pragmatic, to realize that others will see the world differently, to appreciate that apparent difficulties can be turned to advantage, and to know that a full-frontal assault on an issue is not always the most effective way of proceeding.

Dr Paul Blackmore, Director, Centre for Academic Practice, University of Warwick

A view from within

The head of an educational development unit has to engage in a balancing out between managing what happens 'out there', that is across and beyond the institution, and 'in here', within their own team. Here staff working in the Learning Development Unit at Liverpool John Moores University provide a view from within the unit. What follows is a summary of their responses to the question 'what would you hope or expect a leader/manager of an educational development unit to do as part of their role?'

THE 'IN HERE' ROLE

- provide clear goals and expectations for the team in terms of working practices and achievement of targets;
- be a mentor/coach to less experienced team members to help them develop personally and professionally;
- be a manager in terms of the personnel function-appraisal, review, holiday requests, references, etc.;
- provide clear, concise, fair feedback to team members on their performance, abilities as well as on specific materials/activities produced/undertaken by the team member; and
- respond to ideas generated by team members.

THE 'OUT THERE' ROLE

- ensure the unit has a clear remit (that is, has a distinct role compared with other units, for example, staff development);
- advance the case of educational development with senior management in terms of initiatives that unit is involved with;
- represent and champion the ideals of pedagogy, even if these are at odds with other strategic developments;
- raise the profile of learning and teaching amongst all staff;
- network with other people in similar roles in other universities;
- bring in new ideas to the team for action;
- ensure the unit leads by example;
- participate in research/projects either internally or externally so that your own knowledge practice is current;
- network with other managers of a similar level within the institution;
- be the conduit for the advancement of team initiatives and ideas dependent on university structures;
- be knowledgeable about new initiatives/developments in the sector;
- have vision – looking ahead in terms of strategy;
- be up to date in terms of innovative/effective practice;
- be good at networking;
- facilitate groups to work together on projects;
- be strong on ideas – don't necessarily have to implement them;
- summarize key documents/synthesise the information in a user friendly way.

A FINAL WORD

The Premiership model?

Being head of a staff and educational development unit is more akin to being a team manager than a team captain. It's not just about strategy, motivation and scoring goals, it's also about booking coaches and hotel rooms, negotiating pay claims and transfer deals, marketing and getting bums on seats.

Leading an educational development unit is indeed a complex and multi-faceted role. The challenges are many and varied and there is no blueprint for success. The exemplars and case studies described in this chapter are based on the experiences of heads of educational development units and on their own strategies for effective leadership. Is it possible, in concluding, to highlight *one* key strategy? Staff and educational development units have grown in number and in their strategic importance for learning and teaching development. But they can also be vulnerable. They may be dependent on external funding to support their activities; they are likely to have staff on fixed term contracts. They can easily become the casualty of internal re-organization. In this context, a key leadership strategy for heads of educational development units is to have a focus on *evaluating impact.* Arguably it is not enough for the unit to be able to measure its own impact, it is also important that this impact is recognized by others:

> You have to have hard-edged tools that demonstrate 'cost benefits' in the language that institutional leaders and finance directors understand!

> You have to make sure that your allies can and do talk about your work. It is not sufficient that they thank you/the Centre/Unit. They need to be ambassadors for the effectiveness of the unit with other staff, with managers and with other stakeholders.

> We developed the evaluation strategy of the unit as integral to the evaluation model for the institutional learning and teaching strategy. . . . This gives us feedback as well as some sense of how what we do is having an impact. On its own, though, this isn't enough – it's what you then do with this evidence of impact that's important. That's the strategic bit!

ACKNOWLEDGEMENTS

I would like to thank my colleagues in the Learning Development Unit at Liverpool John Moores University and all the leaders in educational development who responded to my informal survey. In sharing their strategies for effective leadership they have greatly informed this chapter. Thanks to:

Carole Baume, Open University; David Baume, Higher Education Consultant; Professor Liz Beaty, University of Coventry and now HEFCE; Dr Paul Blackmore, University of Warwick; Sheila Browning, Kingston University; Professor Diana Eastcott, University of the West of England; Hazel Fullerton, University of Plymouth; Professor George Gordon, University of Strathclyde; Sandra Griffiths, University of Ulster; Dr Steve Ketteridge, Queen Mary College, University of London; Dr Helen King, GEES, LTSN Subject Centre; Richard Latimer, University of Huddersfield; Kristine Mason O'Connor, University of Gloucestershire; Professor Gus

Pennington, Educational Development Consultant and formerly HESDA; Chris Rust, Oxford Brookes University; and Professor Brenda Smith, LTSN Generic Centre

REFERENCES

Andresen, L. (1996) The work of academic development-occupational identity, standards of practice, and the virtues of association, *The International Journal for Academic Development*, 1(1), pp 38–49

Baume, D. (2003a) Far too successful? in *Case Studies in Staff and Educational Development*, (eds) H. Edwards and D. Baume, London, Kogan Page

Baume, D. (2003b) Monitoring and evaluating staff and educational development, in *A Guide to Staff and Educational Development*, (eds) P. Kahn and D. Baume, London, Kogan Page

Blackwell, R. and Preece, D. (2001) Changing higher education, *The International Journal of Management Education*, 1(3), pp 3–13

Buchanan, D. and Badham, R. (1999) *Power, Politics and Organisational Change: Winning the Turf Game*, Sage, London

Buchanan, D. and Boddy, D. (1992) *The Expertise of the Change Agent: Public Performance and Backstage Activity*, Prentice Hall, Hemel Hempstead

Burnes, B. (2000) *Managing Change: a Strategic Approach to Organisational Dynamics*, 3rd edn, Prentice Hall, Harlow

Dearing, R. (1997) *Higher Education in the Learning Society*, Main Report, The National Committee of Inquiry into Higher Education, HMSO, London

DfES (2003) *The Future of Higher Education*, HMSO, London

Gibbs, G. (2000) Learning and Teaching Strategies: the implications for educational development, *Educational Developments*, 1(1), pp 1–5

Gosling, D. (1996) What do UK educational development units do?, *The International Journal for Academic Development*, 1(1), pp 75–83

Gosling, D. (2001) Educational development units in the UK – what are they doing five years on?, *The International Journal for Academic Development*, 6(1), pp 74–90

Land, R. (2001) Agency, context and change in academic development, *The International Journal for Academic Development*, 6(1), pp 4–20

Ramsden, P. (1998) *Learning to Lead in Higher Education*, Routledge, London

4

Leading programmes in learning and teaching

Ali Cooper

BY WAY OF INTRODUCTION

As I start to write this, the phone rings . . . one of the postgraduate participants, anxious to find out whether her submission is good enough to have passed.

Last night I checked my email – a message from a professor with whom I am working on a research project offering an unsolicited and not wholly positive critique of yesterday's Learning and Teaching in Higher Education (LTHE) programme workshop which he attended, letting me know how he would have preferred it to be run.

I marked a portfolio yesterday, and read how valuable the LTHE programme has been for this new member of staff in formulating her beliefs and developing her teaching practices with students, and how thankful she is to have done it, despite it being hard to fit it in.

Earlier in the week a new lecturer tells his Head of Department, who has 'sent' him on the LTHE programme to be 'taught to teach', that he left after one session because it wasn't helping him to teach. The Head of Department publicly declares that this confirms his suspicion that the programme is not appropriate, and that he is willing to advise me on how to improve it for his staff.

A meeting later that day with the colleague in charge of Graduate Teaching Assistants (GTAs) to ask me if we might make part of the LTHE programme mandatory for all GTAs as it is both necessary and valued. Another senior colleague joins us later, to argue that the programme is too long and too good for most new staff – 'a Rolls Royce when they only have the time for a Mini'.

Each day there have been emails requesting information or places on the upcoming LTHE programme from volunteer individuals or heads of department.

This is a not untypical week of diverse responses and sometimes contradictions in the life of an LTHE programme.

Designing and managing a programme for university teachers has felt, for this programme leader at least, both similar and markedly different from the experience of leading and teaching more conventional university courses for undergraduates and postgraduates.

The similarities lie largely in the requirements and conventions of any structured learning programme in any university; decisions to be made about aims and intended learning outcomes, curriculum content and sequence, teaching, learning and assessment methods and the familiar rest.

So, wherein lie the differences between this and any other university course? And how is it that such a programme can seem simultaneously excellent and awful, appropriate and irrelevant, resented and highly valued, chaotic and systematic, nebulous and perfectly clear, over-flexible and over-rigid, prescriptive and open-ended, a trial and a privilege to work on? This chapter emerges from my long-standing interest in the differences between participants' responses, and from my desire to find appropriate responses in the course design and the teaching. The discussion below derives from my experiences of leading two LTHE programmes, one in a post-1992 and one in a pre-1992 UK university. The range of responses within each programme was familiar, despite detailed differences in programme construction.

This suggested to me that many common issues arising for programme designers and course tutors were less to do with the local mechanics or detailed models of individual programmes, and more to do with the experience of learning to teach in a complex and situated context, in which an LTHE programme is only a part. Figure 4.1 illustrates this wider context of perceived inter-related purposes, priorities and desired outcomes, and underlying principles held by a variety of concerned 'stake-holders', which impact on the participants' response to the programme. These various perceptions are expressions not only of concerns and values, but also expressions of potentially competing interests, recurrent or traditional practices, contextual drivers and prior experiences. A distinction also needs to be made between explicit values, such as the need to find a variety of ways to supporting the diversity of students' learning, and those that are more tacit, such as unspoken assumptions made by experienced subject colleagues about how their subject must be taught.

The inter-play between these sources of interest in the LTHE programme often results in contested and competing principles, priorities and purposes which have to be acknowledged and managed. Rather than viewing this as problematic, I believe we need to accept the

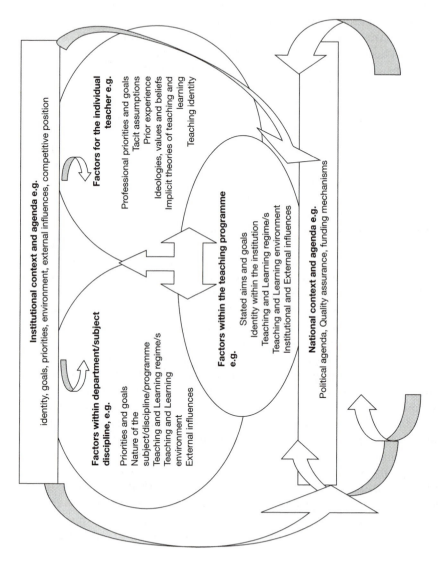

Institutional context and agenda e.g.
identity, goals, priorities, environment, external influences, competitive position

Factors for the individual teacher e.g.

Professional priorities and goals
Tacit assumptions
Prior experience
Ideologies, values and beliefs
Implicit theories of teaching and learning
Teaching identity

Factors within department/subject discipline, e.g.

Priorities and goals
Nature of the subject/discipline/programme
Teaching and Learning regime/s
Teaching and Learning environment
External influences

Factors within the teaching programme e.g.

Stated aims and goals
Identity within the institution
Teaching and Learning regime/s
Teaching and Learning environment
Institutional and External influences

National context and agenda e.g.
Political agenda, Quality assurance, funding mechanisms

Figure 4.1

inherent impossibility of finding, let alone implementing, ideal solutions or even 'best' practices. In so doing, we can then welcome and productively use the tension fields within the LTHE programme as dynamic environments for learning.

I analyse below some of the interesting tensions and dilemmas I have encountered in my work. (For heuristic purposes only I have accentuated the competing nature of these tensions by framing them with the term 'versus'.) These examples derive from my own teaching, and from working with colleagues who lead similar programmes throughout the UK – normally postgraduate certificates professionally accredited by the Staff and Educational Development Association (SEDA) and/or the Institute for Learning and Teaching in Higher Education (ILTHE). These programmes normally seek to develop theory-referenced reflective practice, and are usually assessed by portfolio. Using vignettes to illustrate critical incidents (critical incidents defined here as stimuli for meaning-making) I suggest how the tension fields might be transformed productively and creatively to inform the design and management of an LTHE programme. These vignettes have emerged from fifteen in-depth participant interviews and from tutorials over a five year period.

The categorizing of the tension fields in Figure 4.2 into the three (circled) sections is problematic as they are by nature inter-dependent. Again they are separated here for heuristic analysis only to emphasize key concepts. **Loci for learning to teach** acknowledges that learning to teach takes place in a variety of locations and is perceived as being located differently by individuals and groups. **Approaches to learning to teach** recognizes the diverse perceptions about how learning to teach happens. **Academic identities** emphasizes the central importance of agency in learning to teach, and concerns itself with how academics perceive their role and function as a teacher in relation to their other roles.

The various competing tensions might fit into two or even all three of these categories. As one example, 'Learner as Individual versus Communities of Practice' touches upon issues of identity, loci for learning and approaches to learning. That is, whether learning to teach is seen as more or less of an individual or a socially dependent act relates closely to where such learning can then take place and how one will go about the learning.

EXPERIENTIAL LEARNING VERSUS THE TAUGHT LTHE PROGRAMME

For communities of practice theorists, legitimate peripheral participation in real contexts of practice is the most authentic and effective induction

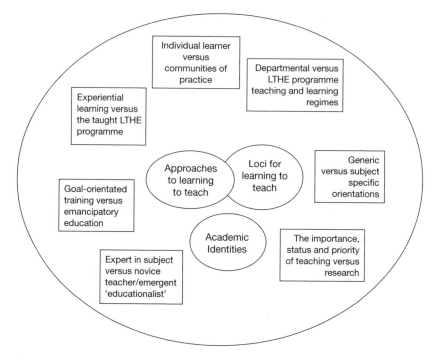

Figure 4.2

procedure into professions (Lave and Wenger 1991; Wenger 2000). However, empirical research into initial school teacher training suggests that training courses are effective in changing conceptions of teaching and thus practice (Entwistle *et al.* 2000). Teaching may be seen primarily as a craft, a process of applying given techniques (a not uncommon view in either novice or experienced HE practitioners). When this view is taken, then learning to teach will be done largely through osmosis, apprenticeship, modelling, imitation, and sheer weight of experience. By contrast, teaching, learning and knowledge-creation may be conceived more as a dynamic meaning-making interaction, in which the construction and analysis of one's own beliefs and practices are taken to be as equally important as mastering techniques. When this view is taken, then an LTHE programme is perceived as appropriate and vital. In order to accommodate this range of views about learning to teach, participants need engage in a variety of activities such as peer observation with colleagues, collecting and interpreting meaningful student feedback, analysing critical moments in their everyday teaching, re-considering their own past learning experiences, positioning themselves as learners during the LTHE programme, critically reading theoretical discussions. Such activities require participants to look through a variety of critically reflective lenses, each of which 'illuminates a different part of our teaching. Taken together, they throw into sharp relief the contours of our assumptive clusters' (Brookfield 1995: 28).

DEPARTMENTAL VERSUS LTHE PROGRAMME TEACHING AND LEARNING REGIMES

Lecturers, like their students, work within an academic environment; this environment includes their discipline as well as the academic department . . . and the institution in which they work. Ways of going about teaching are the outcome of a teacher's perception of the conditions defined by the context of teaching. At the same time, his or her understanding of teaching is influenced by this context.

(Ramsden 1992: 118)

The ways in which teaching and learning are assumed to take place within a discipline are often not rationalized or examined, and are accepted as a set of mutually accepted givens. HE teachers are inducted over a long time into these social processes, first through their own academic experiences as successful students and then as lecturing staff and researchers. Values and practices explored within an LTHE programme can be perceived or experienced by some participants, and often by their non-participating departmental colleagues, as being in potential or actual conflict with the predominant teaching and learning traditions of their department or discipline. This is often because the ideas simply do not fit with what has been termed elsewhere the existing Teaching and Learning Regime within a department.

'TLR' (Teaching and learning regimes) is a shorthand term for a constellation of rules, assumptions, practices and relationships related to teaching and learning issues in higher education.

(Trowler and Cooper 2002: 221)

Therefore, when teaching approaches or principles are suggested by an LTHE programme tutor, they may be dismissed as being simply inappropriate or impossible in a particular subject or context. For example, the use of discursive small-group activities with the lecturer in a facilitative rather than a transmissive role may be seen as only relevant in 'opinion-based' disciplines.

It is sometimes presumed that the LTHE programme cannot be examining different approaches neutrally or critically but must in fact be promulgating a particular and alternative regime to the one which is already known and tacitly accepted by a disciplinary tradition. And indeed this might be the case, either inadvertently or intentionally. The individual's teaching is tightly embedded in a social context that lies outside of the LTHE programme – (Knight 2002; Trowler and Cooper 2002). Individual participants may bring ideas about teaching approaches back to the department to have them soundly rejected as 'not the way we do things round here'. The discourse of the LTHE programme community might be different from that of the department:

F., a postgraduate teaching assistant, was told in no uncertain terms in a department meeting where she shared some ideas about teaching from the LTHE programme that 'we are not teachers; we are academics' and her suggestions were dismissed. The notion of being a 'teacher' was an alien and unwelcome role which did not fit with the sense of identity and conception of academic practice that predominated in this particular university culture.

Change necessitates surfacing and then rethinking aspects such as our teaching identity in relation to students; challenging long-held or tacit assumptions about how learning takes place; and critically analysing traditional practices. This is often a complex and rather disturbing process, which can be discomfiting and even alienating. Contrary practices, views and advice can be confusing and unsettling for inexperienced participants in the early days of their teaching. Replies to questions with responses such as 'well, it depends how you define . . .', can be interpreted as avoidances or lack of specific knowledge and advice, compared with the more assured do's and don'ts offered within the department.

The LTHE curriculum needs to be very carefully constructed, the delivery managed and relationships handled in ways which avoid appearing to promulgate singular regimes or to be negative about those to which participants belong. Instead, the programme's advantage can be in offering analytical tools and activities whereby existing and alternative practices and assumptions can be illuminated, rationalized and tested in an open and neutral environment away from the department where such misgivings can be shared and critically examined for their significance.

INDIVIDUAL LEARNERS VERSUS COMMUNITIES OF PRACTICE

Is learning to teach in HE predominantly an individual endeavour or is it a social activity, situated and inextricably embedded within the practices and beliefs of the academic departmental community? An additional community of practice (Chaiklin and Lave 1993; Wenger 1998) develops within the LTHE programme. Many participants feel that the programme community values and enthuses about teaching in ways that do not happen within a department. They often report that coming at a regular and prescribed time to think exclusively about teaching allows them to devote concentrated and dedicated space to their teaching work, which they would not otherwise do.

Conversely, other participants can find such a 'community' rather alien to their other working environments. They report feeling irritated by a perceived clash in cultures, such as experiencing discussions as too drawn out, open-ended or 'touchy-feely', when what they prefer is to be given definitive facts and knowledge about teaching to take away and apply in as short a time-frame as possible. These differences are often constructed as subject differences – 'medical students are from Mars – business and psychology students are from Venus' (Stevenson and Sander 2002). Such stereotyping is simplistic and inaccurate, as participants discover within a cross-disciplinary LTHE programme that offers the opportunity to construct a complementary community of practice, functioning positively to support its members whilst seeking not to alienate them from other, and stronger, academic communities to which they belong.

THE IMPORTANCE, STATUS AND PRIORITY OF TEACHING VERSUS RESEARCH

Teaching competes with research. Academic reputation, departmental status and individual promotion in many institutions are based on research output (Becher and Trowler 2001: 78). Senior department staff sometimes discourage or block enrolment on a LTHE programme.

J. was told by her Head of Department not to bother submitting an assignment, and M. was asked if she could not speed up or reduce her effort for the assessment submission, because it was interfering with her research priorities. P. did not want his colleagues to know that he was enrolling on the LTHE programme. When experienced lecturers show sufficient interest in their teaching to enrol voluntarily on the LTHE programme, they are sometimes assumed by colleagues to have either poor teaching skills which need remediating, or inferior research capacity which necessitates them concentrating on their teaching. Where institutional policy requires participation in an LTHE programme, more subtle subversion techniques at departmental level can be seen – a little reminiscent of draft dodging.

Explicit discussion of these competing priorities as part of the LTHE programme's curriculum illuminates institutional and departmental cultures and practices. Acknowledging the existence of stronger competitive forces with departments helps to position the programme more realistically. Action-research projects or scholarly articles for external publication, which draw upon or contribute to research practices and departmental concerns, may be more attractive and worthwhile to participants and their colleagues in departments.

J. wrote a piece addressed to her department on how to write appropriate learning outcomes. R. wrote an article addressing a nationally recognized teaching concern for colleagues in her subject which she distributed in her department for comment and information. S. conducted an action-research project on the reasons why non-mathematicians were apparently phobic in areas of his and other subject disciplines.
All three pieces were published within the University.

GENERIC VERSUS SUBJECT SPECIFIC ORIENTATIONS

There is often a perception that LTHE programmes operate within a social science paradigm; as indeed to a large extent they are bound to. Participants, particularly from some hard and applied science departments, often begin the LTHE programme questioning the extent to which they can gain from generic courses or cross-disciplinary dialogue, seeing their own subject as unique and too specialized. Others have less of a problem with this from the outset. But it is not always so:

V., an experienced university teacher of a hard science, welcomed the chance to discuss and compare practices with inexperienced colleagues

> from Women's Studies and Music, whereas both S. and T. from Sociology commented that the approach of the LTHE programme was less relevant to their disciplinary practices.

Most LTHE participants, if not their departmental colleagues, come in time to see cross-disciplinary collaboration as a powerful opportunity to illuminate the traditional practices of their subject or department, challenging assumptions and offering fresh approaches differently from discussions between discipline or departmental colleagues. Peer exchange and peer observation are often cited as the two most powerful elements within the LTHE programme.

However, it is important that the LTHE programme finds ways to cause participants to explore and articulate concepts of teaching and learning in the context of their discipline, to examine the epistemological issues in working with students as well as the pedagogical ones. It is also important that this is seen to be done, in order not to trivialize teaching. Encouraging participants to engage in scholarly and research activities within the LTHE programme, and to seek publication of their investigations into the teaching of their subject in refereed journals (and preferably subject-specific titles), can help to elevate the work and reduce the status gap between teaching and research.

> D. published part of his LTHE programme portfolio, an article which examined the conceptual parallels between the subject matter and the ways of teaching it, in a specialist journal in his discipline. M. had his retrospective examination of changes in teaching his subject over a 20 year period, which he had written as the assessment for the LTHE programme, published in an educational journal.

EXPERT IN SUBJECT VERSUS NOVICE TEACHER/EMERGENT 'EDUCATIONALISTS'

Some participants embarking on the LTHE programme feel themselves to be re-positioned as novices when they are accustomed to being an expert in their field, and find this uncomfortable – especially regarding the assessment of their practice. Others have no problem with this.

F., an international medical researcher, had no difficulty in seeing himself simultaneously as an expert in his field and a beginner in teaching, and deferred entirely to what he saw as the authority of the LTHE programme. H., like F., happily framed the programme and its tutors as 'expert' and himself as 'novice' despite several years' teaching experience; he however was a professional mediator and long-standing social science academic.

A., an experienced sociologist who had taught for just a year, questioned the assessment criteria for the LTHE programme and wished to write her own. She believed herself to be in a better position to judge the quality of her thinking and practice than the programme assessors could be. She saw the criteria as imposing a distorting and disempowering control over her own expertise, needs and interests.

These contrasting responses occurred despite the programme being explicitly positioned as democratic, and born from a constructivist conceptual model of learning and teaching.

Equally, a preconception of teaching where expertise in one's subject equates with the ability to teach it – the more traditional view of university teaching – affects one's sense both of what there is to learn and of how it can and should be learned.

F. believed that many academics are naturally solitary, especially hard scientists like himself. He preferred to learn alone from books and thinking quietly if he had the choice. He was willing to accept that, as a socially constructed activity, teaching was not easily learned in this way, but he was not alone in finding collaborative, discussion-based group activities uncomfortable.

Academics have forged successful and preferred approaches to their learning which they are often reluctant to give up or broaden. Providing some choice and variety whilst retaining some core curriculum and experiences would seem the best compromise. LTHE programme designs need to create opportunities for private study, electronic communication, active group workshops, discussion-based seminars, peer-led learning sets, quiet thinking time in sessions, encouragement to consult and critique literature, experimenting in their own teaching classrooms, action-research enquiry, writing reflectively and analytically, making oral presentations. As with student learning, it is essential that LTHE programme participants feel relatively safe. Excessive exposure or challenge tend to alienate and alarm people, making open-mindedness more difficult to foster.

Drawing – with sensitivity – on the links between the learning of students and of programme participants, encouraging participants to articulate their misgivings and discomforts by framing them up as typical student experiences, can diffuse and redirect negative feelings into constructive learning events. One of the great values of the LTHE programme is to demonstrate and explore the experience of learning and teaching, in the moment. This can also serve to distance and protect the programme tutor's own feelings and responses. Leading and teaching on such a programme can feel very exposing – the programme is very public, the 'students' are articulate adults, they are also one's colleagues, and the subject matter of the course is also the means through which it is being taught – one's own teaching is very much on display. Discontent with an LTHE programme session activity or outcome can be discussed in terms of the diversity of learner responses to teaching approaches, and how this might be accommodated.

> M., a programme participant, used a remark by a tutor in a programme workshop which had offended her as the basis for writing a short critical incident piece for her assessment that helped her to understand her own students. This required her to be frank about the tutor, and she needed to feel safe that such critical analysis would be welcomed and would not disadvantage her at the point of marking. This required the tutors to try to be open-minded and to know their own tolerance thresholds when they invite critical comment.

Participants sometimes resist what they see as a requirement to hand over their autonomy to others; they contest the imposition of LTHE programme or external body principles, values and objectives as irrelevant and 'impertinent':

It is my experience that being on a course and being taught and assessed by people who are, in effect, peers brings out certain behaviours in staff. Suddenly the tables are turned: however much the course leaders may negotiate the content and structure of the LTHE programme, the participants may still experience a sense of loss of power, they feel they are being dropped into a disciplinary environment which is alien to them ('I don't want to become an educational researcher'), with a discourse which they do not share. Some participants, even though they may be intrinsically motivated to do the programme, feel that they should not have to fit into a systematic programme with rules and requirements which are not of their making.

(Wareham 2001)

W. did not see any validity in writing about her teaching at all. V. disliked the external accreditation criteria, describing them as ideologically biased. Such complaints about the appropriateness of the assessment procedures on the LTHE programme can be redirected into a genuine dialogue about power and authority in teaching and learning.

B. took exception to some feedback comments given on her draft submission, regarding them as over-critical and destructive. A difficult situation was defused here by conducting an email conversation about why the feedback appeared to the reader to be so negative when it has not been intended this way by the tutor, and what the implications of this incident were for writing feedback in general. B. went on to develop this into a piece of writing for her portfolio, during which she came to see her own responses as excessive.

A reflective lesson was learnt in this latter discussion by both parties, not just the participant. A tutor has to learn to know when to hold her nerve, and not to cave in to criticism or rejection, and when to accept that there are grounds for adjustment or negotiation.

GOAL-ORIENTATED TRAINING AND ACCULTURATION VERSUS EMANCIPATORY, CHANGE-ORIENTATED EDUCATION

Participants and other stakeholders have diverse goals and expectations of the programme. Some participants start an LTHE programme with clearly defined instrumental goals that they wish to have addressed on a need-to-know basis, and expect their needs to coincide with the programme's curriculum.

A potential participant, Ba., made contact to ask if the LTHE programme would be covering a particular topic, but was disappointed when she found that it was to be covered in the Summer Term, because she thought it should be covered at this point in the year.

Some participants may wish to gain accreditation to aid future job applications. Some want to acquire tips and techniques to apply directly to their current teaching, such as ways of getting students to talk more in seminars. Some bring emerging problems to address, such as expanding numbers and shrinking resources. Others do not anticipate explicitly what they might learn, but still expect a sense of immediate achievement or increased knowledge. Others are happy to explore and think about teaching without an urgent need to apply it to their immediate practice.

> J. said he was avidly storing up the knowledge he was acquiring from the course, which he could not currently use because of his limited postgraduate teaching role, to take back with him to his native country where he expects to be lecturing next year. He had no expectation that everything he would learn would be immediately applicable; he saw the course as a long-term investment.

Some participants have a more emancipatory, change-orientated view to their own learning, having open-ended or unarticulated 'intended outcomes', and wishing simply to engage in a critically dialogical and developmental experience with colleagues.

If a department head has 'sent' a lecturer to the programme, there is usually an instrumental expectation that they will learn new and relevant knowledge and skills to take back to the department, or tangibly improve their teaching performance and the students' learning achievements, or give the department or institution credibility in teaching quality assurance procedures. Very occasionally senior colleagues express a desire to nurture young staff to become critical thinkers who will confront and challenge die-hard attitudes and practices.

Such differences cannot be simply accounted for in terms of departmental cultures or disciplinary approaches:

> G. was frustrated by the course in the first few weeks, believing that it was too slow and ponderous, and asked for a meeting. He proposed that single hour, early morning sessions where tutors delivered what he needed to know which he would then take away and apply would be a more appropriate model. His faculty dean had some sympathy with his view, arguing that this was how industrial and business training occurred. Others were consulted as a result of this meeting, and some adjustments

> were made to the LTHE programme. Both participant and the dean subsequently modified their view.
>
> However Mi., from this same department, having tutored on the LTHE programmes said after some months that he had learned more in this role than in 30 years of lecturing, and wished he could do the LTHE programme and start all over again.
>
> Both expressed surprise at how their expectations and presumptions about how they might learn were different from the actual outcomes. Exploring this explicitly was important to allow tensions to surface and become articulated, and also gave all parties an opportunity to re-examine the influence of learners' expectations and diversity on our courses and teaching practices.

Individuals and groups can hold very diverse tacit assumptions regarding what can be learnt about teaching, and how it can be learnt, and from whom, and what relationship there might be between professional practice and theory. When teaching is seen as largely a craft learned through the acquisition of a set of skills and techniques, then immediacy of application and relevance to current situations become the criteria for judging the course's achievements and the participant's growth. When teaching is seen as more of an art, a way of being and thinking, involving a complex dynamic relationship between learners, teachers and knowledge embedded in a particular context, then what are perceived as successful outcomes are changed understandings and beliefs, requiring longer term, more complex and often less tangible growth. Participants, and also LTHE tutors, will adopt particular approaches to learning to teach according to their goals and views on this process.

When asked at the beginning to articulate their hopes and expectations for an LTHE programme, participants' responses commonly range widely, such as: 'learn how to teach from experts', 'take away lots of new ideas', 'find out how to grade essays', 'find out if what I have been doing is right', 'gain confidence in my teaching', 'work with peers to share ideas', 'feel a sense of community'. Examining and exploring such purposes and expectations can prove helpful in transforming negative tensions, dispelling unrealistic expectations and articulating the ethos of the programme.

Participants also need to be encouraged to feel that responsibility for fulfilling expectations and desired outcomes lies as much in their hands as in the LTHE programme tutors or course structures, for example by being invited to choose their own topics/concern for investigation in a small scale research project. In this way, those with clear goals can feel they are addressing them, and those with a more open agenda can see how their developing understanding is manifesting itself in practice. The LTHE programme needs to offer a variety of learning methods, curriculum and outcomes, aimed both at helping participants to equip themselves with tools and techniques and at encouraging them to be habitually thoughtful and critically enquiring in their approach to students and to learning.

Some participants who have entered the programme in order to develop their own thinking and practice within an exploratory, individualized 'reflective space' (Rowland: 2000: 9) will feel constrained by heavily prescribed criteria; they can better tolerate ambiguity and want to be given the autonomy to explore. Others are deeply irritated if clear, pre-defined requirements, deadlines and instructions are not provided, preferring to have things finite and well-defined. Whilst the programme needs to encourage alternative approaches to be trialled, it is important also to meet participants half way and to acknowledge the often problematic context in which they are trying to pursue the programme. Completion rates appear to increase with greater prescription in attendance, course content and assessment requirements, perhaps because they encourage many participants to engage with the programme in a more pragmatic and instrumental way, allowing a more strategic approach. This may compromise more change-orientated aims, but flexibility and careful negotiation can usually accommodate difference.

A course designer might also experience a tension between wanting to encourage negotiated, individualized 'student-led' criteria and assessment, and being required to write a pre-defined modular programme to conform to institutionally prescribed structures, external accreditation, or internal validation procedures. It is pragmatic not to hand over all the decisions about how to fulfil the programme criteria to the participants. Too much ownership can cause anxiety and irritation, especially for participants whose academic culture is more prescripted.

J., an enthusiastic and very systematic participant, seemed to be becoming increasingly frustrated and despondent. The desire to allow genuinely 'student-led' approaches was consuming precious tutorial time exploring a variety of routes to meet the criteria, but J. reported that she would have been much happier 'getting on with a given task'. As a result of this and other similar experiences, a small number of open-ended activities were subsequently framed, e.g. a critical rationale of a course design, a scholarly piece of writing, and a self-evaluation of teaching progress. These allowed ample room for decisions *within* rather than *between* tasks, with scope for adapting form and content to the local situation whilst addressing the given criteria. This seemed to provide

> a workable compromise that relieved both the participants and the tutor. Completion rates the following year were much higher. This gave the tutor some pause for thought about the relationship between student-led and teacher-led ideologies!

APPROACHING A CONCLUSION

What do these diverse examples of common tensions reveal about the process of learning to teach? How might these accounts help us to design and run an effective LTHE programme?

I identified at the beginning of this piece the potential for differing stakeholder interests in an LTHE programme to compete, cause conflict or create tension fields. It feels problematic to serve and satisfy several masters simultaneously. If the programme is made compulsory within an institution, (an increasing trend which is now advocated by the 2003 UK Government White Paper on Higher Education), it can then be perceived as a institutional vehicle to train its workforce to meet its explicit goals. If the programme is accepted as compulsory by departments, they too will want a stake in the content and the practices of the programme. Individual academics are far less likely to be amenable to an activity they are forced to do – the nature of academic pursuit is to criticize and challenge, and being compelled encourages this response in testing out the programme's validity. However, if it is not compulsory, then it can become a sport for a committed, converted minority.

Such programmes are vulnerable to being 'shot' as the messengers of difficult tidings. For example, staff may feel that they need to be equally outstanding at teaching, research, publishing, income generation, consultancy, entrepreneurship and administration. The programme can sometimes feel as if it is asking more from the individuals than they have to give, instead of being the means of support to help them achieve some of these demands. It is important that tutors make space for participants to explore this tension of normal academic practice, and discuss with them how they might juggle the varying priorities they experience both in their own minds and also those of their colleagues and managers. It is my belief that good academics are well-informed, critical thinkers who can explicitly articulate their rationale for practice, who are committed to their work through in-depth study of the issues that surround them, who know how and where to access further information and ideas. They need to feel supported within a positive and low-risk community of peers where they can test out thoughts and ideas.

The LTHE programme should offer a place where participants can find the space and distance to question, analyse and articulate arguments, a kind of fertile 'retreat' where critical, independent thinkers can be nurtured to challenge existing practices and become change-agents, not simply in their teaching, but in how they manage and integrate the multiplicity of roles they need to play. I regard my primary role as programme leader to be that of critical friend and source of support to those colleagues. This function need not compete with departmental and institutional goals. The programme needs to be well informed, embedded within the culture, but also able to stand at one remove from any single dominant interest. This takes some courage on the part of all the interested parties. It is more useful to seek to align the various interests and perspectives, working more as active players on the same team rather than as stakeholders fighting for their investment. Learning to teach is a social endeavour, not an individual activity. It is not in the gift of any single party – individual participant, programme team, department, institution or government – to ensure good teaching.

Finally, by way of summarizing the issues that have emerged in my discussion above and translating them into practical strategies, I offer below some principled methods which various LTHE programme teams use to help teaching development to become a more socially integrated endeavour.

PRINCIPLES AND METHODS FOR LTHE PROGRAMMES

Embrace diversity

Principles
Acknowledge that a diverse group of learners (of teaching) needs to experience, and critically to observe, a variety of learning and teaching approaches.

Give time for participants to reflect on how different learning and teaching approaches cause them to respond in different ways, and what implications this has for their own students.

Methods
Taught sessions which adopt a variety of approaches – small group discussion, opportunity for debate, practical activities, lecturing with little and some interaction, didactic input, independent investigation, individual study, provision of suggested practical solutions and strategies, clear direction to useful resources, negotiated assignments, unambiguous and highly directive instructions, open-ended tasks that require

decision-making and group negotiation, tightly organized sessions with little room for autonomy, diverse furniture arrangements.

Learn from experience

Principles
Allow adults some space to use, and also be critically aware of, the learning approaches that they have come to find successful in their prior experience.

Methods
Written or oral reflection on their own past learning successes and 'disasters', narratives on how they go about and prefer to learn now and why, investigation into how their subject colleagues and programme peers approach their learning, investigation into how their own students have learned in their past, and how they prefer to approach learning now.

Seek balance

Principle
Open up our practice and the course design for scrutiny, but also recognize our own thresholds of tolerance.

Methods
Sometimes use inevitable mistakes and issues arising with the group (whilst also bearing in mind that this can undermine some learners' confidence in their 'teachers'). Protect ourselves from feeling personally attacked in the ensuing analysis and critical commentary by determining our own limits. Work as a team with others to help to modify our personal responsibility.

Deal with power

Principle
Recognize the inherent power of the teacher role, choosing to use such power with sensitivity and sometimes with explanation.

Methods
Sometimes it becomes necessary to take a degree of control with which adult learners may feel uncomfortable, but is an inevitable part of structured learning and teaching events – e.g. group management, time-

keeping, curtailing of discussion, intervention in a debate, correction of misconceptions or inaccuracies, expression of one's own knowledge or experience.

In employing deadlines, require some precise assignments, create clear assessment criteria. Again these may feel over-directed with academic adults. However, certain parameters give helpful structure to busy lives, instil confidence in some participants who prefer direction to autonomy, and make the running of a programme more practicable.

Acknowledge competing priorities

Principle
Participants can experience a tacit or explicit ambivalence or even indifference to teaching in their departments. So, we should give permission to be committed and enthusiastic about teaching by our own example, whilst recognizing and explicitly acknowledging the competing priorities in participants' local contexts.

Methods
Ask participants to come up with minor triumphs and successes in the past term, describe a positive moment, explore what they enjoy about teaching, talk about what they would really like to see happen in their classrooms/students. Be seen to be juggling the same kinds of plates in our own work.

Enthuse

Principles
Participants enjoy having tutors who see teaching, and talking about it, as a pleasurable and worthwhile activity. They also need to know that tutors are not blind to the constraints, and indeed that they share them.

Methods
Make time and space for discussion of the frustrations around the job, and recognize the complexity of multiple and sometimes competing roles. Make a limited and confidential 'moaning' time. Be constructive through collective exploration and sharing strategies to cope – either in face-to-face or on-line discussion or in written feedback.

Take teaching well seriously

Principle
Treat very seriously the process of learning to teach well, whilst working hard to bring enjoyment, companionship and some lightness of being into that learning process.

Methods
Make time and space to build relationships amongst the group and the tutors. This is a vital part of the teaching strategy on an LTHE programme. It includes paying attention to comfort – timing of sessions, refreshments, furniture layout, group dynamics – not overloading the curriculum with pre-determined content, letting topics run where it feels appropriate even if it means abandoning a bit of the preparation, being open and honest as a tutor, sharing one's own successes and disasters and concerns, trying to find the funny side, telling anecdotes, encouraging participants to meet informally.

Promote conditions for good learning

Principle
Promote and nurture what is known to be true about the conditions in which successful learning takes place, through positive evidence and through opposition to negative practices.

Methods
Sometimes we must voice our own opposition to the erosion of good learning conditions, both institutionally and nationally, rather than appearing to be a tacit spokesperson or merely a training vehicle for existing regimes. Again, this needs to be carefully measured on a more individual basis, as for some this can be undermining, but for others it is a necessary pre-requisite of their being able to trust their tutors' judgement.

Treat teaching as a profession

Principle
Elevate the perception of HE teaching beyond a set of craft techniques. Show the importance of research-led, academic scholarship as a means of improving practice.

Methods
Keep insisting, at institutional and departmental level, on the importance of a rigorous programme and adequate workload allocation for staff to engage in it.

Create assignments which invite small-scale research and investigation and wider reading; invite participants to write for publication on teaching issues; encourage awareness of research literature through given readings, require assessed bibliographies, write scholarship into the assessment criteria. All this needs to be linked clearly to the change agenda – help them to make explicit how such scholarship informs and improves their practice. And, as programme leader or tutor, engage in research-led, scholarly teaching.

Work with departments and disciplines

Principle
Work closely with departments and discipline groups to identify and implement ways to embed understanding and critical reflection into practice at ground level.

Methods
Use subject mentors and experienced colleagues in departments for peer observation; help to develop a peer review scheme within a department which includes programme participants; identify within departments teaching issues which might be addressed by participants; encourage participants to write assignments specifically directed towards a departmental or subject-colleagues audience; devise assignments that require participants to engage in discussion with department colleagues about their teaching, such as how teaching has changed over time, what the key issues are for them, how they believe teaching in their subject should be done, what they enjoy about teaching. Engage in collaborative research and development projects with departments.

Put programme participants first

Principle
Seek always to prioritize participants' needs and interests in planning, teaching and running the programme.

Methods
Seek out evidence of how the programme is being received and responded to, and use this to promote and prioritize the learners' needs over any

requirements by departments or the institution. Informative feedback strategies include anonymous on-line responses to questions or open invitations for comments; Post-it note questions and comments at the end of sessions; 'dear tutor' and 'dear future participant' letters; 'talking wall' mid-course review on flip chart paper; group discussions with a neutral facilitator; listening to what participants say in sessions and in their writing; writing that encourages them to reflect on what they found helpful and problematic during the course and why and the implications for learning in general; revisiting alumni 1–2 years after the programme to explore changes in their conceptions and practices; ask for suggestions of how they would like to see the programme run.

CONCLUSION

Only when educational development is seen as a regular part of academic endeavour will the craft-skills ethos of teaching, a skill might be learned in a few training sessions or on-the-job as a natural adjunct of knowing one's subject, be finally eroded. We need to construct our own specialist persona as a mixture of academic and professional practitioner and teacher–educator within our educational development context – perhaps as nomads travelling amongst and between the territorial tribes within our own institutions and the various discipline based networks, but with our own strong identity. Becher hypothesized that:

> [B]ecause higher education is a field of study, not a discipline in its own right, researchers in that field [and perhaps educational developers too] . . ., like expatriates . . . have abandoned their original context and cut themselves off from its characteristic way of life. It might be said that they lack a culture.
>
> (Becher 1994: 160)

This still may have some truth within a single institution. However, since Becher made this observation, the culture of educational development has strengthened and widened within the Higher Education context. Development colleagues are working across institutions to develop practices and create new understandings, establishing a supportive and critical community of practice. Educational development has already become a field of study and of practice complete with its own culture. Like all new disciplines, what it lacks still is wide acceptance and status. It is imperative that we remain co-learners and academic colleagues: by reflecting critically on our own practice, by prioritizing our own professional development, scholarship and research as a vital part of our work, and by continually developing as learners as well as teachers by critically experiencing learning in formal and informal situations ourselves to revisit what it feels like to be positioned as a learner.

> And when I as a programme leader have done all this, I can turn off my email, transfer the phone, and go home and have a life!
>   Oh, except that being LTHE programme leader isn't my only role. Now, where did I put. . . .

REFERENCES

Becher, T. (1994) The significance of disciplinary differences, *Studies in Higher Education*, **19**(2), pp 151–61

Becher, T. and Trowler, P. (2001) *Academic Tribes and Territories* (2nd Edition), Open University Press/SRHE, Buckingham

Brookfield, S. (1995) *Becoming a Critically Reflective Teacher*, Jossey-Bass, San Francisco

Chaiklin, S. and Lave, J. (eds) (1993) *Understanding Practice*, Cambridge University Press, Cambridge

Entwistle, N., Skinner, D., Entwistle, D. and Orr, S. (2000) Conceptions and beliefs about 'Good Teaching': an integration of contrasting research areas, *Higher Education Research and Development*, **19**(1), pp 1–16

Knight, P. (2002) *Being a Teacher in Higher Education*, Open University Press/SRHE, Buckingham

Lave, J. and Wenger, E. (1991) *Situated Learning: Legitimate Peripheral Participation*, Cambridge University Press, Cambridge

Ramsden, P. (1992) *Learning to Teach in Higher Education*, Routledge, London

Rowland, S. (2000) *The Enquiring University Teacher*, Open University Press/SRHE, Buckingham

Stevenson, K. and Sander, P. (2002) Medical students are from Mars – business and psychology students are from Venus – university teachers are from Pluto? *Medical Teacher*, **24**(1), pp 27–31

Trowler, P. and Cooper, A. (2002) Teaching and learning regimes: implicit theories and recurrent practices in the enhancement of teaching and learning through educational programmes, *Higher Education Research and Development*, **21**(3), pp 221–40

The Future of Higher Education (2003) http://www.dfes.gov.uk/highereducation/hestrategy/

Wareham, T. (2002) Failing teachers, failing students. In *Failing Students in Higher Education*, (eds) M. Peelo and T. Wareham, Open University Press/SRHE, Buckingham

Wenger, E. (1998) *Communities of Practice: Learning, meaning and identity*, Cambridge University Press, Cambridge

Wenger, E. (2000) Communities of practice and social learning systems, *Organization*, **7**(2), pp 225–46

5

Writing for development

Angela Brew

INTRODUCTION

The changing nature of academic development means that I am increasingly using writing as a way of doing my development work. I suspect this is true for many developers. In this chapter I want to explore the ways in which I am using writing for development, and the implications of this for us as developers. I hope that the chapter will provide an opportunity for you to reflect on your own use of writing in development work. I also hope it will let you consider where this might lead. What skills do we need as developers in order to make the best use of this medium? What may we lose by spending time on writing? How we can use writing to enhance our work as developers?

In describing what activities academic and educational developers in his institution engaged in, Andresen (1996: 42) distinguishes the work of developers from what he calls 'regular' academic work. He suggests different or special types of work that characterize academic development: entering teaching spaces to observe and comment on teaching; dealing with confidential evaluation data; participating in judging teaching awards; facilitating public events for teaching development; running accredited programmes for teaching development; studying the research on teaching and learning and higher education; carrying out research and publication about teaching and learning in different disciplines. Each of these activities may engage the developer in some writing. Yet the role of writing in development is rarely mentioned. Indeed, while it might be said that the role I have played with my writing is akin to Land's (2001) notion of the 'vigilant opportunist', the question this chapter raises is whether writing is merely one of a number of tools for development, or whether another role might be added to Land's list of orientations to academic development; namely, that of journalist or script-writer.

It appears to me that my use of writing within my development work has grown. But perhaps it is simply that now I am more aware of, and more consciously use, writing in my development work. It is certainly true that I spend more time in my office sitting at my computer than I did 10 or 12 years ago. The more strategic focus of staff and educational development (see for example Blackwell and Blackmore 2003) means, in my institution at least, that we have had to give up the one to one counselling type of development where an academic staff member comes to discuss a particular problem or issue in their teaching. Now, we give such guidance to people going through our graduate certificate in higher education, and others we direct to a pedagogical expert (usually someone who took the graduate certificate in an earlier year) in their own or a cognate faculty. Yet while I believe that the personal face-to-face contact that we have with academics is less than it used to be, paradoxically, our influence – through our writing – is now wider; extending beyond the individual enthusiast for teaching to senior and other academic managers, to university committees and academic governing bodies as well as to the academic development community itself.

So this chapter is an example of the very phenomenon of which it speaks! I feel like the character Charlie Kaufmann in the film *Adaptation*. He constantly struggles with the idea that you can't write a film about writing a film, yet that is what the film is about! I am faced with the question that writing always poses: how can I reach the people I am writing for? Who are they? How can I write in a way that will engage them? What style of language should I use? – and more specifically in this case, how can I stretch the genre of an academic book to write in a personal reflective style? While I know that there is a vast literature about writing in academic contexts, I am aware that there is almost no academic research literature on writing for academic or educational development. So I am posing questions here, based unashamedly on observations from my own experience, in the hope that they will provide food for thought and perhaps stimulate research questions.

To the fundamental question when setting out on a writing task, who is the audience? Who am I writing for? In academic development work there are essentially four main sets of audiences:

1 Individual academics and groups of academics who are engaging in some kind of development activities – short term activities like one-off workshops, or longer-term activities such as graduate certificates.
2 University managers and academic and other committees.

3 Committees to consider applications of some kind – teaching awards, promotion, etc.
4 The wider academic and staff development community.

These audiences provide the organizing framework for this chapter. My focus is on my own experience. No doubt others will have different, but hopefully similar experiences. In writing about my own experience I raise some more general issues, which are discussed at the end of the chapter.

WRITING FOR INDIVIDUALS

Perhaps the most pervasive and commonest form of writing in relation to development work is the task of capturing attention through event publicity. This is also perhaps one of the hardest. A carefully phrased 'blurb' can nonetheless still bring in the 'wrong' crowd. In the Institute for Teaching and Learning at the University of Sydney, we adopted a format which tried to specify clearly the target audience, yet we often would find that the actual audience was not the intended audience. This was a problem in relation to a workshop on the scholarship of teaching that was held in 2001. The 'blurb' described the workshop as being 'particularly of interest to academics concerned to contribute to their faculty's performance on the Scholarship Index by developing pedagogical research projects or who have a role in encouraging academic staff in their faculty to take up the opportunities provided by this University initiative'. Despite this, according to the evaluations, and also our experience during the workshop, many of the 30 or so academics who attended were unfamiliar with the university's way of 'counting' and rewarding with funding scholarship of teaching outcomes through what is known as the Scholarship Index. Considerable anger and frustration was expressed, confusing us well-intentioned developers with the lack of clarity showed regarding the implementation of university policy at the departmental level. It highlighted the way that colleagues tend to read 'blurbs' for workshops and events within their particular institutional and political context. So we need to take account of that context, and in doing so we can use the publicity to educate our academic colleagues about the phenomenon.

This is illustrated most clearly in relation to publicity for our two-day Showcase of Scholarly Inquiry in Teaching and Learning held in September 2001. We were faced with the task of advertising the event, calling for expressions of interest to present a paper or a poster in an event that was designed to raise issues about the use of inquiry in relation to teaching and learning. We had a title for the event, but who would understand it? This is where the writing came in. It was done for a number of different audiences. From the scholarly literature on teaching and research and the scholarship of teaching, I drew five themes under which people could present their teaching work:

Theme A: Reports of scholarly inquiry into teaching and learning.
Theme B: Examples of teaching that uses evidence from research and scholarship on learning.
Theme C: Examples of using disciplinary research in teaching.
Theme D: Examples of engaging students in inquiry in teaching and learning.
Theme E: Discussions on bringing research and teaching together.

Presentations in Theme A included research projects carried out by departmental academics into students' learning, the first year experience, assessment and evaluation. This theme included work in progress. Presentations in Theme B drew on research from the higher education literature in general, or on work about teaching and learning in relation to specific disciplinary areas. Presentations in Theme C included reports of the development of teaching tools or techniques to engage students in the content of a course or examples of engaging students in the research process in a specific discipline. Presentations in Theme D included examples of problem-based, issues-based curricula and engaging students in inquiry-based learning. Presentations in Theme E included general discussions of the use of inquiry in curriculum design and development, and the way research and teaching can be brought together in specific contexts.

I wrote descriptions of these themes which were then sent to deans and heads of departments to encourage contributions. They were also placed on the Showcase web site:

FURTHER INFORMATION ABOUT SHOWCASE THEMES

This document, prepared by Angela Brew on behalf of the Showcase Advisory Committee, is intended as a helpful guide to the Showcase themes. It provides questions and issues to stimulate the thinking of the University community about what to offer for presentation. Deans, Heads of Schools and Departments and Faculty Teaching and Learning Committees may particularly find it useful. It is not exhaustive and other topics will be considered.

. . . Theme D   Examples of engaging students in inquiry in teaching and learning

In the University there are number of examples of curricula where students learn course content through inquiry or investigation (for example, problem-based and issues-based curricula). Presentations in Theme D would focus on accounts of these kinds of ways of delivering whole courses and/or units of study, or activities within units of study. Hopefully there will be some discussions of feedback about students' responses, or issues involved in setting up such courses and units. Other examples include engaging students in various kinds of individual and collaborative research; for example, independent study projects, problem-oriented project work, field research by students on projects of real significance to the community, work-based learning projects and placements, and inquiry based learning within units of study.

Here are some further questions to stimulate thinking about other ideas that we would like to hear about for the Showcase:

1   Do students have to investigate something using different sources, and evaluate and present the evidence?
2   Does your School or Department have examples of Units of Study where students have the opportunity to engage in research, or where they have to investigate something, perhaps in an innovative way? This might be for the Unit as a whole or for a part of a Unit or for the assessment.
3   Do students participate in an integrative interdisciplinary 'keystone' learning experience where they bring together their studies utilizing research and communication skills learned in the previous semesters?

. . . (continued)

When the abstracts had been submitted and organized a Showcase *Programme and Abstracts* book was prepared. Again the focus was on developing the wider academic community including those 200 or so staff who attended the Showcase, as well as others who did not. The booklet was organized to reflect the themes and they were explored further in the introductions to each section. At this stage it was possible to include examples. At the beginning of the following extract, I have related the theme to the University's Strategic Plan. I also used this writing opportunity to try to move on from the particular examples to think more widely about what the theme might mean in the future.

INTRODUCTION TO THEME D

Examples of engaging students in inquiry in teaching and learning

The University of Sydney aims to 'assist the transition of students into research-based programs through opportunities provided within under-graduate programs.' It also aims to 'support the conduct of outstanding research by both students and staff'. So in Theme D the focus is on examples of curricula (whole courses and/or units of study, or activities within units of study) where students learn course content through inquiry or investigation. Feedback about students' responses, or issues involved in setting up such courses and units, is included in most presentations focusing on this theme.

The use of problem-based and issues-based curricula has been growing in the university over the last few years. As the presentations in Theme D now demonstrate, the use of such approaches has gone beyond medical and social work contexts in which this method of teaching originated, into mainstream teaching.

Basil Baldwin's students (BALD02) in the Faculty of Rural Management investigate and then create plans for property development and manage-ment that are ecologically sustainable whilst meeting business goals. Edmund Balnaves in Computer Science (BALN03) emphasizes the importance of reproducing the research process of data collection and analysis and theory building in an Arts Informatics Systems unit of study, while Christine Crowe (CROW85) has developed an inquiry based learning unit of study in 'Social justice, law and society' for a large class of Sociology students. In the Scenario-based approach of Fred Wong and colleagues in the Department of Pharmacy (WONG81) students have to investigate and present a new drug formulation report, on behalf of a pharmaceutical company, for permission to market the drug. Their paper is the result of a collaborative initiative including general as well as academic staff and students. This illustrates the way in which moving into inquiry based learning ultimately breaks down distinctions between different categories of people in higher education . . . (continued)

How much of the success of the Showcase was due to these writing strategies is impossible to say. Academic Board noted:

> that the Vice-Chancellor's Showcase of Scholarly Inquiry in Teaching and Learning took place on Thursday 27 and Friday 28 Sept and was well attended, with participants commenting favourably on the collegial nature of the event. The Chair noted that presenters addressed key strategic issues relating to teaching and learning in

the University and attendees developed a clearer understanding of what was meant by scholarship in teaching and learning.

(Minutes of the meeting on 10 October 2001, p. 3)

It seems the work had its intended effect.

I have discussed this example in detail to show that writing publicity for an event can be a non-trivial task. It can be effective in itself promoting development.

WRITING FOR THE SCREEN

Nowadays it is usually possible to provide publicity information via web sites or through web-based development work. Indeed, the Internet provides perhaps the largest single source of writing work for the academic developer. Much of this is targeted at the individual academic. As well as the provision of information about services, events, and courses the academic development centre web site is becoming an important source of more general information for faculty academics. This is not the place to review web site usage, and clearly different centres have differing ideas about the role of their web site for development as any survey of such sites will demonstrate. What I want to focus on here is the issue of audience and the writing challenges of web based development.

A survey of academic development web sites carried out in 2000 indicated that the most common usage of the site was for the provision of information (Kandlbinder submitted). Yet there are a number of ways of viewing the work of providing information. At the University of Sydney we try to provide information in what is otherwise called an audience or 'student-focused' way; i.e., through thinking through how the audience is going to read and respond to the information, rather than taking a 'teacher-focused' perspective and giving information without such considerations, rather like giving a lecture without considering the learning needs of the student. Getting the balance right between being 'audience-focused' without being patronizing is difficult.

At the beginning of our graduate certificate programme, we find that very few of the academic participants will have studied the course outline on our web site. This illustrates an important point about writing for development; that much may fall on blind or deaf eyes or ears.

I recently had the pleasure of writing a web-based module for our postgraduate supervisors' development programme. This is a flexible programme including six on-line independent study modules as well as face-to-face workshops. One section of the programme web site is intended to provide resources for a wider range of supervisors who choose not to study the programme as a whole. The problem was, how were we going to tell whether supervisors had completed the programme modules and had in fact learnt from it? How do you assess a professional development programme which itself is aimed at improving supervisors' skills so their students pass their examinations (e.g. gain a PhD)? Our solution has been to devise what we have called the 'Recognition Module' (Brew and Peseta submitted), considered immediately below.

WRITING FOR LEARNING

Writing for learning poses particular challenges and I am grateful to my background and training in the distance education context of the British Open University when it comes to writing course outlines for Internet use, or course materials for academic development such as the Recognition Module. This module takes supervisors through the various stages of writing a critical case study of their own supervision practice:

Stages in writing your case
Preparing your descriptive account
- Write your supervision autobiography
- Identify your supervision issues
- Prioritize your list of issues
- Write paragraphs on your key priority areas
- Obtain feedback
Preparing your reflective account
- Attend to feelings
- Identify dilemmas and contradictions
- Identify issues or themes
- Develop your Case Study plan
Preparing your Case
- Draft your case
- Critically evaluate your case
- Identify strategies for improving your practice
- Finish and publish your case
- Obtain written feedback

Not only did this present a writing challenge to us as developers; the structure we adopted also presents writing challenges for supervisors as they first present their supervision autobiography and then develop a supervision case study. Along the way we provide written feedback, which presents yet another writing challenge for us. We are able to see the effects of our feedback on supervisors' development when they subsequently present their case study. For example, in outlining one of his key issues a supervisor presented a view of supervision as the supervisor deciding the direction of the project and the way the supervision was to proceed for the student. The following is an extract from the feedback which I wrote collaboratively with a colleague. (I have used a fictitious name.)

Dear Mike,
It was great to read your supervision autobiography and see the way your thinking is developing. Thank you for being so open and frank in your work for this Module. This feedback is intended to move your thinking forward, to deepen the learning that you do in preparation for your Case Study, so we hope it fulfils that purpose.

We can see that your supervisory practice is successful in meeting your needs for supervision, including successful completion of the thesis, a list of useful publications and the acquisition of a set of employability skills for your students leading to success in gaining jobs. That's fantastic. But what we notice about the way you describe all this is that it is from what we would call a teacher-focused perspective. These are your goals for the candidatures. What about the students' goals? True they are likely to want some of the same things, but recognizing that each student is different, with different needs, and also different aspirations, what we're wondering is, how would your thinking be different if you took a student-focused perspective? Would this focus more on what they are learning and perhaps less on what you are supplying; more on their learning outcomes and less on yours for them, we wonder?

You mention the two students who failed to complete their studies and clearly that experience has influenced how you now supervise. We wonder if there is anything you now feel you could have done which would have prevented the students from leaving before completing their theses. You mention you now take a 'less ad hoc' approach. What precisely does this mean? It could lead to adopting a uniform approach for all students. This would not necessarily be a good thing, would it? . . .

Finally Mike, thank you for sharing your reflections and issues with us. We hope you find these comments helpful and wish you well with completing the remainder of the Recognition Module.

The feedback resulted in a shift in this supervisor's ideas about supervision as demonstrated when he wrote in his case study about the importance of students being able to negotiate the topic and the way supervision proceeds and that students should be seen as 'active participants' in prioritization and in decision making. In the case study he wrote about the importance of avoiding undue teacher-centredness (Brew and Peseta submitted).

Some feedback is given in the context of formal learning, as for example on this programme or on our Graduate Certificate assessment projects. We see the giving of formal feedback as part of the teaching of supervisor or teaching skills and understanding, but we are frequently engaged in providing feedback via email for a vast array of circumstances. Some feedback is part of the everyday work based learning of academics in our own institution and some is external to it. So for example, I was recently asked to write comments on an initiative designed to encourage research on teaching that had been running for a few years in the Health Sciences Faculty. My comments were included as part of a report to the Dean of the Faculty.

One example of the ad hoc feedback which forms an increasing part of our repertoire as a developer in my institution is the provision of feedback on applications for teaching awards, promotion applications, research grant applications and the like. Here it is important to set the right tone, avoid being patronizing but also being clear and precise so the applicant can improve the application. Where possible I do this face-to-face but this is not always possible.

I have recently had the experience of examining several PhD theses. Here, comments can provide valuable feedback to the candidate, but the examination report also has to speak to the committee making decisions on whether to award the degree. Sometimes it is also important to provide signals to the supervisor to aid future supervision. The report therefore is in a very real sense a teaching document. I ask myself what do I want to say to the committee, the supervisor, the candidate and try to do all this in my report. This may involve gently pointing out to the committee that the thesis is not as non-traditional as it suggests, or to the supervisor that the candidate would have created a better thesis had they not been so tightly constrained.

WRITING FOR THE ACADEMIC COMMUNITY OF MY UNIVERSITY

One aspect of the developer's work which has been significant over the years is the preparation of materials for workshops. The writing of workshop notes is an important aspect of this. However, one part of this that I particularly enjoy and which participants find valuable is the writing of semi-fictitious scenarios to provide triggers for discussions. Here is an example:

SCENARIO A

Carin is a first year student studying economics. She went to Sydney Girls' High School where she excelled in all subjects. Her parents wanted her to go to Sydney Uni because they themselves were graduates of the place. Her father is a successful accountant in the city and her mother looks after the home and Carin's younger brother and sister.

During the first semester, Carin attended the lectures and made lots of notes. She didn't like many of the lectures as there were about 500 people in the lecture theatre and she didn't know any of them. The few girls she knew from school were all doing arts. So many of the lecturers went too fast in their lectures and she had difficulty taking down all the notes. There was only one piece of assessed work in this unit of study and although she was worried, there was no one to ask how many of the books on the reading list she should read. She liked reading so she read lots of them. Anyway reading was a way of coping with the loneliness she felt. She knew she could always find a little corner in the library. Then she sat down to write the essay. This was difficult because she kept on thinking she probably hadn't read the right things. The question wasn't straightforward because when she read one book she got one answer and when she read another she got a different one.

When she got the essay back she was devastated because it was 59 per cent. She had never had anything less than 70 per cent at school and she didn't know what her parents would say. She read the feedback in tears. What will she say to her parents?

Scenarios or case studies such as this provide useful opportunities for participants to reflect on the issues being discussed (in this case the first year experience). This example is one of three case studies each of which raises different issues. Different groups can work on different scenarios and then share their observations and reflections. It is interesting how the use of a creative scenario like this can encourage creative ideas on the part of the participants who then tend to speculate on other aspects of the work, character, personality and/or family circumstances of the fictitious student!

Many academic development units produce a regular newsletter. The Institute for Teaching and Learning at the University of Sydney is no exception to this. We produce a magazine called *Synergy* which is designed to provide a forum for discussion of teaching and learning across the university. *Synergy* has proved to be a useful way for academics to write about their teaching and sometimes it is the very first time that a faculty academic has submitted teaching ideas for publication. The sharing of good practice in this way helps to stimulate development and provides a vehicle for the scholarship of teaching. A number of academics who publish in *Synergy* often go on to submit articles on teaching and learning to scholarly refereed journals.

WRITING FOR COMMITTEES

An increasingly important part of my work as a developer is writing reports and drafting policies for university committees. I regard this as a key way in which I am able to influence the wider university community. The way a report is presented can move the thinking of individuals on the committee to which it is presented away from their current conceptions towards new ways of thinking. It is in this sense writing for development. Sometimes the written word is the only way in which a developer can reach this audience.

I recently had occasion to give a five-minute presentation on research-led teaching and the scholarship of teaching to our university's Teaching and Learning Committee. This committee is a sub-committee of Academic Board, so I knew that whatever I could do to develop the committee's knowledge about the varieties and forms of research-led teaching might end up in a minute that would be read by all members of the Academic Board. Specifically, I was seeking endorsement of the Academic Board for the setting up of a cross-faculty working group to progress our university wide project on this issue. Five minutes is not much time for this, so I chose to write a short paper to underscore what I said. The paper provided the background to the project in terms of the university's strategic priorities, the project aims and activities undertaken so far. It then went on to explain what was meant by research-led teaching and outlined a vision for its development. Finally the paper set out some recommendations and the next steps to be taken to progress the initiative. Following the recommendation of Teaching and Learning Committee, Academic Board endorsed the establishment of the Working Group. This writing has already led to significant developments on this issue. The Working Group has subsequently set up performance indicators for research-led teaching, examined beginning students' perceptions of research in the university, investigated the extent to which research-led teaching is prevalent in their faculties and established a statement on what the university under-stands by research-led teaching. One of the next tasks will be to develop a policy on the relationship between teaching and research. I will be involved in drafting that policy and seeking endorsement of the working group to recommend to the Academic Board that it be adopted as university policy.

Increasingly it seems these days, academic developers are called upon to write applications. I have been involved over the past few years in writing applications for teaching awards, for research grants, for promotion and applications for funding for new initiatives. Not only does writing applications develop a particular style of writing, and learning what style is appropriate is a major task in itself, but it also provides valuable experience when discussing and providing feedback to academics in regard to their applications for the same sorts of initiatives.

WRITING FOR MANAGERS

Sometimes my writing takes me into the world of university management. This has included reporting on aspects of academic practice, writing responses to correspondence and writing briefing notes. Again I see each writing task as an opportunity to engage in development. As far as the Showcase of Scholarly Inquiry in Teaching and Learning was concerned (see above) I wrote the speech for the deputy vice-chancellor to open the Showcase. While he put his own spin on what I wrote, essentially the speech opened up to him, and then later to the audience, ideas about scholarly inquiry in teaching and learning that came from the forefront of the literature on this topic. A number of positive comments were made about the speech. I kept quiet, as I imagine political speech-writers do too!

THE WIDER COMMUNITY

And so it comes full circle. I am now writing a book chapter about writing as development. Writing chapters, refereed journal articles and, indeed, books is an extension of the development role to the wider community. By engaging in these activities, our writing reaches beyond the confines of our own university, contributing to the ongoing dialogue about academic development, teaching and learning and the role and functions of the university.

CONCLUSION

When I set out to write this chapter I thought it would be a simple matter to put together the kinds of writing that I had been engaging with as an academic developer. It was not until I sat down to explore the different kinds of writing that my development work has entailed over the past few years that I realized the extent and scope of the writing. I have found it essential to have skills to cope with different genres, to be sensitive to cultural issues and the use of language that is inappropriate in some contexts.

I have not referred here to, for example, the use of fictional writing for professional development such as Bolton (1994) describes. Nor have I referred to the development of writing for research or other purposes (see for example, Lee and Boud 2003). These offer different opportunities for writing and for development. Although wide-ranging, the writing that I have discussed in this chapter is somewhat limited. It is confined to the pragmatic; to supporting the role of the 'vigilant opportunist' (Land 2001). It is teacher-focused (Prosser and Trigwell 1999) where it is used to convey information, and student-focused in feedback to academics on aspects of their work and in course materials. However, it has rarely been emancipatory. Rowland (2000: 77) suggests that teaching in higher education might be 'imprisoned by the language that describes it'. Might we perhaps, through our writing, go beyond such 'imprisonment' to develop new forms of expression and new understandings of teaching and learning and of our role as academic and educational developers in higher education?

This leads us to question where, in the future, writing might take us in our development work. What are the possibilities for its development? How can this medium be exploited and what happens if we take seriously writing as a developmental activity both for us and for the academics with whom we engage? What would happen, for example, if we were to engage in the kind of fictional writing as a way of exploring development issues such as Bolton (1994) suggests? Autobiographical writing is increasingly being recognized, not only as a tool for research but also as a way of understanding who we are and how we might develop (Bolton 1994). We might move away from a focus on writing to achieve a particular outcome for a particular audience, to a focus on writing as a developmental process in and for itself. I hope so, because writing has the power to challenge and change both the writer and the reader, and surely that is what we are about as academic and educational developers?

ACKNOWLEDGEMENT

I would like to acknowledge the help and advice of my colleague Tai Peseta in preparing this paper.

REFERENCES

Andresen, L. (1996) The work of academic development: occupational identity, standards of practice and the virtues of association. *International Journal for Academic Development*, **1**(1), pp 38–49

Blackwell, R. and Blackmore, P. (Eds) (2003) *Towards Strategic Staff Development in Higher Education*, Society for Research into Higher Education and the Open University Press, Buckingham

Bolton, G. (1994) Stories at work: Fictional-critical writing as a means of professional development. *British Educational Research Journal*, **20**(1), pp 54–69

Brew, A. and Peseta, T. (submitted) Changing supervision practice: a programme to encourage learning through feedback and reflection [refereed journal article]

Kandlbinder, P. (submitted) Peeking under the covers: on-line academic staff development in Australia and the United Kingdom. *International Journal for Academic Development*

Land, R. (2001) Agency, context and change in academic development. *International Journal for Academic Development*, **6**(1), 4–20

Lee, A. and Boud, D. (2003) Writing groups, change and academic identity: research development as local practice. *Studies in Higher Education*, **28**(2), pp 187–200

Prosser, M. and Trigwell, K. (1999) *Understanding Learning and Teaching: the experience in higher education*, Society for Research in Higher Education and the Open University Press, Buckingham

Rowland, S. (2000) *The Enquiring University Teacher*, The Open University Press and the Society for Research in Higher Education, Buckingham

6

The impact of staff development programmes and activities

Holly J. Smith

INTRODUCTION AND OUTLINE

The primary aim of this chapter is to explore how we can investigate the impact of programmes of professional development in learning and teaching in higher education. Much of what I say about investigating the impact of programmes can also be adapted and applied to shorter, less formal staff development activities. I shall briefly outline various ideas about defining impact and about approaches and methods that could be used. I shall go on to consider the implications that choices of methods have for the understandings that we seek and claims that we can make about our professional development programmes and activities.

Why do we need to know the effects of professional development programmes? Baume (2003) suggests three main sets of reasons to evaluate any staff or educational development undertaking. These are to *account* for monies and effort and expended, deliverables delivered, goals achieved; to *improve* the project as it proceeds; and to *understand* the undertaking, the reasons for its effects, successes and failures. Those funding a professional development programme may want those running it to be able to account, in some terms or another, for the use of resources and the effects that the programme has. Those running the programme will certainly want to be able to improve it, and, as academics, those running it will also want to understand how and why the programme produces the reactions and has the effects that it does. The same applies, on a correspondingly smaller scale, to most staff and educational development activities.

In considering professional development programmes I focus on centrally run (rather than departmentally based) and credit bearing (rather than less formal) programmes, whether these are accredited institutionally or nationally by the Staff and Educational Development Association (SEDA) or the Institute for Learning and Teaching in Higher Education) ILTHE, or all three. Such accredited programmes lie at one end of the long spectrum of staff and educational development activities that most of us undertake, and thus raise more issues than apply to identifying and understanding the effects of smaller courses and activities. The greater investment in more extended programmes; by developers, participants and institutions; has made them a more frequent subject of evaluation. This chapter will be illustrated with a case study of a qualitative evaluation of such a programme at Liverpool John Moores University.

As this book intends to be both a practical and a scholarly guide, this chapter is structured around the processes required for you to examine the impact of your own professional development programmes. Sue Thompson's and Ali Cooper's chapters (3 and 4) in this book both make very clear the importance of context and the complexity of its effects. Because of the importance of context, case studies are likely to provide a useful complement to generalizations. If you want to know about the impact of your own programmes then a piece of scholarly investigation would be one possible next step. The chapter by Ashwin and Trigwell (Chapter 7) offers some useful ways forward.

The processes of investigating the effects of your own professional development programme can usefully be considered in three stages:

1   Defining impact: What is being evaluated?
2   Approaches to analysis: How do we come to know?
3   Data collection methods: What can we know?

An author naturally hopes that a reader will work through the chapter in the order in which the chapter is presented, following the evolving argument and making connections as they go. However, this author accepts that you may be more or less interested in each of the three topics listed above and the case study of the evaluation of a programme, and has tried to construct the chapter so that you can go straight to the topic which most concerns you, reading or skimming the others as required.

DEFINING IMPACT: WHAT IS BEING EVALUATED?

The idea of impact needs to be operationalized before it can be assessed. The HESDA project[1] 'Evaluating the impact of professional development courses in teaching and learning for associate teachers in UK Universities' did some useful work on this. The HESDA project team suggested that the impact of professional development courses can be conceptualized in terms of their impacts on the following.

The organization

Over a period of years the individuals participating in courses and other educational development activities might be expected to share ideas or practices with colleagues, or to take on new roles within the institution as their careers develop. Those educational developers responsible for courses might also feed back their experience, perhaps using it to inform institutional policies or Teaching and Learning Strategies. In such ways there may be effects at an institutional level, but they may be difficult to evaluate and studies of this have not yet been reported in the UK. The collection of anecdotes or production of case studies would provide indications of such effects.

The department

The influence of individual course participants on their colleagues or departments can greatly magnify the impact of any course. Course development, team teaching and peer observation schemes can all provide mechanisms for such influence. Educational developers usually work with individual staff drawn from many departments within the institution, but sometimes specific development courses or one-off activities are carried out in collaboration with a department. Each type of activity may impact a department in a different way.

The experience of the students taught by participants

An international project is under way (the proposal is described by Gilbert and Gibbs 1998) which examines participants on professional development courses and their students. Some preliminary findings have been reported by Coffey and Gibbs (2000). They used a modified version of the Student Evaluation of Educational Quality (SEEQ) questionnaire developed by Marsh (1982) with six rather than the original nine subscales. They found that student ratings of their teachers increased significantly on four of the six subscales of the SEEQ: learning, enthusiasm, organization and rapport. This is an indication of positive effect on students taught by course participants. The project also asked students to complete the Module Experience Questionnaire (MEQ) based on the Course Experience Questionnaire (CEQ) developed by Ramsden (1991). Participants completed the Approaches to Teaching Inventory (ATI) developed by Trigwell and Prosser (1996) and the Teaching Methods Inventory developed by Gibbs, Gilbert and Coffey.

The careers of participants

The widespread availability of professional development courses is such a recent phenomenon that there is as yet no longitudinal evidence on this issue, but it is an area worthy of investigation. The case study reported in this chapter found evidence for various impacts on careers, from individuals who felt the qualification was a career asset to one who reported that the experience of the course had helped them to reach a decision to leave academia. However, while graduate destinations surveys from professional development courses may provide some information, there is no published research on this issue.

The individual participant

This is the route through which all the other possible impacts are made, and has been the sole focus of most evaluations to date. I would suggest that individual impact is likely to be mediated by participants' prior learning, their implicit theories about teaching and learning, their expectations about the course, and their working context. The HESDA team suggested that the impact on the individual could be conceptualized in terms of impact on:

- self-perception (confidence, self-esteem) – *how you feel;*
- conceptions of teaching, conceptions of learning – *what you believe;*
- teaching practices – *what you do;* and
- knowledge and understanding of pedagogy – *what you know.*

It also seems reasonable to expect that impact should have some relationship to the aims and intended outcomes of the educational development programmes. Certainly the stated aims and outcomes of a professional development programme should provide a useful frame of reference in determining impact. Almost all UK professional development programmes for university teachers are within the SEDA Teacher Accreditation/Professional Development Framework and/or accredited by the ILTHE. The two schemes share many features. They specify outcomes or activities required of programme participants and the professional values that must underpin their practice. As these schemes provide a common basis for many diverse programmes they might form a useful starting point for considering the impact of programmes (SEDA 2003; ILTHE 2003).

If the aims of a programme do provide a frame of reference for thinking about impact, then it is worth considering in more detail how those aims have been conceptualized. Gibbs and Coffey (2000) interviewed 11 UK programme leaders about the intended aims of their professional development programmes. They acknowledged that all programme leaders interviewed held multiple intentions, which they categorized as follows:

1   Training to develop skills and competence (a behavioural change model like that of Murray 1997).
2   Training to develop reflective practitioners (based on the Schön (1983) model of the reflective practitioner).
3   Appreciating the complexity of teaching and developing a language and form of discourse to discuss and analyse it (Sprague and Nyquist (1991) suggest that experience alone is not enough to enable teachers to discuss their practice, they must also acquire a vocabulary with which to do so).
4   Moving teachers from a teaching-centred to a learning-centred conception of teaching (based on Trigwell *et al.*'s (1994) distinction between teacher-focused approaches with an intention to pass on knowledge and student-focused approaches where there is an intention to help students to develop their own knowledge).
5   Orientating teachers to value and pay attention to teaching.
6   Developing confidence to teach and innovate.
7   Launching teachers on a trajectory of continuing professional development.
8   Hybrids and flexibility.

The fact that the various aims above are not mutually exclusive raises questions about the relationships between the aims. For example, if a programme aims to bring about both behavioural change and conceptual change in participants, there may (or of course may not) be, in the mind of those teaching the course, a model, implicit or explicit, of the relationship between behavioural and conceptual change. This model might be that conceptual change and behavioural change are independent; that conceptual change could cause behavioural change; or that behavioural change might cause conceptual change. The model would affect the design and operation of the course. Ho's work (2000) suggests that conceptual change will bring about improvements in teaching practice, and describes an approach to staff development based on this view. Social psychologists have observed that it is somewhat uncomfortable, but nonetheless entirely possible, to believe and act in ways that are not logically compatible. I believe that such inconsistency is an important aspect of human behaviour. Educational development is unlikely to be an exception to this, as Murray and Macdonald (1997) have shown.

It is also interesting to consider how the classification of aims maps against models of teacher development. There are a number of such developmental models, in addition to Sprague and Nyquist (1991) and Trigwell *et al.*'s (1994) mentioned above. Kugel (1993) describes a number of stages within Phase I where teachers have an emphasis on teaching and Phase II where they have an emphasis on learning. Biggs (1999) specifies hierarchical levels of development with a teacher focus at Level 1, What the student is; at Level 2, What the teacher does; at Level 3: What the student does. McLean and Bullard (2000) provide a useful synthesis of several models of teacher development. All this leaves a variety of possibilities to conceptualize and evaluate impact. I would suggest examining these models of teacher development as a potential framework for any evaluation. But these models are diverse, and ultimately you must choose how you wish to define impact for your own purposes in assessing it.

Despite the extreme paucity of evidence in this area, Rust (2000) has published a small-scale evaluation of a professional development programme at Oxford Brookes University. Rust concluded that individual participants achieved both behavioural change and conceptual change and developed as reflective practitioners, and also that the impact of the programme went beyond teaching and learning issues to inform other aspects of the roles of participants, as well as providing support, induction and networking for participants. He also speculated that some of these changes may be more obvious to participants in retrospect. This raises issues about the timing of evaluation of such programmes.

APPROACHES TO ANALYSIS: HOW DO WE COME TO KNOW?

Next in the process of coming to know the impact of professional development programmes are epistemological questions. Silverman (1999) suggests asking yourself the following questions early in the process:

What status do you attach to your data?
Is your analytic position appropriate to your practical concerns?
What claims will your analytic position and data collection methods permit you to make about your research?

In answering such questions you need to consider the different traditions and schools that have shaped thinking on these issues. In recent decades there has been a great divide between what I will call realist approaches and constructionist approaches. (The terminology can be confusing. Cohen *et al.* (2000) use the terms objectivist and subjectivist approaches, and Smith and Hodkinson (2002) use the terms neo-realist and relativist to describe broadly the same schools of thought.) Depending on your disciplinary background, you might think such consideration is elementary, or you might wonder if such abstruse issues are relevant to investigating what works in staff development. I would argue that these issues and questions are important, because, unless you consider them, you cannot answer Silverman's questions. And failure to address these questions does seriously undermine the evaluation of impact. If your disciplinary background already leads you to a commitment to an analytic position, you might jump forward to the next section.

In the realist, empirical tradition, researchers believe that data gives largely unproblematic access to reality. In the constructionist, interpretative tradition, researchers contend that reality is socially constructed and remains unknowable except through those (principally linguistic) constructions by which we create shared understandings of reality. Within these two opposing traditions of course there is a huge variety of approach. Realist approaches with a generalizing tendency, such as quantitative content analysis, privilege the researchers' account and gloss over differences between individuals. Alternatively, realist approaches such as feminist standpoint research privilege the authenticity of personal experience. But these approaches remain realist in the sense that they assume that words can describe experience.

Within constructionist approaches, some varieties of Discourse Analysis (DA) consider issues of power and identity outside the text. Therefore they can explore the implications of accepting the accounts of reality that are deconstructed. Another constructionist approach, Conversation Analysis (CA) is much narrower, and strictly considers nothing outside the text, focusing on the detail of organizational features of interaction. There is no reason why any analytical approach should not be used to examine the impact of staff and educational development, as long as the approach is appropriate to your practical concerns, and lets you make the kinds of claims you wish to make. There has been a tendency to use only realist approaches to measure the effects of educational interventions, because I believe there is a pressure to make claims to justify educational development in quantifiable terms of cost and time as Baume (2003) highlights in his description of the accounting function of evaluation. However, this is somewhat strange in universities where colleagues would decry such simplistic reductionism in their own disciplines. A committee of social scientists might well wish to deconstruct claims that any realist evaluation might make. I think our colleagues might find other analytical approaches applied to our work as developers more compelling. However, Unger

(1998) has argued that if you accept the relativist position that no paradigm is intrinsically of more or less value than any other, perhaps you should take the pragmatist position that realist, empirical work is a very high-status discourse and you need to engage in it to be heard within the academy. Discourses for courses, perhaps.

Of course you are free (within any local and institutional constraints) to choose the approach or approaches that you and those for whom you are undertaking the evaluation find most appropriate. Remember, too, that many researchers work within different analytical frameworks at different times or on different projects. If you are new to research within this field, I suggest that you start with an introductory textbook on research methods such as Richardson (1996), Silverman (1997), and Silverman (2001) which outline a range of approaches. Once you have decided on an approach, you can then move on to the specialist literature which details the background and practicalities of how to go about your chosen method. Finally, you would need to do a bibliographic search to identify published research on your area of interest using your method.

For example, you might want to know how Graduate Teaching Assistants (GTAs) felt about their sudden change of status from undergraduate student to postgraduate student and teacher of undergraduate students. From a general research methods text you might select grounded theory as most appropriate for you to explore the issue in your particular context. You could then go to Strauss and Corbin (1998) to get started on planning your evaluation, and finally you would search among abstracts on ERIC[2] to find other studies taking a grounded theory approach to the area. Your choice of a qualitative analytical framework would mean that you could not make quantitative claims such as that 65 per cent of GTA experienced problems with their teaching role in their first year. However, such a realist approach would enable you to generalize, so that you could be reasonably confident that your description of the process of role transition would be meaningful to any GTA, not just your sample. But if your key stakeholders wanted numbers, a questionnaire survey would provide these. A pluralist approach to determining impact may well be politically realistic as well as academically respectable, as Unger (1998) argues.

DATA COLLECTION METHODS: WHAT CAN WE KNOW?

Of course you may be very pragmatic and choose your methods on the basis of what data are available and then consider what the implications are for the analytic framework and claims that can be made! However, logically, the method of data collection should follow from your choice of approach. So, for example, if you decide to use DA you might decide not to collect any new data at all but use teaching portfolios written by programme participants as data (McLean and Bullard (2000) have done so within a different analytic framework). Because these are often written explicitly as accounts of development or justifications for certain practices they could be an ideal source to examine how participants construct their own theory of accounts of learning and teaching. Possible data collection methods include the following.

Interviews and focus groups

Interviews have the advantage of allowing subjects to be explored that have not been anticipated by the researcher. The rapport that a face-to-face interaction produces, and the fact that a researcher is prepared to listen intently to what the interviewee has to say, can lead interviewees to disclose a great deal more than they might in a less personal form of data collection. Your approach to analysis dictates whether interviews involve actively challenging the interviewee's constructions, or, in the realist tradition, just neutrally reflecting and reformulating their words to confirm your comprehension of what they are saying. But even in the latter case, where interviewers provide no critical comment, interviewees can use the interview to develop or clarify their own thinking on a topic in a way that they might not have done before. Therefore, it is inevitable that participating in the interview process will change the way that both interviewer and interviewee understand the topic under discussion. Focus groups add another dimension to interviews; here, the participants can stimulate and provoke each other, although when this happens the group dynamics and power structure within the group bring their own effects.

Interviews and focus groups share the major disadvantage that, prior to any kind of analysis, some processing of the raw experience is required, whether the writing of field notes or verbatim transcription from audio recording. This can be immensely time-consuming. Your approach to analysis will determine the level of detail required in a transcript. If you want to do CA you will require a very much more detailed transcript than for quantitative content analysis. A word-processed transcript is likely to take up to 10 hours of transcription time for each hour of interview tape, and many more hours to analyse. And you may need to check back with the tape in order fully to understand the transcript – even a verbatim transcript does not fully capture a conversation!

Questionnaires or inventories

Open-ended questionnaires are a stimulus to respondents to produce short directed pieces of writing, and so are considered in writing below.

Closed questionnaires require respondents to make ratings (such as Agree, Strongly Disagree) or forced choice responses (such as Male or Female) in a way that usually permits some kind of numerical scoring. The main advantage of rating scales is that such scoring can allow the use of descriptive and inferential statistics to answer questions (such as, is there a gender difference in the amount of time lecturers spend on staff development activities?). Obviously such questionnaires do not permit unanticipated responses, and so rarely reveal new insights into an issue.

The most common mistake in the use of questionnaires or inventories is failing to decide how the data will be analysed to answer research questions in advance of data collection. This can lead to a huge amount of wasted effort. For many topics, there are existing inventories that have been validated (such as the Approaches to Studying Inventory (ASI) Entwistle and Ramsden 1983). Where none exists, you can develop one if you have a set of questions that you believe are relevant to the issue. Exploratory factor analysis tries to identify underlying structure, or factors, from the matrix of correlations between question responses. It could be that highly correlated items are measuring the same factor. Tabachnick and Fidell (1996) provide a clear introduction to factor analysis. Questionnaire items can be removed, rewritten or deleted to try to tap the factors identified and improve reliability. However, such an approach may be subject to the criticism that it is blind empiricism, and cannot produce meaningful results without any theoretical underpinning. Exploratory factor analysis rarely produces a clear factor structure accounting for a substantial amount of the variance. Even within a realist analytical framework it has been argued that dimensions should be generated from theories and factor analysis used to confirm or reject. In either case, very careful reporting of measures of internal reliability and some attempt to measure validity are needed.

Observation

Systematic observation and participant observation offer radically different approaches to data collection. Participant observation requires the observer to find some role, perhaps as a student in a lecture. Then, in the tradition of anthropology or sociology, the observer tries to understand the situation from that perspective. Detailed field notes need to be written, either during observation or immediately afterwards. In systematic observation, categories of behaviour predefined by the researcher are observed using time-sampling or counting frequency or duration. This permits quantitative analysis to answer questions such as, do lecturers who have completed training ask students more questions than those who have not? Observation is potentially very powerful, with high ecological validity as it takes place in naturalistic settings. However, it does not guarantee greater authenticity of interpretation, it just shifts the responsibility for interpretation from the participant to the researcher.

Email or computer-mediated conferencing (CMC)

This has the great advantage of the raw data being ready transcribed, and usually also formatted, in a way that permits manipulation and so facilitates analysis. This is extremely useful for any kind of textual analysis. Some forms of CMC with real time interaction also maintain some features of conversation, so they can be somewhat similar to focus groups.

Writing

Many kinds of writing can be used as data; those already existing, such as a Learning and Teaching Strategy document or an assessed teaching portfolio, or those written specifically to generate data to address a research question. Writing has the advantage of allowing participants time to collect and draft their ideas, unlike an interview where they must respond immediately, so writing may be more complex and complete. Writing is also immediately available and accessible, and can be subject to many forms of analysis.

Concept mapping

Concept mapping as a technique was originally devised by Novak and Gowin (1984). It requires participants to identify important concepts in a given domain and to specify relationships among these concepts by arranging them visually into a map so that links between concepts equate to propositions. Concept mapping can provide insights into the personal theories of the participant. There are various procedures for scoring concept maps which permit quantitative analysis, but perhaps it is most useful as a qualitative method, unusually a qualitative method that is not discursive.

Teaching process recall

This technique involves video recording a teaching episode, then replaying it with the teacher concerned while they think aloud, trying to describe their thought processes as they acted. It is particularly useful for examining teacher thinking, providing access to reflection-in-action or decision-making moment by moment, which isn't usually accessed by the methods above that are more likely to elicit generalizations or personal theories. It is time-consuming and intrusive for participants and so requires commitment to work with the researcher in examining their practice.

LIVERPOOL JOHN MOORES UNIVERSITY CASE STUDY

In order to illustrate the processes set out above, I will use a case study[3] which examined the Post Graduate Certificate in Learning and Teaching in Higher Education (PGCLTHE) at Liverpool John Moores University (LJMU).

Defining impact

Initially impact had been defined in terms of improving teaching and learning within the institution, and meeting the needs of participants. This was then operationalized as changes in the:

- behaviour of individual programme participants;
- behaviour of colleagues and departments;
- experience of students taught by participants; and
- beliefs about their role of individual programme participants.

It was also important to the PGCLTHE team to ask for feedback on the programme in a detailed but open-ended way.

Approach to analysis

Addressing the epistemological questions of Silverman (1999):

What status do you attach to your data?
The study adopted a realist perspective, acting on the belief that respondents have real or true internal states or beliefs, and accepting that participants' written and verbal statements can represent them. However, the project also accepted that beliefs are unique to the individual, although language will allow some common understandings. We also anticipated that individuals will have diverse and contradictory views.

Is your analytic position appropriate to your practical concerns?
The realist approach did seem to meet the practical needs of the programme team to evaluate the PGCLTHE after three cohorts had been through it and as the team prepared for a validation event. The team had a strong preference for qualitative methods, because gathering ideas

about what sort of effect the PGCLTHE might have would be pre-requisite to quantifying these effects. However, in retrospect, a constructionist approach could have been extremely interesting. A DA approach could have examined the discursive repertoires the participants drew on to construct their accounts of their own role, and how this had changed during the programme.

What claims will your analytic position and data collection methods permit you to make about your research?
The realist but entirely qualitative approach would not permit us to make generalizations from the sample of respondents to a larger group, but it would illustrate possible impacts and allow issues previously not considered by the programme team to emerge. Our approach privileged the researcher's interpretation, so it would allow us to make links between individual respondents and allow some grouping of ideas through thematic analysis (Miles and Huberman 1994).

Data collection methods

There were already a number of sources of relevant data in existence, which could have been analysed in a variety of ways:

Hopes fears and expectations
An exercise undertaken at the beginning of the programme had involved each participant writing one 'hope' one 'fear' and one 'expectation' about the programme on a post it for sharing.

Talking wall
A mid-course evaluation had involved responding to a number of questions posed by the programme team. Each of these questions was written at the top of a very large piece of paper and placed around the room. In the absence of programme team members, but with a facilitator, participants walked around the room, writing responses and then responded to each other's responses.

'Dear Tutor' letters
Mid-course all participants were invited to write a letter to the programme team, about whatever they wished and which was read by their tutors.

In addition to these some further data collection was designed to address the conceptions of impact outlined above congruent with the analytic approach set out above:

Questionnaires
An open-ended postal questionnaire sent to the 74 current and past participants in the PGCLTHE. Twenty-five responses were received. The questionnaire was in three parts designed to elicit examples of changes in behaviour and beliefs and also feedback on the programme.

Individual interviews
Individual interviews were conducted with seven programme participants, using the questionnaire as the basis for a semi-structured interview with further prompts. Participants were selected in order to sample new and experienced academics and support staff. Individual interviews were also conducted with three mentors who also held strategic roles within the institution as Teaching and Learning Co-ordinators (TLCs) and Directors of School.

Group interviews
Group interviews to bring together participants, mentors, TLCs and Directors of School were held in three Schools sampling arts and sciences.

Findings

The evidence of impact might best be structured as it was conceptualized above, as changes in:

Behaviour of individual programme participants
In their questionnaire responses, participants described a variety of changes in practice which were congruent with the aims of the programme team, such as producing more lesson plans, using more varied teaching methods and different forms of assessment, using more student activities in large group lectures, providing more support materials for students, thinking more about learning outcomes, and negotiating learning more with students. However, this doesn't fully capture the increased confidence in their own practice that these changes produced.

> 'I feel more confident! Changed to a student participation style of teaching.'

> 'I feel much more confident in my teaching ability and the variety of methods I am able to use.'

School Directors, TLCs and mentors also reported in interviews that PGCLTHE participants had acquired the language and knowledge to talk and write about teaching, which they saw as an advantage for Teaching Quality Assessment (TQA) as it then was.

> 'I'm less anxious about our impending TQA because the PGCert got me used to being observed and talking about my teaching.'

I would suggest that participants appear to be gaining both *declarative knowledge* about educational theories and *procedural knowledge* of teaching methods on the programme to achieve *functioning knowledge* (kinds of knowledge described by Biggs 1999) which increased their confidence.

Behaviour of colleagues and departments

Evidence for impact at an institutional level came from participants' questionnaire responses and more directly from interviews with School Directors, TLCs and mentors. Some participants were sceptical about any impact on their colleagues or changes in the practice of their department:

> 'No interest shown.'

> 'None to my knowledge.'

> 'Not much.'

However, there were contrary examples, and, especially where participants worked with other past or current PGCLTHE participants, changes in colleagues' practices were described, such as giving more student feedback, improving small group work, using alternative assessment strategies and gapped handouts:

> 'I doubt I've influenced anyone, except those who have been on the PGCert.'

> 'I and a colleague who also completed the PGCert have redesigned and team taught courses, thus spreading ideas.'

Perhaps programme participation was functioning to create a new sub-culture within departments. This might also be indicated by the spontaneous suggestion from an interviewee that regular teaching seminars, rather like research seminars, should be established, which would be a forum to discuss practice with colleagues.

School Directors and TLCs interviewed cited TQA grades, and attributed success in some measure to the participation in the PGCLTHE of some of their staff. They suggested that participation in peer observation during the programme led participants to become positive models for the value of peer observation as schemes were set up in departments.

Experience of students taught by participants
No direct evidence was available on this, but, in the questionnaire responses, participants suggested that that they paid more attention to student feedback, tried to see things from the perspective of their students and believed that students were happier, experiencing more variety, learning more and giving more positive feedback.

'Hopefully their experience is just better!'

'I believe students' experience is more exciting and more useful to them, and the feedback from them is pretty positive.'

Beliefs about their role of individual programme participants
In participants' questionnaire responses there appeared to be a wide-spread change in their view of their own role. This was frequently expressed as an acceptance of the role of professional teacher, and contrasted with their identity as a researcher. Several participants explicitly used concepts from the programme such as reflection, deep and surface approaches to learning, student centred learning and facilitation to describe their role. There was some divergence between the minority who had always seen teaching as central to their role and the majority for whom the PGCLTHE had been a stimulus to rethinking their role:

'See my role as encouraging a deep approach rather than inputting knowledge.'

'Became more professional towards teaching rather than viewing it as a means to fund research.'

'Before the PGCert I had not considered myself as a teacher, but as a researcher who gave lectures.'

'It changed my view that my role is as a provider of information (in an interesting way!) to thinking of myself as someone who facilitates learning.'

This rethinking of their role, reported by participants after the completion of the programme, is particularly interesting when contrasted with the 'hopes, fears and expectations' exercise completed at the very start of the programme. In this, participants expressed anxiety about their role beyond the programme, about their research, publications, work-load, administrative tasks, employment status and time management. There was also a widespread expectation that the programme would provide tips or skills that would enable more efficient teaching:

'To become great deliverer.'

'To pick up some tips on teaching in HE.'

'To become a competent HE lecturer.'

'Learn use of flashy media for impressive lecturing.'

Participants were not asked at that point to make explicit their personal theories of teaching. But I conclude that one impact of the programme was to help participants to articulate their own theories of teaching, and in doing so at least some shifted their view of their role as a teacher from Trigwell *et al.*'s (1994) teacher-focused to a student-focused conception.

Because a wide variety of data collection methods was used and some free responses were sought, some issues emerged beyond the conceptualization of change. Some of these issues might be considered as barriers to or difficulties in achieving impact:

Lack of recognition of achievement in completing PGCLTHE
There was a divide in opinions about the incentives or rewards for completing the PGCLTHE. In particular there was a contrast between Directors of School who saw no problem in lack of rewards, and new, part-time, temporary or sessional staff who felt very anxious about employment and saw their completion of the PGCLTHE as only benefiting LJMU, or only benefiting themselves in applying for new jobs elsewhere. There was a unanimous feeling that successful completion of the PGCLTHE would be of benefit to individuals in seeking future employment. Some participants attributed subsequent success to their successful completion of the PGCLTHE; others complained of lack of recognition of teaching as against research.

Participants are self-selecting
It was observed that only those already committed to improving the quality of learning and teaching volunteer for the PGCLTHE, and those who might benefit most will not volunteer for the programme. Such people could also be destructive in the role of mentor.

Mentors
Both mentors and mentees reported some instances of confusion and difficulty with the role of the mentor. The problems cited included lack of contact, that mentors were untrained as they were unable to attend training events, and that mentors felt confused or anxious about being responsible for the subject-specific input on the PGCLTHE.

Teaching as subject specific versus generic
Opinion was very divided on the issue of the subject-specific nature of teaching, but all agreed that the core of the PGCLTHE must be generic. The three Directors of School interviewed suggested that some of the programme could be organized around subject-specific issues. In contrast very few participants mentioned this and many described the added value of interdisciplinary contact between staff.

Compulsion
Institutional plans to make the PGCLTHE compulsory for new staff or a condition of successful completion of probation were overwhelmingly welcomed by all. Many participants went further and suggested it should be available or even compulsory for all existing staff.

Feedback on the programme
The PGCLTHE was considered appropriate and useful by all respondents, surprisingly regardless of their role or experience, and even by those who had subsequently left teaching. However, all participants interviewed had felt pressure of time had been a problem on the PGCLTHE.

CONCLUSION AND SUMMARY

I hope that this chapter has raised the kind of questions that you will need to answer in any attempt to evaluate the effects of your staff development work. I also hope that it has helped you to find ways to answer these questions. To reiterate, the issues that I hope you will consider in planning your evaluation are how you conceptualize impact, the implications of your analytic approach, and then appropriate data collection methods.

I expect that the time you spend considering how you conceptualize and then measure impact will be inseparable from thinking about what the intended outcomes of the programme were. The SEDA and ILTHE frameworks, Gibbs and Coffey's (2000) taxonomy of programme leaders' aims, and the models of professional development of teachers in higher education all provide potential frameworks for thinking about what impact might mean for your programme. I also hope that, having read this far, you will feel confident about the planning of a project to research the professional development of teachers in higher education, and more confident about the claims you might make and challenges that others might make about such a project.

The context of staff and educational development work is extremely complex. In universities of all places, a sophisticated and scholarly approach will be required to examine the many and various interactions between our activities as staff and educational developers and the complex system of the university in the wider world.

Baume (2003) suggests *accounting, improving* and *understanding* as the main reasons for evaluation. I would suggest, that if one takes seriously the intention to understand, then good evaluation is really research. Among many other functions research should allow unintended consequences of educational development to be examined. Identifying unintended effects, and seeking to understand the processes through which both intended and unintended consequences occur, will form a vital part of the evolving scholarship of staff and educational development. I believe that this growing body of scholarship will be vital to enable us to engage with our colleagues in the university in debate about staff educational development and how development contributes towards attainment of the purposes of higher education.

ACKNOWLEDGEMENTS

Many thanks to David Baume and Peter Kahn for their editing, and also to Martin Oliver for comments on an earlier draft.

NOTES

1   The HESDA project 'Evaluating the impact of professional development courses in teaching and learning for associate teachers in UK Universities' ran from September 2001–December 2002. The project team of programme leaders consisted of Holly Smith at University College London, Ali Cooper at the University of Lancaster, Sue Clayton at the University of Sussex, Carol Maynard at Liverpool John Moores University and Jessica Claridge at the University of Exeter.
2   ERIC is the world's largest source of education information, with more than 1 million abstracts of documents and journal articles on education research and practice. The searchable database is updated monthly and provides free access to ERIC Document citations at http://www.eric.ed.gov/.
3   The case study reported here was carried out by Holly Smith for a LJMU Teaching Fellowship into the impact of the PGCLTHE on teaching and

learning at Liverpool John Moores University in Semester 2 1998, under the direction of the course leader Sue Thompson and Ali Cooper.

REFERENCES

Baume, D. (2003) Monitoring and evaluating staff and educational development. In *A Guide to Staff and Educational Development*, (eds) P. Kahn and D. Baume. Kogan Page, London

Biggs, J. (1999) *Teaching for Quality Learning in Higher Education*. OUP/SRHE, London

Coffey, M. and Gibbs, G. (2000) Can academics benefit from training? Some preliminary evidence, *Teaching in Higher Education*, **5**(3), pp 385–9

Cohen, L., Manion, L. and Morrison, K. (2000) *Research Methods in Education*. 5th Edition, RoutledgeFalmer, London

Entwistle, N.J. and Ramsden, P. (1983) *Understanding Student Learning*. Croom Helm, London

Gibbs, G. and Coffey, M. (2000) Training to teach in higher education: A research agenda, *Teacher Development*, **4**, pp 31–44

Gilbert, A.K. and Gibbs, G. (1998) A proposal for a collaborative international research programme to identify the impact of initial training on university teaching. Paper presented at HERDSA conference, Auckland New Zealand

Ho, A.S.P. (2000) A conceptual change approach to staff development: A model for programme design, *The International Journal for Academic Development*, **5**(1), pp 30–41

ILTHE (2003) About the ILT: Membership, ILTHE. *http://www.ilt.ac.uk/249. asp#jump09* Accessed 7 August 2003

Kugel, P. (1993) How professors develop as teachers, *Studies in Higher Education*, **18**, pp 315–28

McLean, M. and Bullard, J. E. (2000) Becoming a university teacher: Evidence from teaching portfolios (how academics learn to teach), *Teacher Development*, **4**(1), pp 79–101

Marsh, H.W. (1982) SEEQ: A reliable, valid and useful instrument for collecting students' evaluations of university teaching, *British Journal of Educational Psychology*, **52**, pp 77–95

Miles, M.B. and Huberman, A.M. (1994) *An Expanded Sourcebook: Qualitative Data Analysis*. 2nd Edition, Sage, London

Murray, H.G. (1997) Effective teaching behaviours in the college classroom. In *Effective Teaching in Higher Education: Research and Practice*, (eds) R.P. Perry and J.C. Smart. Agathon Press, New York

Murray, K. and Macdonald, R. (1997) The disjunction between lecturers' conceptions of teaching and their claimed educational practice, *Higher Education*, **33**, pp 331–49

Novak, J.D. and Gowin, D.B. (1984) *Learning How to Learn*. Cambridge Press, New York

Ramsden, P. (1991) A performance indicator of teaching quality in higher education: The Course Experience Questionnaire, *Studies in Higher Education*, **16**, pp 129–50

Richardson, J.T.E. (Ed) (1996) *Handbook of Qualitative Research Methods for Psychology and the Social Sciences*, BPS Books, Leicester

Rust, C. (2000) Do initial training courses have an impact on university teaching? The evidence from two evaluative studies of one course, *Innovations in Education and Training International*, **37**(3), pp 254–61

Schön, D.A. (1983) *The Reflective Practitioner: How Professionals Think in Action*. Basic Books, New York

SEDA (2003) Professional Development Framework Handbook. Birmingham, Staff and Educational Development Association. *http://www.seda.ac.uk/pdf/index.htm* Accessed August 7 2003

Silverman, D. (Ed) (1997) *Qualitative Research: Theory, Method and Practice*. Sage, London

Silverman, D. (1999) *Doing Qualitative Research: A Practical Handbook*. Sage, London

Silverman, D. (2001) *Interpreting Qualitative Data: Methods for Analysing Talk, Text and Interaction*. 2nd Edition, Sage, London

Smith, J. K. and Hodkinson, P. (2002) Fussing about the nature of educational research: The neo-realists versus the relativists, *British Educational Research Journal*, **28**(2), pp 291–6

Sprague, J. and Nyquist, J. D. (1991) A developmental perspective on the TA role. In *Preparing the Professoriate of Tomorrow to Teach: Selected readings in TA Training*, (eds) J. D Nyquist, R. D. Abbot, D. H. Wulff and J. Sprague. Kendall-Hunt, Dubuque, IA

Strauss, A. and Corbin, J. (1998) *Basics of Qualitative Research: Grounded Theory Procedures and Techniques*. 2nd Edition, Sage, London

Tabachnick, B. G. and Fidell, L. S. (1996) *Using multivariate statistics*. 3rd Edition, Harper and Row, New York

Trigwell, K. and Prosser, M. (1996) Congruence between intention and strategy in university science teachers' approaches to teaching, *Higher Education*, **32**, pp 77–87

Trigwell, K., Prosser, M. and Taylor, P. (1994) Qualitative differences in approaches to teaching first year university science, *Higher Education*, **27**, pp 75–84

Unger, R. K. (1998) *Resisting Gender: Twenty-five years of feminist psychology*. Sage, London

7

Investigating staff and educational development

Paul Ashwin and Keith Trigwell

INTRODUCTION

In the last few decades, the practice of staff and educational development has been the subject of more scrutiny, research, investigation and debate than ever before, as the extent of development activity has also grown. Publications such as this book have benefited from, and aim to contribute to, this continuing growth. A significant component of the contribution has come from investigations of staff and educational development *by* staff and educational developers. It is this topic that we have taken as the focus of this chapter. (Approaches to investigating the impact of staff development programmes are considered in Chapter 6.) We acknowledge the contribution to investigating of staff and educational development made by those outside staff and educational development, and also by those within who have conducted investigations in related fields, but these are not areas we pursue further in this chapter.

A part of the growing debate about staff and educational development (hereafter sometimes simply called development) is the role of research. The purpose of this chapter is not to provide a guide on how to do research. Many guides are available that are suitable for research into development. They cover a variety of research paradigms (for example, Cohen *et al.* 2000; Silverman 2001; Knight 2002; Robson 2002). Instead, our purpose is to present an argument for a scholarly approach to educational development which has the investigation of practice as a core (and necessary) component. The approach that one takes to scholarship defines the sort of investigative questions one is interested in asking, the methods one adopts, the actors and collaborators involved in the investigation, and the developer's conception of the situation they are investigating. (We write here as if an individual developer is acting alone. We do this for simplicity, rather than because we see development as necessarily an individualistic activity, which we do not.)

In the pages that follow, we argue that investigation of practice (but not necessarily research) is an essential component of professional activity. We identify three qualitatively different aims of investigation of practice: investigations that develop personal knowledge, those that develop local knowledge and those that develop public knowledge. We argue that these different types of knowledge are associated with different standards of evidence and of ways of collecting that evidence, and they will have a different range of implications. Research, an investigation that develops public knowledge, is thus just one form of investigation. We argue that, unlike investigation that leads to the development of personal knowledge, research is not a necessary condition for the scholarship of staff and educational development.

In the last part of the chapter we give examples of different investigations that we have undertaken. We use these examples to illustrate the different types of knowledge produced from investigations into development. We conclude by arguing that engaging in scholarly educational development can facilitate the development of each of the different types of knowledge (including publishable research) that can result from investigating development.

INVESTIGATION AND SCHOLARSHIP OF STAFF AND EDUCATIONAL DEVELOPMENT PRACTICE

The scholarship of university teaching has received much attention in the last decade (see for example Boyer 1990; Kreber 2001; Shulman 1993, 1997; Trigwell *et al.* 2000). Much of what has been written on the scholarship of University teaching also applies to the practice of educational development. As we do with teaching, we take the view in this chapter that investigation into aspects of educational development is an essential part of the scholarship of the practice of educational development, and is also fundamentally related to other parts of the practice of educational development.

The idea of the scholarship of professional practice has been previously described (Trigwell and Shale in press) as having three temporal components: *awareness* of relevant aspects that inform the practice, the conduct of the *practice,* and the *outcomes* of that practice. Each component is strongly related to the other two and is described as being defined by a set of elements. For the practice of educational development, the three components, and key elements, are shown in Figure 7.1.

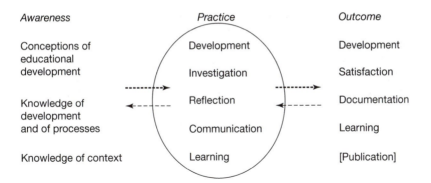

Figure 7.1 *Components of a model of scholarship of staff and educational development practice*

The key elements of awareness include the conceptions of practice, knowledge of the content and process of development, and awareness of the context in which the development activities occur. The five key elements that are associated with the practice of development are the development activities, investigation of and reflection on that practice, communication with others about the practice, and learning about development. The outcome elements include adding value through the practice (development), an affective aspect (satisfaction with the practice), artefacts such as documentation (planning documents, participant details, reports, etc.), and learning (that which has been learnt by the developer).

The focus of the scholarship of educational development practice is on adding value (the developmental gains) through action (the development process). Doing this job professionally involves an awareness of the elements listed, including being informed by the relevant research and accumulated experience, and the use of all five elements (circled) that constitute the practice. Some of these elements, particularly the development activities, are topics of discussion in other chapters and in other books. Here we concentrate on just one of them – the investigation of practice.

Our definition of investigation ranges from those personal reflections on issues or problems that produce little more than a small insight or a sign through to research published in international journals. The significance of the differences across this range is the topic of following sections. We consider the investigation of practice, in any form, to be an essential component of the scholarship of educational development practice. However, we argue that research, and publications that may result from that research, are not an essential component, although we accept that there may be other reasons (such as the UK Research Assessment Exercise, curiosity or job satisfaction) why staff need to research and publish. The two main reasons why we have taken this position are (a) that we are aware of highly professional, scholarly educational development practices that do not include research and publication and, (b) because there are staff employed on conditions, and in development units, where such research and publication are very difficult to achieve.

Investigation of practice is an integral part of the model of the scholarship of educational development practice. As such it is seen as being (a) informed by the three elements of awareness, (b) a co-element of practice that can support and be supported by the other elements of practice, and (c) a contributor to all five outcome elements. Considerable attention in the scholarship of teaching literature has been given to two of the awareness elements: the knowledge needed to conduct an investigation, and the importance of the context in which investigation is conducted. As with the scholarly investigation of teaching, we argue that a scholarly educational development investigation would need to make use of existing knowledge, both from the literature (both that of a disciplinary and a pedagogical nature) and from relevant experience.

The element of awareness that seems to have attracted much less attention is an awareness of conceptions of development used to inform practice (Trigwell 2003; Webb 1996). The variation in the conceptions of staff and educational development that are adopted is rarely articulated. For example, is development seen as fundamentally about creating contexts that make development possible? Or is it seen as the development of staff? And if it is the latter, is it seen as being based on changes in ways of thinking and doing or on simpler theories that say that if we add extra skills to each person's repertoire, then we will get better performances? And, in any of these qualitatively different conceptions, is it the ideas from experience and from the literature that informs practice, or the expressed development wishes of the 'client' that is the focus? A range of such conceptions is reported in Chapter 6.

None of the conceptions described above is absolute. They can be combined in various ways. Further, there is little or no evidence that some of these conceptions are better or worse than others. Notwithstanding all this, it is fundamental to staff and educational development, as well as to teaching, that whatever conception is held suggests how activity is related to outcome – for example, how teaching is related to learning, or how developing relates to development. In this chapter we assume the use of such a conception. We build on this conception to suggest how investigations into staff and educational development can be conducted. Such a conception equally underpins other similar processes, such as the management of educational development.

To summarize, our model of the scholarship of development practice suggests:

(a) that some form of investigation of practice is an essential part of the scholarship of educational development practice; and
(b) that activities associated with the investigations, as with the practice as a whole, are:
   • underpinned by a clear conception of how development activity relates to the outcomes of development (i.e. a model of how change takes place);
   • informed by relevant research; and
   • informed by the developer's experience of development work.

This is our starting point, and what we take as the minimum position in regard to the professionalism of development. Investigation of the form prescribed above is achievable in all staff and educational development units and by all development staff. Where we see the variation is in the nature of the investigation being conducted – both in the area being investigated and in the purpose of the investigation. It is this variation that is the topic of the remainder of the chapter. It is this variation that to some extent is also dependent on the conditions of appointment of development staff, and on the objectives of the development unit.

INVESTIGATING EDUCATIONAL DEVELOPMENT

We have organized this section around the idea that a developer who is interested in investigating their practice can engage in investigations at three qualitatively different levels depending on the type of knowledge that they are seeking to produce.

The three levels of investigation are:

1 An investigation to inform oneself about an aspect of educational development. This will result in the production of *personal* knowledge.
2 An investigation to inform a group within one or more shared contexts (typically development unit, subject department or faculty, institution) about an aspect of development. This will result in the production of *local* knowledge.
3 An investigation to inform a wider audience about an aspect of development. This will result in the production of *public* knowledge.

These three types of knowledge are similar to Rowland's (2000) distinction between the personal, shared and public contexts of knowledge, which

Table 7.1 Levels of investigations showing relations between the
purpose, process and outcomes of that investigation

Level	Purpose of investigation	Evidence gathering methods and conclusions will be	Investigation results in
1	To inform oneself	Verified by self	Personal knowledge
2	To inform a group within a shared context	Verified by those within the same context	Local knowledge
3	To inform a wider audience	Verified by those outside of that context	Public knowledge

he argues are resources that academics could draw upon in learning about their teaching (p. 61). Table 7.1 summarizes the characteristics of the different levels of investigations into development that define the qualitative differences. The three levels of knowledge that can result from the investigations form an inclusive hierarchy: that is, an investigation to inform a wider audience (what is commonly thought of as research) that results in the production of public knowledge will also lead to the development of personal knowledge and, unless the work is done in total privacy, local knowledge. It may be clear that, in undertaking research into staff and educational development and contributing new public knowledge, the developer will also gain new personal knowledge. It is not so obvious that this will also lead to the development of new local knowledge (however the local context is defined) as our focus in this chapter is on investigations that are carried out *into* educational development *by* educational developers. If a developer is reporting research into educational development outside of their context, then they also have a responsibility to make these results known to those involved in the development activity and thereby contribute to the development of local knowledge.

Developers could as part of their practice be engaged in all three types of investigation, producing personal, local and public knowledge. But they will not engage in all three types of investigations in all aspects of their practice. In some cases, only an investigation to inform oneself will be appropriate (although the possibility of sharing the investigation and its outcomes to at least the local context, the development unit, should always be considered). In other cases the developer will need to inform themselves and a group within a single (local) context, and the results may not be suitable for a wider audience. We see these decisions about which level is relevant in different aspects of a developer's role as professional decisions, to be made by individual developers or organizational groups. But we argue that this decision about which level of investigation is appropriate is one that generally needs to be made prior to the investigation taking place.

Investigations carried out at Level 1 result in the development of *personal* knowledge. This is knowledge born out of personal and professional experience (see Eraut 1994, pp. 104–7 and Rowland 2000, p. 55). The focus of such an investigation can be seen as the learning of the developer. The evidence gathered as part of this type of investigation, as well as the processes used to gather the evidence, will be verified by the developer and will have implications for the practice of the developer. The developer will do what they need to do to satisfy themselves of the validity of their conclusions. This can be seen as a form of reflective practice. Examples of the activities that are undertaken in this type of investigation include the developer undertaking personal reviews of the literature, monitoring and reflecting on the processes of educational development, and individual reflection on group discussions. Examples of artefacts that reflect the development of personal knowledge include reflective journals and diary notes.

Level 2 investigations are undertaken to inform a group (that includes the developer) about their shared context, and results in the development of *local* knowledge. Group in this context refers to functional groups, which have come together for a defined purpose, in this case relating to development. The processes of investigation and the evidence gathered as part of this type of investigation will be verified by the functional group as a whole as well as by the developer, and will have implications for the context in which the development is taking place. The investigator needs to satisfy others of the validity of their conclusions, and this may require more than is needed to satisfy only themselves. Examples of activities that result in the production of local knowledge include literature reviews that examine how a development might fit within a particular context; the evaluation of a development within a particular context; or the evaluation of a context prior to the implementation of a development activity. Examples of the outcomes of this type of investigation can be found in portfolios of courses in learning and teaching in higher education as well as in conference papers and reports, in departmental papers and reports and in some publications by societies, for example the Staff and Educational Development Association (SEDA), the Higher Education Research and Development Society of Australasia (HERDSA) or in Canada the Society for Teaching and Learning in Higher Education (STLHE).

Level 3 investigations are undertaken to inform a wider audience about some aspect of the development in which the developer has been involved. The evidence gathered and the meanings drawn from this, as well as the ways in which evidence was gathered and the meanings drawn, will be verified by people from outside of the context through the peer review process. The outcomes of research will have implications that go beyond the context in which the investigation was conducted, and the investigator needs to satisfy this wider audience of the validity of their conclusions. Examples of research activities include the full range of social science research approaches. The outcomes are found in research journals in higher education such as *The International Journal for Academic Development, Studies in Higher Education* and *Teaching in Higher Education.*

We re-emphasize that our view of scholarship implies that investigations undertaken at all of these levels will need to meet the criteria of what counts as scholarly educational development practice. That is, all levels of investigation will be based on a conception of how development activity leads to development outcomes, will be informed by relevant literature relating to educational development, and will draw upon the developer's experiences of development.

In the next section we give examples of investigations into educational development. Each illustrates the differences and relations between personal, local and public knowledge. Each example addresses a different investigation focus: a focus on the *people* involved in the development activity, including the developer; on the *development activity*; and on the *context* in which the development takes place. This distinction is an artificial one, and all areas might be involved in some studies. We use it here as a device to help to illustrate the qualitative differences between the three types of knowledge that can be developed through investigating educational development.

EXAMPLES OF INVESTIGATIONS INTO EDUCATIONAL DEVELOPMENT

Each of the following three examples examines how personal, local and public knowledge were developed and why we describe the example as a scholarly investigation of educational development. Our intention in doing this is to allow the reader to experience the variation in each example between the different types of knowledge. We have drawn on our own practice because examples of the development of personal knowledge and local knowledge are largely invisible within the research literature.

Example 1: an investigation focused on people who are involved in educational development

The first example is of an investigation that focused on the people who supported the development of academic staff at the University of Technology, Sydney, Australia. A decision in the late 1990s by the Engineering Faculty to turn their traditional programme into a graduate attributes-based programme with a core module on sustainability was to have a profound impact on academic staff. Four communications staff from the Faculty of Humanities' English Language and Study Skills Assistance Centre agreed to team-teach the module with engineering staff. Four teams of four each worked with a quarter of the 270 students on one of four engineering themes (clean power, space, transport, pollution) with the common aims that students would develop a critical appreciation of the concept of sustainability, appreciation of the importance of advocacy, and formulation of reasoned arguments in writing and speaking (Trigwell 2000).

KEITH TRIGWELL WRITES

The investigation into the needs of academic staff teaching in the newly designed sustainability module had three aims: (a) to ascertain for myself what development needs were arising out of the team-teaching context involving staff from two different disciplines, (b) to provide information for use by the teaching team in discussion and review sessions, and (c) to yield data which could form the basis of a research publication. The investigation was conducted by interviewing 14 of the 16 academic staff involved (11 of 12 engineers, and three of four communications staff). The interviews focused on their experience of the teaching they had just completed (at the end of the first year the subject was offered). They were asked about the nature of their preparation, approach to team-teaching, engagement with the literacy and writing components, problems that they had experienced, and where they felt more support was needed.

With respect to the first aim, the focus of the analysis of the interviews was on the content of the last two areas (problems and support), but within the context of their response to the other questions. The knowledge generated from the analysis was fed back to individual members of the teams in personal discussions. It was also used to develop the material for the team discussion sessions. This part of the investigation was conducted at Level 1. No artefacts in the form of reports or the like were produced in this process. This investigation, based on sound interview processes with questions derived from the literature on team-teaching could have been the end of the story. In this case it was not.

The second aim (at Level 2) was addressed through an analysis of the responses to questions about how the team felt about the way it had worked. While these data were focused on use for the development of the teams, they were presented in the form of a report in conjunction with other data collected from the student evaluation of the subject. The students' perspective in this report was also the subject of conference paper (Trigwell and Yasukawa 1999).

A phenomenographic analysis of the interviews with the 11 engineering staff was conducted for one publication from the research component (Level 3) of the investigation. Four qualitatively different descriptions of the teachers' experience of teaching Engineering for Sustainability were reported in an engineering education journal (Trigwell 2000). These results constitute a contribution to understanding educational development through an increased awareness of the variation in ways of experiencing cross-disciplinary team-teaching.

Example 2: An investigation with a focus on the educational development activity

The second example is of an investigation that was focused on the development activity, and is about the implementation of peer learning schemes. These schemes were introduced across a college to provide structures in which students could support each other in their learning. The development involved working with students and teachers to introduce peer learning across a range of courses (Ashwin 2002).

PAUL ASHWIN WRITES

This example is based upon my work in developing a strategy for the implementation of peer learning across an organization. In investigating this implementation strategy, I was interested in developing my understanding of how to implement peer learning (Level 1). I was also concerned to examine how the implementation of peer learning developed within that context (Level 2) as well as how this might relate to the implementation of peer learning in other contexts (Level 3).

I developed my understanding of the implementation of peer learning through discussions with the students and teachers involved in peer learning, through an examination of the literature on implementing peer learning and organizational change as well as more general literature on teaching and learning in post-compulsory education, and by reflecting on the relations between these and my experiences of implementing peer learning. An example of how my personal knowledge developed was a change in the way that I thought about the relation between peer learning schemes and the context in which they operated. Before starting my investigation, I saw peer learning initiatives as entities that were entirely separate from the courses and institutions in which they operated, which meant that they could be implemented in a fixed way regardless of that context. As a result of my investigation into peer learning I began to see the implementation of peer learning initiatives as an example of organizational change. This changed view implied that any implementation of a peer learning initiative needs to fit with the context of the courses and institution in which it is being implemented.

As well as developing my understanding of the implementation of peer learning, I also needed to provide the institution with evidence about the development of peer learning. As part of this level 2 investigation, I examined how the implementation of peer learning developed within the institution by examining how the take-up and awareness of peer learning of students and teachers changed over time. The development of this local knowledge was reflected in a report to the college in which I concluded that the implementation strategy had been successful in encouraging more students and teachers to become involved in peer learning (Ashwin 1997). These findings were verified by those within the shared context in which peer learning was being implemented. The results were meaningfully interrogated and actions taken to investigate their validity by those within that organizational context. The implications were for the particular context in which peer learning was being implemented. The specificity of the report and its developmental focus meant that it was not suitable for publication outside of the context in which it was written.

Having been struck by the absence of literature on implementing peer learning across organizations, I also included an investigation at Level 3. I examined how the implementation of peer learning in the college might be related to the implementation of peer learning in other contexts by examining the changes to the implementation strategy in terms of the literature on organizational change (Ashwin 2002). By using this literature, as well as a mixture of the local and personal knowledge I had produced, I developed a model for the implementation of peer learning across organizations that had implications that went beyond the initial context in which peer learning had been implemented. This was verified through the peer review process and published in a research journal.

Example 3: An investigation with a focus on the context of educational development

The third example is of an investigation that was focused on the context of educational development. In early 2001, the Senior Tutor of a college of the University of Oxford requested an evaluation by the Institute for the Advancement of University Learning of the perceived learning context of his college.

PAUL ASHWIN AND KEITH TRIGWELL WRITE

The focus of the investigation was to be on how students in one Oxford college experience their learning environment. Instruments such as the Course Experience Questionnaire (CEQ) (Ramsden 1991) were available, but their appropriateness in a context as different as an Oxford college had not previously been ascertained. In addition we were both new to Oxford and to how educational development might be conducted at Oxford. We saw this request as an opportunity: (a) to develop our understanding of the Oxford context, (b) to provide information to the college that could be used for development purposes, and (c) to test the appropriateness of the CEQ by conducting a research study of the relations between its scales and students' approaches to learning. Following discussions with the Senior Tutor and representatives from the college's student body, the Junior Common Room (JCR), we modified the CEQ according to our understanding of the college context, added another 45 items that were a combination of items requested by the college and those added by us to test the CEQ, and distributed it to all 400+ undergraduate students.

The process of developing the modified and additional items for the questionnaire served as a part of our learning about Oxford (Level 1). To support this process we collected and reviewed the literature on teaching and learning at Oxford (Oxford University 2000), and held informal discussions with experienced teachers and developers. At the same time, as part of another project, we were each interviewing students at other colleges about their learning experience, and we discussed and compared our learning from those interviews (though the analysis of the interviews was not completed in time to inform this evaluation). However, most of our learning from this process came in the analysis of the students' response to the questionnaire.

A confidential report containing the students' response to the questionnaire was produced for the college (Senior Tutor and JCR) (Level 2). This report included an analysis of the CEQ scales and of individual items requested by the college and an analysis of the open-ended questions, linked where possible to distributions and means of the quantitative components. This report focused on a description of the learning context – the context of the development activity.

The analysis of the CEQ in the Oxford context, and the testing of new, Oxford-specific scales, formed the basis of a research publication (Trigwell and Ashwin 2002). One of the new scales we tried contained items that were specific to Oxford, but we conceived of them as being part of an evoked conception of learning (a conception of the learning task evoked by a specific situation) scale. Our research hypothesis was that evoked conceptions of learning would show meaningful relations with the scales of the CEQ and with students' approaches to learning. The results, which were consistent with this hypothesis, gave further insight into how the development of teaching and learning could be enhanced. These conclusions and data on the new scale were deemed appropriate for a wider audience.

We noted earlier that scholarly investigation by educational developers happens most at Level 1, and least at Level 3. A common feature of all three of these examples is that the investigation was conducted at each of the three levels. Another common feature, and the one we wish to emphasize, is that in all three examples all three levels of investigation were planned before the investigation began. This is necessary (though often overlooked) if the data gathered, and the processes used to gather them, are going to be of a sufficient quality to be verified by those within and outside the context of the investigation. As the examples above show, the question behind a personal investigation is likely to be of a very different form to the question that informs an investigation that results in the development of local knowledge. The question is likely to be different again to the type of research question that is to be the basis of a study with implications that go beyond the context in which it has been conducted. This is true irrespective of the focus of the investigation (on people, the development activity, or the context) and of the timing of the investigation (before, during or after the development activity).

CONCLUSION

In this chapter we first argued that educational development is a scholarly activity and that investigation is an essential part of this scholarly activity. We argued that this investigation can be undertaken at three different levels, and that investigations at these three different levels result in the development of three different types of knowledge: personal, local and public knowledge. Further, we argued that, whilst all developers will be involved in the development of personal knowledge, and nearly all in reporting their activities within their institutions (the development of local knowledge), it is not a necessary condition of the scholarship of educational development practice that practitioners engage in the production of public knowledge through research. Which level of investigation is appropriate depends on the aims of the particular task and is a decision for individual developers and development groups. This decision needs to be made at the planning stage of the investigation, as without such planning it may be difficult to turn a Level 1 investigation into Level 3 (research) investigation.

Conducting educational development in a scholarly way, along the lines set out in our model, more closely aligns personal, local and public knowledge. If personal knowledge is based on an explicit conception of how development operates, is based on the relevant literature and on personal experience, then it is easier to see gaps in the research literature, to see how investigation of process has relevance in a wider context, and to plan to make the personal implications of learning relevant to those inside and beyond the context of development.

REFERENCES

Ashwin, P. (1997) *Peer Support Annual Report 1996–7*, Newham College, London

Ashwin, P. (2002) Implementing peer learning across organisations: the development of a model, *Mentoring & Tutoring*, **2**(3), pp 221–31

Boyer, E.L. (1990) *Scholarship Reconsidered: Priorities of the Professoriate*, The Carnegie Foundation for the Advancement of Teaching, Princeton, NJ

Cohen, L., Manion, L. and Morrison, K. (2000) *Research Methods in Education.* Fifth Edition, RoutledgeFalmer, London

David, M.E. and Woodwards, D. (1998) *Negotiating the Glass Ceiling: Careers of Senior Women in the Academic World*, Falmer, London

Eraut, M. (1994) *Developing Professional Knowledge and Competence*, The Falmer Press, London

Knight, P.T. (2002) *Small Scale Research. Pragmatic Inquiry in Social Science and the Caring Professions*, Sage Publications, London

Kreber, C. (Ed) (2001) *Scholarship Revisited: Perspectives on the Scholarship of Teaching*, Jossey-Bass, San Francisco

Oxford University (2000) *Learning and Teaching at the University of Oxford*, http://www.learning.ox.ac.uk/iaul/IAUL+3+2+1.asp

Prosser, M. and Trigwell, K. (1999) *Understanding Learning and Teaching: The Experience in Higher Education*, SRHE and Open University Press, Buckingham

Ramsden, P. (1992) *Learning to Teach in Higher Education*, Routledge, London

Robson, C. (2002) *Real World Research.* Second Edition, Blackwell Publishers, Oxford

Rowland, S. (2000) *The Enquiring University Teacher*, SRHE and Open University Press, Buckingham

Shulman, L.S. (1993) Teaching as community property, *Change* (**Nov/Dec**) pp 6–7

Shulman, L.S. (1998) Chapter 1 in *The Course Portfolio: How faculty can examine their teaching to advance practice and improve student learning* (ed.) P. Hutchings, American Association for Higher Education, pp 5–6

Silverman, D. (2001) *Interpreting Qualitative Data. Methods for Analysing Talk, Text and Interaction.* Second Edition, Sage Publications, London

Trigwell, K. (2003) Awareness of variation in ways of experiencing academic development, in *The Scholarship of Academic Development* (eds) R. Macdonald and H. Eggins, SRHE and Open University Press, Buckingham

Trigwell, K. (2000) Student-focused programmes: challenges facing engineering academic staff, *British Journal of Engineering Education*, **1**, pp 21–6

Trigwell, K. and Ashwin, P. (2002) Evoked conceptions of learning and learning environments. Paper presented at the Improving Student Learning Symposium (Theory and Practice – 10 Years On), Brussels, 4–6 September

Trigwell, K. and Shale, S. (in press) Student learning and the scholarship of university teaching (August 2004)

Trigwell, K. and Yasukawa, K. (1999) Learning in a graduate attributes-based engineering course, *Research and Development in Higher Education, http://herdsa. org.au/vic/cornerstones/tocnewcurriculum.html*

Trigwell, K., Martin, E., Benjamin, J. and Prosser, M. (2000) Scholarship of teaching: A model, *Higher Education Research and Development*, **19**, pp 155–68

Webb, G. (1996) *Understanding Staff Development*, SRHE/Open University Press, Buckingham

8

How do professionals learn and develop? Implications for staff and educational developers

Rhona Sharpe

INTRODUCTION

Universities are heavily involved in both the initial and the continuing education and development of professionals, in fields as diverse as law, medicine, engineering, social work, nursing and of course, teaching. There is now a growing body of literature concerning this education and development of professionals within higher education (e.g. Barnett 1992; Boud *et al.* 1985; Eraut 1993, 1994; Morrison 1996; Yelloly and Henkel 1995). The idea for this chapter started with the thought that as staff and educational developers, we might usefully draw more on the existing literature of professional learning, education and development in our work with higher education teachers.

This chapter draws particularly on theoretical approaches to professional learning and development, although the benefit of the sharing of stories of good practice is also fully acknowledged. It is important for educational developers to make use of models and theory for at least two reasons. The first is the inherent value of theories and models as devices to help us understand and extend our work. The second is that using theories and models is a vital part of the professionalizing of our own work. We believe in and promote notions of scholarship. We expect the teachers we work with to know and apply theories of teaching and learning in their work. This chapter aims to use professional learning theory as a hook to understanding our own practice.

In this chapter, the aspects of professional learning which might be relevant to the developer are organized around the *what, how, where* and *when* of professional learning. Starting with the 'what', models of knowledge and competence are reviewed. For the 'how', a critical stance is taken on the influence and application of experiential learning and reflective practice. Discussion of the 'where' focuses on recent theoretical developments in social learning, emphasizing the importance of the concepts of communities of practice and non-formal learning situations. Finally, the 'when' discusses initial and continuing professional development and how they might link with developing conceptions of learning and stages of teacher's development.

WHAT PROFESSIONALS LEARN: KNOWLEDGE, VALUES AND COMPETENCE

This section concentrates on the links between professional knowledge, values and competence and the important role of developers in the professionalization of teaching. In earlier years we ran short 'how to teach' courses, where the emphasis was on practical skills, tips and tricks. However, staff developers have found that such an approach alone does not lead to teachers improving their practice (Biggs 1989; Gibbs 1995). As we have moved towards professionalizing teaching, we have incorporated what we consider to be the knowledge, values and competences which underpin teaching into our professional development courses and this is reflected in current accreditation schemes for higher education teachers (Baume and Baume 1996; Bucklow and Clark 2000).

Professional knowledge

It is important that, in order to provide the best possible professional development, we understand something of professional knowledge, its characteristics and its acquisition. Professions have traditionally been thought to demand a substantial specialist knowledge base which requires a long period of formal training to acquire. We are familiar with academic's expertise being defined by their knowledge of their subject, but not until recently by their knowledge of their teaching of that subject. However, we do now expect teachers to apply to their practice knowledge of models of student learning and motivation and of curriculum development.

Schön characterizes one view of the knowledge base of the professional as 'specialized, firmly bounded, scientific and standardized' (Schön 1983 p. 23). It is the explicit knowledge found in text books – the codified knowledge of academic papers – the knowing that. How is this knowledge acquired? Following on from a long-established and still much practised model of teaching as the relatively unproblematic handing over of knowledge from teacher to learner, a more recent model of knowledge acquisition, heavily promoted in schools and more recently in higher education, has been constructivism. Constructivism is based on the notion that learners construct their own meanings, and that learning opportunities should be designed to allow them to do this through student-centred, active learning experiences, working with others and with concrete problems. Learners use their prior knowledge, combined with their learning environment, to construct individual and idiosyncratic meanings – which may or may not be the meaning intended by the tutor! There is no obvious reason why a constructivist approach should not be just as effective for teachers who are learning to teach, and there are many examples of such an approach from teacher education (see Richardson 1997).

Applying professional knowledge in practice

In addition to the 'knowing that', models of professional knowledge include an assumption that such knowledge is there for a purpose – to be used. Knowing that is not enough; you also need to know how. Michael Eraut, who has conducted the most comprehensive recent review and analysis of professional knowledge, states that 'professional knowledge cannot be characterized in a manner that is independent of how it is learned and how it is used' (Eraut 1994, p. 19). Professionalism then isn't just about having a knowledge base, but using knowledge to respond effectively in professional roles. Taking this even further Eraut describes his realization that 'learning knowledge and using knowledge are not separate processes but the same process. The process of using knowledge transforms that knowledge so that it is no longer the same knowledge' (p. 25).

Qualitative studies support the recognition that teachers have a solid knowledge base about their teaching. Asking teachers about how they think and work:

> revealed that 'good practitioners' had an enormously complex and highly personal knowledge base, constructed from experience but used in a fairly intuitive way. . . . Moreover, much of this complex knowledge-base was tacit rather than explicit, so that practitioners could not readily articulate what they did or how they did it.
>
> (Eraut 1993, p. 224)

Externalizing tacit knowledge

One of the most important findings which Eraut refers to above is that the knowing how is frequently tacit. Polanyi (1967) first defined tacit knowledge as 'that which we know but cannot tell' and later studies have found that professionals consistently find it difficult to explain what they do. For example, Dreyfus and Dreyfus (1986) in studies with pilots found that these experts relied on tacit knowledge; they made fast intuitive decisions that they found hard to put into words. Dreyfus and Dreyfus termed this 'unconscious competence', and a string of research has confirmed that often we just don't know, as in cannot articulate, what we know. So professionals, including professional teachers, rely on two types of knowledge: explicit knowing that, and tacit knowing how.

One aim, then, of professional development is to make the expert's tacit knowledge explicit – to interrogate tacit knowledge to construct explicit knowledge. In practice developers can support individual professional development by encouraging teachers to share their knowledge about teaching; to make it explicit, to reflect on it, interpret it and use it as a step towards further learning. We thus prompt, guide, challenge and encourage action. Indeed, as part of more recent work in social cognition, tacit knowledge has been recognized as a phenomenon found not just in expert individuals, but also in professional groups or communities (Brown and Duguid 2000). For example, Nonaka and Takeuchi (1995) conducted research into organizational learning with workgroups in Hewlett Packard. They suggested that knowledge is created from the interaction of explicit and tacit knowledge through socialization; that tacit knowledge may be gained on the job but externalized through dialogue; and conversely that explicit knowledge may be internalized to become tacit through practice. The four processes of socialization, externalization, combination and internationalization (the SECI model) work in a spiral of knowledge creation and transfer from individual, to group, to organization and on. So externalizing knowledge benefits not just the individual but the whole professional community. This idea led to a massive growth in publications in the field of knowledge management.

Professional values

Since the professional typically has some power over their client, professions find it right to espouse some basis of principles or values to inform and underpin their practice. In UK higher education, the Staff and Educational Development Association's (SEDA 2003) Professional Development Framework expects the work of those who support learning in higher education to be underpinned by the commitments to:

- an understanding of how people learn;
- scholarship, professionalism and ethical practice;
- working in and developing learning communities;
- working effectively with diversity and promoting inclusivity;
- continued reflection on professional practice; and

- the development both of people and of educational processes and systems.

Similarly, the Institute for Learning and Teaching in Higher Education's (ILTHE) scheme for higher education teachers asks them to demonstrate the following professional values:

- a commitment to scholarship in teaching, both generally and within their own discipline;
- respect for individual learners and for their development and empowerment;
- a commitment to the development of learning communities, including students, teachers and all those engaged in learning support;
- a commitment to encouraging participation in higher education and to equality of educational opportunity; and
- a commitment to continued reflection and evaluation and consequent improvement of their own practice.

The Canadian Society for Learning and Teaching in Higher Education also provides a lengthy description of their ethical principles on their website (STLHE 1996).

An essential aim of professional development is to incorporate these values into development programmes in such a way that professionals not only know about them, but also use them to drive their practice.

Two interesting Codes of Practice, containing some elements both of professional values as I have been considering above and of professional competences to which we turn next, have been published by the UK General Social Care Council (2002). I mention them here to suggest that the distinction proposed in this Chapter between professional knowledge, values and competence may itself shift over time.

Professional competences

The competence approach starts by defining specific outcomes and behaviours to describe what various professionals do in the workplace. For example, it has offered a comprehensive overview of what managers do, and thus helped management developers decide what to include in their programmes. In the UK, the National Council for Vocational Qualifications prompted the updating of courses to emphasize student performance and outcomes and their assessment in the real work environment. The Management Charter Initiative management standards (MCI 1991, 1995) were quite influential in their attempt to map more advanced skills into a competence framework. They produced a detailed statement of all the competences required for satisfactory performance of a generic management post. These were used as a basis for analysis of specific management roles e.g. in school management (Earley 1992).

There has been some debate within the competence approach about the balance between the skills and performance, which were the starting point for defining competences, and personal qualities, knowledge and understanding. The MCI standards do state that their standards should be supported by a body of knowledge, but this receives less emphasis than the skills and qualities.

In devising competences for UK higher education teaching, both SEDA and the ILTHE require their areas of work (outcomes) to be underpinned by core knowledge and values. The emphasis is on what professionals do with their knowledge and how they can demonstrate what they do for the purposes of assessment. This approach has helped to define and standardize the work of higher education teachers and it has provided a way to accredit and reward satisfactory performance. Overall, the competence approach has confirmed the importance of both knowledge and values, not for their own sake, but for how knowledge and values are used to underpin professional performance.

Implications for developing professional knowledge, values and competences

Those of us supporting the professional development of teachers might find it helpful to understand how teachers construct knowledge like any other learners, but that *professional knowledge* has its own special character- istics. This review shows how ideas about professional knowledge have changed. Professional knowledge is no longer viewed as just consisting of a standardized, explicit and fixed knowledge base. It is now seen as knowledge which exists in its use, is ethical in its use and is changed by experience. The distinctive nature of professional knowledge lies in the interplay between its construction and use. When teachers use their knowledge, use changes what that knowledge is. This can lead us to design professional development activities which:

- allow for knowledge construction both individually and in collabora- tion with others e.g. inquiry based learning, problem-based learning, action research;
- encourage knowledge to be applied effectively within professional roles allowing the 'knowing that' to be updated;
- encourage learners to interrogate and engage with their developing knowledge in order to externalize and make explicit the 'knowing how', so that it can be shared and learnt from, to the benefit of both the individual and the organization; and

- Incorporate the values and ethical practice of the profession to reaffirm how knowledge is used in practice.

HOW PROFESSIONALS LEARN: LEARNING FROM EXPERIENCE

Having established that professional learning is more than knowledge acquisition, but is about *externalizing* and *applying* knowledge, we now move on to the processes by which professionals learn. Research in the field of adult learning has provided a large body of evidence that self-directed learning takes place in all sorts of informal situations, not just formal courses. It seems that adults learn from their experiences. Following this view, much of the work on professional learning has concentrated on the links between experience and knowledge.

Reflection as a process of learning from experience

David Kolb is committed to the idea that most human learning is from experience rather than from formal education. Kolb has promoted Lewin's (1951) ideas about the cyclic nature of learning widely in education and training. Kolb describes effective learning as consisting of four stages in an experiential learning cycle: concrete experience, reflective observation, abstract conceptualization and active experimentation (Kolb 1984). In order to learn successfully, people must have opportunities to have an experience, reflect on it, make generalizations about it to place it in a conceptual framework and use this to plan to

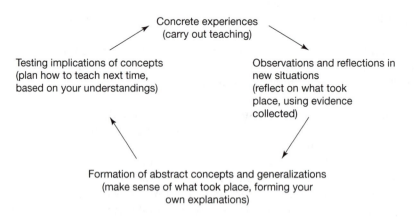

Figure 8.1 Kolb's cycle of learning and its application to teaching (adapted from Kolb (1991) and H850:Teaching and Learning in Higher Education, Open University)

tackle a new situation. This has given developers of higher education lecturers, particularly in the UK and Australia, a simple but useful structure around which to base their programmes (e.g. Pill *et al.* 2001).

Donald Schön's notion of reflective practice has been similarly influential as a process for learning from experience. The ideas in Schön's books (Schön 1983, 1987, 1990) have been widely taken up by teacher education (e.g. Zeichner 1995; Morrison 1996); higher education teaching (e.g. Barnett 1992; Boud *et al.* 1985) and social work (e.g. Yelloly and Henkel 1995).

Schön was arguing against the dominant culture of the time, which he termed 'technical rationality'. This was the belief that professionals solve problems through scientific application of knowledge and rational analysis of the outcomes. Schön observed that, for many professionals, problem solving is messier than this, and professionals don't actually use such logical processes in their work. He argued that you can't have a techno-rational plan for every situation, so that applying rational decision making in the 'swampy lowlands' of professional practice would lead to only partial solutions. Instead, Schön described the 'professional artistry' of noting what is happening at the time (reflection-in-action) and considering it after the event (reflection-on-action).

For example, when a student asks a question, the teacher reflects in action. They consider whether they've understood the question correctly or whether they need to clarify it; how they are going to phrase their answer; what they know about the questioner and how this knowledge might affect their answer. They might answer a bit of the question, gauge the reaction, and then continue. Schön terms this questioning and experimenting on the spot reflection in action. After the session, the teacher might make time to consider how the session went, what kinds of questions were raised, why certain misunderstandings might have occurred and how they could be avoided next time. The teacher here is reflecting on action. In relation to the previous discussion on tacit knowledge, reflection is clearly a key process by which tacit knowledge becomes explicit.

> Through reflection, he can surface and criticise the tacit under-standings that have grown up around the repetitive experiences of a specialised practice, and can make new sense of the situations of uncertainty or uniqueness which he may allow himself to experience.
>
> (Schön 1983)

Schön's work has been studied widely and in great detail. Inconsistencies have been noted in the way he uses the term reflection-in-action, and the distinction between this and reflection-on-action (Moon 1999b; Eraut 1994). Schön may have used his own terminology ambiguously, but more worrying are the questions about whether there is really time to reflect in action (Court 1988) and the lack of actual evidence for reflection-in-action in classroom teaching (Eraut 1995). Reflection-in-action is described as a tacit and automatic process, and as such is going to be difficult to study and promote. Schön originally saw the application of his work for the education of professionals as the creation of a virtual 'practicum' where participants could be faced with new situations and practise their reflection-in-action and responses to them. Instead, staff development has tended to focus on the theoretically and practically easier concept of reflection-on-action to make formal education settings more practice based. There is now a great deal of practical guidance to support professionals to continually develop themselves through their usual work, using techniques to promote reflection-on-action, such as dialogue and facilitation (Brockbank and McGill 1998), journal writing (Moon 1999a) and action learning sets (McGill and Beaty 1995).

Cowan (1998) introduces a third type of reflection – 'reflection for action'. He uses everyday language and examples to explain his concept of professional learning as a process of analysing and evaluating personal experiences and generalizing from them. Analysing is asking the question 'how do I do it?' (similar to reflection-in-action); evaluating is extending this to 'how well can I do it?' (similar to reflection-on-action); and generalizing is summarizing the relevant bits which might inform future practice. So, the additional anticipatory type of reflection – reflection for action – is the 'reflection which establishes priorities for subsequent learning by identifying the needs, aspirations and objectives which will subsequently be kept prominently in the learner's mind' (p. 37). He models the learning process as including all three types of reflection, and therefore as requiring three types of learning activity. Cowan (2003) explores and illustrates many ways to use, within staff development, these and other ideas about learning from reflection.

However, the speed and fervour with which many professions have adopted the rhetoric of reflective practice have alarmed some, and caused them to question how it is applied in practice. Some writers have criticized teacher education for using the notion of reflective practice to give training programmes credibility without any real ideological consistency or depth (Ecclestone 1996). In particular, reflective practice has been criticized for being ineffective when it is contentless (what knowledge do you bring to the process?), when it doesn't lead to action (what is the outcome of the reflection?) or when it is poorly defined (as a tool for contemplation or to direct action?). Boud and Walker (1998), in an honest and challenging paper, argue that reflection is highly context-specific and has been used inappropriately, even unethically, in some educational programmes which have adopted the rhetoric of reflective practice. Many of their examples are of reflective activities being applied in inappropriate contexts, be that in preparation for assessments that are non-reflective, or in encouraging self-disclosure which staff are inadequately prepared to deal with. They also refer to reflection being turned into mechanistic exercises, reflective activities that are unrelated to any learning or lead students to adopt an uncritical acceptance of their experiences. The key, then, is context. There is little point in:

> promoting the use of reflective journals when formal assessment is based on competitive, cognitively-orientated examinations, or encouraging the exploration of personal identity when anti-discriminatory practices are not well established within an institution.
> (Boud and Walker 1998)

Boud and Walker encourage developers to engage in an honest appraisal of how their reflective activities are designed appropriately for each unique group and professional education programme, and to develop a level of trust commensurate with the level of disclosure expected.

Implications for promoting learning from experience

We are now building a more complete picture of professional learning. This picture includes not only the externalization and application of professional knowledge in practice but also some learning from these experiences through a process of reflection. The original ideas of Lewin, Kolb, Schön and others have been widely used and extended. Those of us supporting the professional development of teachers might also find it helpful to explore and clarify what we mean by reflection and how different types of reflection can be promoted through our development activities. This might lead us to design professional development activities:

- where participants can learn from experience in informal settings;
- which take into account cycles of action and reflection by giving opportunities for learners to engage in different types of activities at different times;
- which give opportunities and structures to facilitate clearly defined different types of reflection: reflection in action, on action and for action; and
- which are clear about the type of reflection expected, its alignment

with assessment, the expected degree of personal disclosure and academic critique.

WHERE PROFESSIONALS LEARN: SITUATED LEARNING AND COMMUNITIES OF PRACTICE

The social aspects of learning have come to the fore recently with the emergence of the field of situated learning which recognizes and emphasizes the importance of context in learning. These social approaches see the individual as part of a system which includes other people, places, materials and tools. The much cited Lave and Wenger (Wenger 1988; Lave and Wenger 1991) were primarily interested in learning in work situations, and their ideas have become influential in the field of education. They saw such systems as consisting of discourse communities (from scholarly discipline groups to particular student cohorts) which provide cognitive tools (ideas, theories, concepts) that individuals use to make sense of their experiences. They also presented us with the notion of the 'community of practice' which has embedded in it knowledge about, say for example, a certain professional practice. Professional learning is seen as the process of entry into that community of practice.

For many of us, these influential ideas of situated learning are already with us, even if we haven't adopted their terminology, in that we have been promoting social approaches to teaching in higher education. For example, some of the implications for education are that classroom activities should be authentic in that they are close to what practitioners really do; that they should foster important life skills; and perhaps that they aim to enculturate students into their specific academic or professional communities. The situated approach asks us to consider 'how to help students develop deep understanding of subject matter, situate students' learning in meaningful contexts, and create learning communities in which teachers and students engage in rich discourse about important ideas' (Putnam and Borko 2000). This approach may well already feel familiar.

Locating professional development

These advances in situated learning apply particularly well to development work since, for many professionals, including teachers, their learning and development mostly takes place in non-formal learning situations within communities of practice. The situated perspective argues that *all* knowledge is situated, so one question for professional development is how various settings might give rise to different kinds of knowing.

In academic life, staff are likely to be part of more than one community of practice, being peripheral in some and central to one or more others. They might be part of the community of their discipline, their school or department, their course team, even their peer group on a professional development course. Part of the skill of the developer would then be in locating development activities within the appropriate community.

For example, Jenkins (1997) has argued that academics have their strongest allegiance to their discipline, and that, for educational development activities to have impact, they should be based in the community of the discipline. (Determining the impact of development is the subject of Chapter 6.) Jenkins has promoted the development of discipline based workshops for new lecturers (Clark *et al.* 2002). The discipline based approach has been adopted widely in the UK with the creation of the 24 Subject Centres which form the Learning and Teaching Support Network and the Institute for Learning and Teaching for Higher Education's requirement that its members know about discipline-specific pedagogical issues as well as generic ones.

Similarly, Knight (2002) has argued that the importance of context has been insufficiently appreciated in teacher education. Knight finds little support from professional development activities for the notions of situated cognition, noting that the centrally run courses tend to be formal and to be removed from the primary discourse communities of the staff. Where Jenkins (1997) and Clark *et al.* (2002) proposed that development activities to take place in the community of the discipline, Knight calls for the community of the department to be the site for professional development. Conducting development alongside lecturers in their classrooms should make it more likely that what they learn will influence their practice. Here we can situate their learning in a meaningful context for them to aid its transferability, e.g. by mentoring or coaching. Action research is another good example of context-based development activity; here a group of professionals research a common problem from their practice in spirals of evaluation, planning and action (Carr and Kemmis 1986).

On other occasions we are less interested in development as the transfer of specific techniques or skills, and more in development as fostering innovation and new knowledge. Here the situated perspective might lead us to temporarily taking staff out of their usual community in order that automatic and resistant patterns of thought accepted by that community have less influence. Boud and Walker (1998) talk of creating a local context which can act as a kind of oasis, a space where the environment is deliberately designed to be different from that which surrounds it. Centrally run professional development courses could create their own atmosphere where staff can resist the dominant culture of the institution and try out different attitudes, values and practices. Putnam and Borko (2000) agree that different situations can be used to promote different development goals. This suggests using approaches where the developer works alongside an academic to facilitate their adoption of specific practices, away days to promote new ideas and a mix of both approaches when aiming for multidimensional change in teacher's thinking.

Implications for deciding where professionals learn

In summary, since all learning is socially situated, we need constantly to be aware of the influences of culture and context, and use these influences as we plan our staff development. Some implications:

- Professional development can be carefully located within one of a number of appropriate communities, depending on the aims of that particular activity. At times this might mean entering the disciplines or departments, at other times it might involve deliberately staying removed from them.
- To work effectively in the communities of discipline, department, institution and educational development itself, we need to be adaptive, to be aware of the languages of these communities and to learn to speak (or at any rate hear and respect) them all!
- If we work within communities then we have the power to change them. Guiding members of a department through a professional development programme should change the characteristics of that community.

WHEN PROFESSIONALS LEARN: FROM INITIAL TO CONTINUING PROFESSIONAL DEVELOPMENT

This section begins to bring together the previous sections on knowledge, learning and communities to show the importance of each at different times in a professional's career. The idea of professionals moving through a number of stages has long been an appealing notion. There have been various attempts to model this progression from novice to expert (Dreyfus and Dreyfus 1986; Benner 1984). In work with higher education teachers, characterization of such stages has focused on individual's concerns, their conceptions of and approaches to teaching and learning. Both Nyquist's work with teaching assistants in the United States (Nyquist and Wulff 1996) and McKeachie's review of his more than 50 years of experience with new lecturers (McKeachie 1997) agree that teachers develop from an early anxiety about their survival and lack of teaching skills (teacher centred) through to later concerns about how students are learning (student centred). Similarly, Prosser and Trigwell have identified conceptions of teaching, conceptions of learning and approaches to teaching in university teachers. Broadly, each of their dimensions moves from a teacher centred approach to a student centred one (see Prosser and Trigwell 1999 for a review). There are obvious implications here in devising relevant professional development activities which meet groups' needs at a particular time. For example, Sharpe (2000) collected the concerns of teaching assistants who were at different stages of their careers, found support for the stages in Nyquist's model, and went on to describe a framework for the development of teaching assistants which meets their changing needs.

Perhaps this area of research could also help with the difficult question of whether professional development should start with teaching skills or with challenging conceptions of teaching and learning. The work of Nyquist and of Prosser and Trigwell suggests that, if we take a traditional approach to planning staff development, we would be aiming to design sessions which are congruent with teachers' existing conceptions and concerns, that is, that start with the teaching centred view, e.g. on methods for lecturing well or running effective tutorials. Despite this area being fraught with methodological difficulties of trying to classify changing conceptions in the complex world of teaching and professional development, studies do appear to show inconsistencies between teachers' conceptions and their approaches to teaching. Murray and MacDonald (1997) found that, although teachers may hold student centred views of learning, they find it more difficult to practice student centred teaching. Similarly, McLean and Bullard (2000), in examining teachers' portfolios, found that novice teachers held firm student centred conceptions but not all were able to operationalize these. Ho (2000) tackles this problem by promoting the use of professional development programmes specifically to achieve conceptual change in higher education teachers. She describes a model of a programme at Hong Kong Polytechnic University which starts by encouraging participants to analyse their existing conceptions of teaching, confronts them with the inconsistencies between these conceptions and their teaching practice, and offers more appropriate alternative conceptions and supports teachers as they plan changes in their teaching based on their developing conceptions. This group of studies suggests that higher education teachers move relatively quickly from espousing teacher centred to student centred conceptions. However, the explicit use of their theories in action requires more support. Perhaps this could be achieved by going back and challenging and confronting their conceptions rather than by promoting methods and skills for student centred teaching.

Lave and Wenger also tackle this progression from novice to expert. They suggest that individuals move from the edge of a community when they are novices, to the centre where they make decisions and have influence, as their expertise expands and they become more skilled (Lave and Wenger 1991). Interestingly, although it isn't commented on in Sharpe's paper above, her framework for graduate teaching assistants also moves individuals through development activities based with the community of their department to a secure and closed community of other teaching assistants from a range of departments and then to a generic certificate course with other teachers and teaching assistants from all disciplines seeking different awards. This could be seen as starting in the periphery and moving towards the centre of the educational development community of practice.

The discussion of professional knowledge at the start of this chapter is derived in the main from work with experts, and it's not clear how much it can tell us about beginning teachers. Teachers have long used the notions of constructivism in their teaching, and have made the small jump to applying constructivism to teacher education. Winitzky and Kauchak (1997) tried to apply the cognitive theory of constructivism to their teacher education programme and to follow the development of knowledge in their student teachers. By asking the student teachers to draw concept maps at various points in the course, they found that initial knowledge is fragmentary and unstable, but that structural knowledge does increase both through the programme and beyond. They found that this growth of knowledge is uneven and idiosyncratic. Once a knowledge base is developed, it has been found that experts have more organized knowledge structures than novices and that, as a result, experts perceive, organize and remember more details of a situation than novices (Bruning *et al.* 1995; Berliner 1994). This might lead us to work with beginning teachers much in the same way as we do with students – by providing active, social constructivist learning environments in which to develop a body of knowledge. Indeed, initial education in many professions does follow the apprenticeship model which focuses on the learning of body of knowledge which will see the newcomer through their early days of practice. However, this tendency to concentrate on knowledge acquisition through constructivist learning can go too far. Eraut (1994, pp. 13–14) argues against the frontloading of theory in initial training 'regardless of students' ability to digest it and use it', and against syllabi which are 'notoriously overcrowded because they attempt to include all the knowledge required for a lifetime in the profession'. Indeed he finds little of value in the initial/continuing development distinction, and reminds us that the acquisition of professional knowledge is dependent on its application and use.

At present there are moves across all sectors of education to encourage teachers to engage in continuing professional development (CPD) throughout their career. The review of the literature on expert knowledge would seem to suggest that CPD should concentrate on developing reflection on practice in order to encourage the skills of learning from experience. CPD currently tends to be based on individuals conducting their own needs analyses, setting their own targets and selecting or creating opportunities for development related to their plan.

Implications for deciding when professionals learn

In summary, there is evidence that there are differences in the concerns, beliefs and knowledge of teaching, and approaches to learning in beginning and expert teachers. Some implications of these differences:

- Initial professional development can also focus on creating active, constructivist learning environments to support novices to develop and apply knowledge about teaching and learning.
- Continuing professional development can concentrate on developing the reflective skills in order to access the tacit knowledge of experts.
- Initial professional development can be targeted to match teacher's immediate concerns. However, longer term improvements in teaching may be achieved by concentrating on conceptual change.
- Both initial and continuing development will be influenced by the community you are in, and development activities may have the explicit aim of moving individuals into a new community.

CONCLUSIONS

The hope behind this chapter was that delving deep enough into the literature of the education of other professions would locate and highlight useful theoretical and practical implications to bring to developers of higher education staff. It is interesting to note the recurrent themes in this chapter which reinforce notions of effective professional development, including:

1 Cycles of development – the idea that development is iterative, cyclical and likely to involve planning for action – is found in all of the models of learning from experience.
2 Individual construction of meaning – that as part of this process individuals need to interpret, make generalizations and construct their own meanings and conceptions – is a theme which occurs in the

notions of knowledge construction, the learning cycles of Kolb and Cowan and the more recent work of Gibbs, Trigwell and others on conceptions of teaching and learning.

3 Working with others – the notion that professional knowledge cannot be acquired in isolation but is inextricably related to its use – is made explicit in Eraut's work but also underpins the competency approaches and the recent work by Knight and others on the location of staff development.

4 Making tacit knowledge explicit – in order to promote construction of meaning and working with others, tacit knowledge needs to become explicit so that it can be reflected on, shared and ultimately assessed. This is likely to be increasingly important as we work more with experienced staff for their continuing professional development.

Although this review has confirmed many of our existing practices, it has also led me to a sense of dissatisfaction with the dominance of reflective practice as too easy a solution for the full complexity of professional learning. The focus of reflective practice on individual improvement sits uncomfortably with principles of social learning and the importance of context and community which has emerged out of each of the discussions here. The importance of context was seen in the discussion of the acquisition of professional knowledge, which is dependent on the creation of constructivist learning environments which allow for professional knowledge to be used and built and transferred among individuals and groups. Reflection is effective when it is related to experience and linked to action and guidelines for good practice, demonstrating the importance of context to learning and to practice. Communities of practice are suggested to have powerful influences on the appropriate location of development activities; and even the labels 'novice' and 'expert' are placed differently depending on the particular context being considered. From constructivism to communities of practice, it seems that we need to encourage development opportunities in groups in order to change the individual and their community.

This is illustrated in Figure 8.2 (from Sharpe and Tait 2003) which attempts to bring together the literature reviewed here. Here the outer circle – context – literally embraces the circles representing professional knowledge and experience. I remain convinced that, in order to move forward as a profession, it is as important for us, the developers, to model and problematize our work. Although there are beginnings (Ho 2000; Cheetham and Chivers 1998; Kreber 2001), there is not yet an accepted model for the professional development of teachers in higher education. Perhaps this chapter goes some way towards this by bringing together the wide literature on professional learning and development summarized in

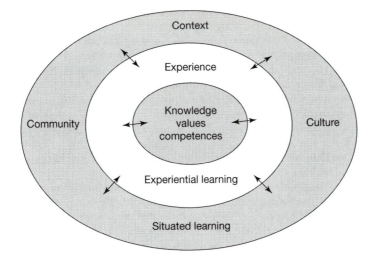

Figure 8.2 *How professionals learn. Important factors and their interactions.*

Figure 8.2. If we can bring together our understandings of individual learning and of the vital importance of context to learning and practice, we surely have the focus for the next stage of our work on professional learning and development.

REFERENCES

Barnett, R. (ed.) (1992) *Improving Higher Education*, SRHE/OUP, Buckingham

Baume, C. and Baume, D. (1996) A national scheme to develop and accredit university teachers. *International Journal for Academic Development*, **1**(2), pp 51–8

Benner, P. (1984) *From Novice to Expert: Excellence and Power in Clinical Nursing Practice*, Addison-Wesley, Menlo Park CA

Berliner, D.C. (1994) Expertise: The wonder of exemplary performances, *Creating Powerful Thinking in Teachers and Students: Diverse perspectives*, in J.N. Mangieri and C.C. Block (eds) Harcourt Brace Publishers, Fort Worth, Texas

Biggs, J. (1989) Approaches to the enhancement of tertiary teaching, *Higher Education Research and Development*, **8**, pp 7–25

Boud, D. (1999) Situating academic development in professional work: using peer learning, *International Journal of Academic Development*, **4**, pp 3–10

Boud, D., Keogh, R. and Walker, D. (1985) Promoting reflection in learning: a model, in *Reflection: Turning Experience into Learning*, (eds) D. Boud, R. Keogh and D. Walker, Kogan Page, London

Boud, D. and Walker, D. (1998) Promoting reflection in professional courses: The challenge of context, *Studies in Higher Education*, **23**(2), pp 191–206

Brockbank, A. and McGill, I. (1998) *Facilitating Reflective Learning in Higher Education*, SRHE/OUP, Buckingham

Brown, J.S. and Duguid, P. (2000) *The Social Life of Information*, Harvard University Press, Cambridge, MA

Bruning, R., Schraw, G. and Ronning, R. (1995) *Cognitive Psychology and Instruction: Second Edition*, Merrill, New Jersey

Bucklow, C. and Clark, P. (2000) The role of the Institute for Learning and Teaching in Higher Education in supporting professional development in learning and teaching in higher education, *Teacher Development*, **4**(1), pp 7–13

Carr, W. and Kemmis, S. (1986) *Becoming Critical: Education, Knowledge and Action Research*, The Falmer Press, London

Cheetham, G. and Chivers, G. (1996) Towards a holistic model of professional competence, *Journal of European Industrial Training*, **20**(5), pp 20–30

Cheetham, G. and Chivers, G. (1998) The reflective (and competent) practitioner: a model of professional competence which seeks to harmonise the reflective practitioner and competence-based approaches, *Journal of European Industrial Training*, **22**(7), pp 267–76

Clark, G., Healy, M., Jenkins, A., Wareham, T., Chalkley, B., Blumhof, J., Gravestock, P., Honeybone, A., King, H. and Thomas, N. (2002) Developing new lecturers: the case of a discipline based workshop, *Active Learning in Higher Education*, **3**(2), pp 128–44

Court, D. (1988) Reflection in action: some definitional problems, in *Reflection in Teacher Education*, (eds) P. Grimmett and G. Erikson, Teachers College Press, New York

Cowan, J. (1998) *On Becoming an Innovative University Teacher*, SRHE/OUP, Buckingham

Cowan, J. (2003) Learning from experience, in *A Guide to Staff and Educational Development*, (eds) P. Kahn and A.D. Baume, SEDA/Kogan Page, London

Dreyfus, H.L. and Dreyfus, S.E. (1986) *Mind over Machine*, Blackwell, Oxford

Earley, P. (1992) *The School Management Competences Project: Final Report*, School Management South, Crawley

Ecclestone, K. (1996) The reflective practitioner: mantra or model for emancipation? *Studies in the Education of Adults*, **28**(2), pp 146–61

Eraut, M. (1993) The characterisation and development of professional expertise in school management and teaching, *Educational Management and Administration*, **21**(4), pp 223–32

Eraut, M. (1994) *Developing Professional Knowledge and Competence*, Falmer Press, London

Eraut, M. (1995) Schön schock: a case for reframing reflection-in-action, *Teachers and Teaching*, **1**, pp 9–22

General Social Care Council (2002) *Code of Practice for Social Care Workers* and *Code of Practice for Employers of Social Care Workers*, General Social Care Council, London

Gibbs, G. (1995) Changing teachers' conceptions of teaching and learning through action research. In *Directions in staff development* (ed.) A. Brew, Society for Research into Higher Education and Open University Press, Buckingham

Ho, A. (2000) A conceptual change approach to staff development: A model for programme design, *International Journal for Academic Development,* **5**(1): pp 30–41

Jarvis, P. (1994) Learning practical knowledge, in *Professional Development for Education Management,* (eds) L. Kydd, M. Crawford and C. Riches, Open University Press, Buckingham

Jenkins, A. (1997) Discipline based educational development, *International Journal of Academic Development,* **1**(1), pp 50–61

Knight, P. (2002) A systematic approach to professional development: learning as practice, *Teaching and Teacher Education,* **18**, pp 229–41

Kolb, D. A. (1984) *Experiential Learning: Experience as a Source of Learning and Development,* Prentice-Hall, Englewood Cliffs, NJ

Kolb, D. A., Rubin, I.M. and Osland, J. (1991) *Organizational Behaviour: an experiential approach,* Prentice-Hall, Englewood Cliffs, NJ

Kreber, C. (2001) The scholarship of teaching and its implementation in faculty development and graduate education, in *Revisiting Scholarship: Identifying and Implementing the Scholarship of Teaching,* (ed.) C. Kreber, New Directions for Teaching and Learning, no. 86. Jossey-Bass, San Francisco

Lave, J. and Wenger, E. (1991) *Situated Learning: Legitimate peripheral participation,* Cambridge University Press, Cambridge

Lewin, K. (1951) *Field Theory in Social Science,* Harper and Row, New York

Management Charter Initiative (1991) *Management Standards Implementation Pack,* MCI, London

Management Charter Initiative (1995) *Standards for Managing Quality,* MCI, London

McGill, I. and Beaty, E. (1995) *Action Learning: A Guide for Professional, Management and Educational Development,* 2nd Edn, Kogan Page, London

McKeachie, W. J. (1997) Critical elements in training university teachers, *International Journal for Academic Development,* **2**, pp 67–74

McLean, M. and Bullard, J.E (2000) Becoming a university teacher: evidence from teaching portfolios (how academics learn to teach), *Teacher Development,* **4**(1), pp 79–102

Moon, J. (1999a) *Learning Journals: a handbook for academics, students and professional development,* Kogan Page, London

Moon, J. (1999b) *Reflection in Learning and Professional Development: Theory and Practice,* Kogan Page, London

Morrison, K. (1996) Developing reflective practice in higher degree students through a learning journal, *Studies in Higher Education,* **21**, pp 317–32

Murray, H., Gillese, E., Lennon, M., Mercer, P. and Robinson, M. (2003) *Ethical Principles in University Teaching,* STLHE. *http://www.tss.uoguelph.ca/stlhe/ethics. html* Accessed 8 August 2003

Murray, K. and McDonald, R. (1997) The Disjunction between Lecturers' Conceptions of their Teaching and their Claimed Educational Practice, *Higher Education,* **33**, pp 331–49

Nonaka, I. and Takeuchi, H. (1995) *The Knowledge Creating Company,* Oxford University Press, New York

Nyquist, J.D. and Wulff, D. H. (1996) *Working Effectively with Graduate Teaching Assistants*, Sage, Newbury Park

Parker, S. (1997) *Reflective Thinking in the Postmodern World*, Open University Press, Buckingham

Pill, A., Ryan, S. and Fuller, M. (2001) Who dares develops, *Innovations in Education and Teaching International*, **38**(1), pp 54–62

Polanyi, M. (1967) *The Tacit Dimension*, Doubleday, New York

Prosser, M. and Trigwell, K. (1999) *Understanding Learning and Teaching*, SRHE/OUP, Buckingham

Putnam, R. and Borko, H. (2000) What do new views of knowledge and thinking have to say about research on teaching? *Educational Researcher*, **29**(1), pp 4–15

Richardson, V. (ed.) (1997) *Constructivist Teacher Education*, Falmer Press, London

Ryle, G. (1949) *The Concept of Mind*, Hutchinson, London

Schön, D. (1983) *The Reflective Practitioner: How Professionals Think in Action*, Basic Books, New York

Schön, D. (1987) *Educating the Reflective Practitioner*, Jossey-Bass, San Francisco

Schön, D. (1990) *The Reflective Turn: Case studies in and on educational practice*, Teacher's College Press, New York

SEDA (2003) Staff and Educational Development Association, Birmingham: SEDA. Available at *http://www.seda.ac.uk/pdf/index.htm* Accessed 24 July 2003

Sharpe, R. (2000) A framework for training graduate teaching assistants, *Teacher Development*, **4**(1), pp 131–44

Sharpe, R. and Tait, J. (2003) Understanding the developers' roles: heuristics that help. Paper presented at the *SEDA conference: The Scholarship of Academic and Staff Development*. University of Bristol. April 2003

Wenger, E. (1988) *Communities of Practice: Learning, Meaning and Identity*, Cambridge University Press, Cambridge

Winitzky, N. and Kauchak, D. (1997) Constructivism in Teacher Education: Applying cognitive theory to teacher learning, in *Constructivist Teacher Education*, V. Richardson (ed.), Falmer Press, Bristol, PA

Yelloly, M. and Henkel, M. (1995) *Learning and Teaching in Social Work: towards reflective practice*, Jessica Kingsley, London

Zeichner, K. (1995) Conceptions of reflective practice in teaching and teacher education, in *Action and Reflection in Teacher Education*, (eds) G. Harvard and P. Hodkinson, Ablex, New Jersey

SUGGESTED FURTHER RESOURCES

If you are interested in the topics touched on in this chapter then read . . .

Schön, D. (1983) *The Reflective Practitioner: How Professionals Think in Action*. Basic Books, New York. And Schön, D. (1987) *Educating the Reflective Practitioner*. Jossey-Bass, San Francisco: Schön is an educationalist and it is a pleasure to read these original sources to illustrate and clarify the underlying message of his work

Cowan, J. (1998) *On Becoming an Innovative University Teacher*. SRHE/OUP, Buckingham. I love this book and recommend it whenever I can. It has an up to date and practical take on reflection for HE teachers with lots of examples and ideas for practice

Eraut, M. (1994) *Developing professional knowledge and competence.* Falmer Press, London. Michael Eraut has been a dominant and challenging thinker and has published widely on professional knowledge, learning and development. This book brings together his thinking around professional education up until the mid 1990's and is a good starting point for accessing his more recent works

O'Reilly, D., Cunningham, L., Lester, S. (1999) *Developing the Capable Practitioner: professional capability through higher education.* Kogan Page. An edited collection of practitioner's examples of how they have applied their understanding of professional learning to their courses for managers, occupational therapists, further education lecturers and other professionals

9

Careers within staff and educational development

Peter Kahn

INTRODUCTION

Whilst staff and educational development as a field for scholarly and professional practice is receiving more attention than only a few years ago, careers within staff and educational development receive far less attention. For example neither Prospects (2003) nor Blaxter *et al.* (1998), both concerned with careers in higher education, mention the field. Development is certainly a highly specialist profession, but then so are many other areas of work in higher education. Even within the specialist literature on staff and educational development, the tendency is to concentrate on becoming and being a staff and educational developer, and on establishing professional identity within the field (see for example Andresen 1996; Issacs 1997; Kapp *et al.* 1996; and O'Leary 1997), rather than on the *range* of careers that are possible within the field. Holmes (2003) provides perhaps the richest currently-available account of a career within staff and educational development, whilst Graham Webb in Chapter 10 of this book identifies some of the capabilities and qualities developed through working in development and shows how these can inform further work within and beyond development.

This chapter seeks to open discussion on the nature of advanced roles within staff and educational development for more experienced developers. Indeed, a clear understanding of the possibilities is important if one is to set, and subsequently achieve, goals for one's career. We have already seen in the companion volume to this text (Kahn and Baume 2003) that clearly articulated goals form an essential element in shaping any programme of personal and professional development (Kahn 2003). In saying this we do not deny the parallel need for the developer to stay alert to exciting and un-anticipatable opportunities that will undoubtedly crop up! But it remains useful, when setting career goals, to appreciate the characteristics and challenges of some of the more demanding roles within the field.

At the same time, we are also concerned in this chapter with looking at how someone might position himself or herself to move into any of these roles. Rather than attempting a more generic approach, this chapter presents five case studies. These case studies offer an appreciation for what each role involves, and hopefully also a view of how one might prepare for any of these roles that appeal. These are not of course the only five possible roles, but between them they cover a representative range.

The first case study is provided by Charles Juwah. Charles' role includes leading a development programme in learning and teaching for new academic staff alongside other responsibilities. Leading such a programme might constitute a realistic initial career goal for a relatively new developer, particularly for one on a short-term contract. (Ali Cooper gives a detailed account and an analysis of leading such a programme in Chapter 4.)

We then look at a role where development work helps to underpin an academic career. Paul O'Neil considers how a concern for development is important for those responsible for organizing teaching at a departmental level. Academics who have developed an initial interest in development may see this as a possible way forward.

In recent years we have seen the creation of many more educational development units. Managing one of these units is, as has already been suggested, an obvious role to which a developer might aspire in the longer term. Gwen Van der Velden looks at the demands of this role, and the support that one needs to prepare for this kind of position. (Sue Thompson explores the leadership of an educational development unit in greater detail in Chapter 3, and Fred Percival and Gill Tucker show how a head of educational development can work productively with a senior university manager in Chapter 2.)

Working as a freelance consultant is another role that might attract many developers. While it may be difficult to establish oneself as a consultant, such a role offers a great deal of freedom to choose work that one finds appealing. James Wisdom's case study takes a realistic look at what is involved.

Finally, in the UK we have also seen in recent years an increase in the number of national roles for developers. Richard Blackwell considers a variety of issues relevant for developers who aspire to such a role, which evidently has many overlaps with the role of an independent consultant.

In outlining these five roles, we are not seeking to trace the full range or length of a career within the field. Indeed, patterns of employment within higher education are now so unpredictable that the concept of a career may no longer be relevant, as Taylor suggests (Taylor 1999, pp 107–8). The careers of the women in senior management roles that David and Woodwards (1998) describe are evidently not wholly planned. Nor are we suggesting that the roles that are outlined in the case studies are mutually exclusive. One role might well lead to, or in some cases overlap with, another – for example a national adviser might usually expect first to have been a leader within an institution. The case studies instead seek to introduce the range of more senior roles that are possible within the field, incorporating critical reflection on what is entailed in undertaking these roles to offer insight into their nature.

LEADING A DEVELOPMENT PROGRAMME

Charles Juwah, The Robert Gordon University, Aberdeen
This personal account very briefly highlights my role as the Senior Educational Development Officer and Deputy Head, Centre for the Enhancement of Learning and Teaching (CELT) at The Robert Gordon University, Aberdeen. I here outline my current role as an educational developer, including the challenges I encounter, how I came into the job and what might help someone else move into this role.

My role is mainly to manage and co-ordinate the University's Educational Development and Training programme for the accreditation of academic staff to achieve qualified higher education teacher status and membership of the Institute for Learning and Teaching (ILTHE). I also take on other responsibilities, including leadership of and teaching on the Postgraduate Certificate Higher Education Learning and Teaching (a multidisciplinary Masters Level course); facilitating continuing professional development programmes in teaching, learning, assessment and research supervision; and contributing to the Centre's educational research.

Challenges within the role

This role has allowed me to work with colleagues across the institution in different learning and development contexts, with some success. It also presents a variety of challenges. The challenges include:

- Strategically positioning educational development to gain credibility with most academics, and to be on a par with other academic disciplines with renowned scholarship and languages of discourse. In my view, the comparative lack both of status as a discipline and of a grounded scholarship of educational development are main reasons why some academics do not want to engage with educational development. This situation has serious implications for the efforts of developers to enhance the quality of teaching and students' learning experience.

- The low uptake by academic staff of and engagement with continuing professional and personal development in the areas of teaching, learning and assessment is a further issue. Lack of assured high-quality, ring-fenced time for professional development is the main reason often given by academics for their low participation or their non-engagement.
- Also of concern is the lack of engagement of part-time teaching staff in development activities.
- The lack of parity of recognition and reward between discipline research and research into teaching and learning results in inadequate engagement by staff in the latter. This has a knock-on effect in reducing the development and promotion of the scholarship of teaching and the enhancement of reflective practice.

Transitions

I came into my current role of academic management as a career move from the further education sector, where I had a strong background in teaching, training and professional development. I had trained as a scientist, and taught at a further education college with a diverse student population of mixed abilities drawn largely from non-traditional academic backgrounds. It was a real challenge to cater effectively for the individual needs of each student in a learning context that was a mix of academic, vocational, multi-disciplined and work-based. To enable me perform my role effectively as a competent practitioner (teacher, assessor, learner support, manager, consultant, etc.), I both saw the need to and was required to undertake a postgraduate course in educational technology. I quickly followed that up with a teaching qualification and with other professional development. Without doubt, the knowledge I gained from, and the skills I developed during, the teacher training and professional development courses stood me in good stead to meet the learning needs of students, work-based professionals and institution colleagues.

To move into the educational developer's role, one needs to be nurtured through an integrated personal and professional development programme. However, the individual must have an interest and a commitment to professional development related to enhancing students' learning. A commitment to collegiality and to a multi-disciplinary focus, as well as good organizational and interpersonal skills, are also all important. The nurturing of an individual to an educational developer's post can, in my view, be achieved via situated learning in a community of practice. In such a setting, the apprentice learns from and with experienced peers, and through discourse and reflection on practice proceeds towards mastery. Appropriate mentoring to provide guidance and support (when one is low and unsure) and (when one feels more secure) to challenge, and also coaching to facilitate learning and to engender superior performance and achievement of competency, are both essential. Such nurturing should cater for the personal, technical, professional and social development needs of the individual.

UNDERPINNING AN ACADEMIC CAREER

Professor Paul O'Neil, University of Manchester
As the Associate Dean for Medical Undergraduate Studies and Professor of Medical Education, I act as the Programme Director for the undergraduate medical course at the University of Manchester. I had not, however, originally planned to centre my career around teaching to quite the extent that has now occurred. I completed my MD researching into breathlessness, and subsequently moved into Geriatric medicine, as a Lecturer and then Senior Lecturer. Part of my rationale for moving into Geriatric medicine was the collaborative approach that typifies this field. At this point in my career, a hospital responsibility for teaching opened up and the Dean suggested that I take it on. I had always liked teaching, so it seemed natural to take up his suggestion. However, I soon found that moving into this role meant my stepping off the traditional academic road. The break became particularly clear when my clinical colleagues moved to a different hospital and I stayed in place.

A focus on development

The main focus to my role is on development rather than on administration. There is a difference between simply taking on the role of associate dean and using that role as a springboard to initiate change. Similarly, more attributes are required than simply liking to teach. I still of course gain satisfaction from teaching; I enjoy seeing people come through the programme, and then in some cases go on to work with me as doctors. But it is also necessary to focus on the development of teaching as well as just on teaching. So I initially developed expertise in assessment, acting as a resource for the department in this area.

You need a particular mindset for leading in education, one that encourages others to engage in development work as well. It is important to build a team – other people need space to own the idea, and to take it on board. They need to be able to adapt things if they are to gain a sense of ownership. It therefore makes sense for the development of staff to feature alongside developments in teaching and learning. The unit I am responsible for now runs an extensive programme of workshops for NHS clinicians with the principle of building capacity. The emphasis is on organizational development as well as educational and staff development.

Project work is also an important aspect of my role. In 2001 I became the holder of a National Teaching Fellowship. The project funded by that Fellowship is going well, setting up online assessment in a problem-based learning context. This involves working with a virtual managed learning environment, recognizing the fact that our students now study all over the North West of England. The funding has enabled me to gather together a project team. Another project in which I am currently involved is a Fund for the Development of Teaching and Learning Phase 4 initiative that involves setting up a question bank. It is important to me that the projects that I undertake involve research into learning and teaching, because research is an essential underpinning for any academic career, whether the field is learning and teaching in higher education or Geriatric medicine.

Support to step off

I found that several factors were important in supporting my transition into a development role. The collaborative dimension is essential; in my own case a group of us were able to offer mutual support. The organization also has to be ready for change. On the undergraduate medical course, the leadership was supportive in a facilitative rather than directive way. In addition, my experience is that mentoring from others is critical, as are role models – a Professor of General Practice was particularly helpful. If you step off the mainstream academic career track, you need people to support you – otherwise it is easy to end up isolated. If sympathetic colleagues are not present within your own institution, then seek them out elsewhere. Find your own community of practice.

Courses are also important. Newer colleagues who are seeking to develop in this area will increasingly need a formal qualification. In 1994 a group of us went to Maastricht for a summer school on problem-based learning. Since then I have continued to seek out a number of courses, and in 1996 I went to Harvard on a course that they run. I now go back twice a year as a member of staff on the programme, which includes a focus on issues such as personal change, leadership and curriculum development – on how to make things happen. All of these courses enable you to step out of role for a period and to take stock.

In practice, it is often harder to build up expertise within educational work at the start of your academic career. It becomes easier to do this when you reach a more senior grade such as Senior Lecturer. Part of this difficulty stems from our lack of expertise in analysing excellence in teaching. However, it is evident that greater credit is still given for primary research, so promotion in many cases is difficult. Fortunately this is changing with the increased number of opportunities to take on educational development roles.

A MANAGEMENT ROLE

Gwen Van der Velden, University of Kent at Canterbury

My role as head of an educational development unit builds on skills and capabilities in three main areas. First of all I need to spot and evaluate innovations in teaching; this involves keeping an eye on national initiatives, and on developments in the teaching of specific areas. I then need to develop strategy and implementation processes. An example of this is taking a lead in writing the University's Learning and Teaching Strategy, followed by working with others to determine who should champion specific causes and how they should approach their activity. Finally there is the managerial element to my work. I need to manage the members of my own team, the projects that we have taken on, the contacts and networks we have with academic departments and the funding of the unit. In addition to abilities in these three areas, the head of an educational development unit also needs a good measure of professional conviction and confidence.

It is relatively straightforward to learn how to manage both people and projects, and you would hardly be an educational developer unless you enjoyed spotting innovations. It is the strategic level that is perhaps the most challenging to address. Strategic sense does not develop in a vacuum; my experience is that you need to draw on the way strategy is developed and implemented in a variety of settings if you are to be effective in this area. You also need to be flexible, and willing to think 'outside the box'. Some of my team's best achievements were borne out of quite extraordinary projects, initially deemed likely to fail.

Developing strategic sense

How might you develop the strategic sense that is needed to manage a unit? Strategic sense in this context means that you know how what you want to achieve fits with the agendas of others (teaching staff, funding masters, senior managers, your institution's governing body, Heads of

Departments, etc). It means you need to understand the bigger picture in which they function, and what their drivers and obstacles are. In most cases you will not have had enough access to such people when you were on your way to becoming head of an educational development group.

My main advice is to find an informal mentor – I have found such mentoring invaluable. A mentor ideally needs to be more experienced and in a more senior position than you are, and to have had experience of more than one institution. I have had three or four such mentors over the last few years. Insight into the workings of other institutions opens up your eyes to a wide range of possible courses of action within your own work. Mentors can introduce you to situations you will not have been in before. Prepare for some sitting in and watching of situations that may go well above your head, and discuss afterwards with your mentor the processes of what you observed. I have been surprised how often really straightforward messages can be wrapped up in terribly intimidating meetings.

If you want to find a mentor, you need be clear about what you wish to achieve. And then take a risk and ask them if they will mentor you, rather than hoping that they will offer. If asked, people are usually willing to support you, particularly if you offer to do some leg-work for them in return. I have found that some of my mentors were surprised and flattered to be asked, but once I explained what I felt I could learn from them, some of them felt that mentoring would be a learning experience for them too. In any case, make sure you ask them for input about all major relevant aspects of their work, and for feedback on topics and concerns that you bring from your own work.

Another avenue to gain the strategic sense needed to manage a unit is to offer consultancy in other institutions. This provides you with insight into the workings of other educational development units, enabling you to understand how organizational and power structures vary between institutions. External consultancy helps you to think outside the structure that you are working in yourself. Working on a national project or initiative is a further way to acquire this experience. I gained valuable experience of other units as a consultant on the Teaching and Learning Technology Programme. An added bonus is the fact that you can build up strong national networks through this type of initiative. Years later, I still benefit from those networks.

However, such consultancy is not always so easy to acquire, so an alternative is to move between jobs or institutions. Within the past few years I have stayed at the same institution but averaged a different job almost ever year. I was lucky in that the University gave me new challenges and learning opportunities in quick succession. Had that not been the case, I am well aware that I would have had to move institutions to gain the skills I wished to gain. This means that you need to take some risks with your career, but then risk taking is inherent to educational development work.

Confidence and conviction

I was about two years into my career as an educational developer when a colleague who had begun to act as a mentor towards me said that I lacked trust in my own abilities. I needed more 'guts'. I put this down to English not being my first language, and therefore my being inhibited to express myself, but he said this was irrelevant. Not long afterwards he invited me to a presentation with an external audience. Twenty minutes before the presentation was due to start he told me that I had to present the topic and gave me some slides. He had carefully chosen a subject on which I knew a great deal. Although I felt terrified initially, I had no option but to deliver. When I realized that the audience appreciated my contribution, I realized that I had become an expert and that I should do my job with confidence. The whole experience may not have been one of the best examples of staff development, but it certainly was a great confidence builder. And confidence in my professional expertise is essential to my role.

Once you have developed confidence, supported by constructive evaluation of your work, you need to become publicly clear about what you are trying to achieve. In my case, it is developing the potential that students have, and making them critical professionals. I want to see more all-round learning in their studies, regardless of where they come from. And that often makes me quite critical of much current Higher Education. It is easy to change your tune from one committee to the next, tailoring your message to your audience; easy, but unwise. Instead, having chosen your message to meet the strategic goals of your university, you need to carry your message forward wherever you go, rather than trying to change it all of the time to please those you work with. Leadership means that you need to give a clear lead, not simply try to follow those around you, while still avoiding 'bloody-mindedness'. Sometimes you will win the battle, sometimes you will lose. I don't worry too much if I lose. I try to figure out what has gone wrong, to learn how to play it better next time. The good thing about education is that there will always be another chance, as the process of change and development in learning and teaching is mostly cyclical.

CONSULTANCY IN HIGHER EDUCATION

James Wisdom, independent higher education consultant

This case study comes with a health warning – do not follow its advice unless you are prepared to take on a precarious life. Consultancy in higher education is not a career change you should take on lightly. In particular it is nothing like as financially rewarding as the title 'consultant' may suggest. Consultancy is often commissioned by people with relatively little discretionary funding. People on part- or full-time salaries in universities, or staff who have taken early retirement, are sometimes willing to offer consultancy at modest rates. The result is that, in the UK at least, it is hard to charge much more than half the standard rate for consultancy in many other professional sectors. It is no wonder that my accountant is shocked!

So why then do I actually work as a consultant? The simple answer is that consultancy is the most enjoyable work I could do; it allows me to carry out a range of development work on a freelance basis. It is true that it is possible to engage in a variety of development work within an institution, and I have been lucky enough to do a lot of this in my career. However, it typically takes approaching two years to learn how to operate effectively in a new institution, and this is true even for those who have had experience of several moves between institutions. While this length of time may reduce as institutions are better managed, it will always be the case that institutions differ in culture from each other. I found that, at the stage in my career when I became a consultant, I did not want to invest that time in becoming familiar with yet another new institutional culture when there were so many more interesting things to learn. A further factor was that I wanted to develop in this area while still young enough to enjoy doing it. I have had many colleagues whose last years before retirement have been hard and tiring, particularly if they have felt trapped within their institution.

How then does one become a consultant? First of all, you must genuinely want to – motivation is critical. After that, you actually need to make the change. It is often the case that people do not want to leave an existing job until they have defined their new one. By contrast, I found that I could not define my new role until I had left my old one. It probably takes as much effort to leave a job as it took to get it. My advice, once you have made the decision, is step off the plank; you can then, after a short and perhaps alarming drop, start to swim. There are of course strategies to help ease the transition – one of my colleagues left his employment on a tapering contract, reducing his hours progressively over a period of three years. An arrangement like this can offer a relatively low-risk strategy for making the change.

Work as a consultant, of course, is centred around offering services to clients. So I would suggest that, when starting out, you do not make major changes that take you away from your existing network. This is the group which will support you and through which you will find your opportunities. If clients recommend you, you know you must be doing a reasonable job.

I do not think it is wise to define yourself in a restrictive way, which is one of the dangers of rushing to advertise yourself through a brochure or a website. If you define yourself around one interest then you may preclude yourself from carrying out other forms of consultancy. It may help to get someone else to describe you to yourself in terms of what you might offer. We can easily think about ourselves in fixed terms, but I think it is more interesting for consultants to think of themselves in fluid terms – which of course then allows for one's own further professional development. Approaches will come from a variety of different directions.

In terms of the actual day-to-day business of consultancy, there are a few factors that I would like to highlight. Clients often present you with a commission that soon turns out not to be their central problem. Hence you need to be sensitive towards what you are being asked to do. You may need gently to help them to refine their account of what they need from you – another reason for maintaining a flexible approach. This life can seem quite hard if you fall into difficulty, so maintain your network of colleagues and stay close to your clients. Time management can also be an issue, as there is a tendency in consultancy work for feast to alternate with famine – clients' timetables can change and – like buses – several jobs can start or end at once. This is work that expands to fit the time available for it, and you will have to work quite hard at the business of not working.

Educational development work is often challenging – whether you are working with a group of colleagues within an institution or as a freelance visiting a variety of institutions – but it can be hugely worthwhile, and consultancy is one more way of contributing to the development of its practice.

NATIONAL ADVISERS

Richard Blackwell, Senior Adviser, Learning and Teaching Support Network (LTSN) Generic Centre
I write this case study as a senior adviser in the Learning and Teaching Support Network (LTSN) Generic Centre based in York. My role includes managing four national projects in the UK and liaising with a group of LTSN Subject Centres. This case study is for those considering movement into a similar role. At the time of writing, I had been in the role for just

over two years after nearly 10 years in staff development at the University of Nottingham, five of those years being spent as Director.

The experience and some lessons

The first two years in the job have been an incredibly rewarding professional development experience. My project work has enabled and required me to engage much more with the intellectual basis for staff and educational development than previously, for example, in the areas of change and the scholarship of teaching and learning. However, my role goes well beyond interacting with the staff and educational development community. I have enjoyed the challenge of starting afresh, making new contacts in national agencies such as Universities UK and the Higher Education Funding Council for England. I have found it necessary to earn the right to be heard anew, especially within the organization, and this can be psychologically challenging (as they say!). My experience is that the work is inevitably more driven by short-term funding (I am on a fixed term contract, as is the organization) and measurable outputs. Sometimes it seems that producing tangible products is more important than the real business of ensuring longer-term impact on practice.

I work mainly from home and, taking advice from academic colleagues who frequently worked at home before taking up my post, I established a separate office, in my attic. I have found the transition to working at home much less problematic than I expected, although the lack of ready support (e.g. when the computer breaks down) and of peers in adjacent rooms are downsides. The latter particularly is important if, like me, you seek and benefit from peer input in developing proposals, projects and events. Such input needs to be acquired in other ways, often on the telephone. The organization is small (although that may change if national agencies in the UK are brought together as a result of the considerations of Teaching Quality Enhancement Committee) and the administrative infrastructure feels slim compared to that of higher education institutions.

The work is highly political in nature, both in the micro-political sense of involving working with and bringing together sometimes competing interests and in the macro political sense that progress is of interest to funding councils and the Department for Education and Skills. This can lead to real and perceived external pressure to accommodate particular policy priorities which some may find uncomfortable. There is also another kind of politics not far below the surface. As much of the national work is currently fixed term (the new fixed term contract regulations might change that) there is inevitably a certain amount of positioning for the future by individuals, including colleagues. Sometimes team working and individual competitiveness go together to a greater extent than I experienced within institutions.

Transitions

Moving into a national role can be difficult. As well as excellent work within institutions at a senior level a degree of national profile and demonstrable success also appears to be required, such as leading successful national projects or contributing to the development of national organizations.

Anyone moving into such a national role also needs to pay attention to their own development. I have acquired both formal and informal mentoring support in my current role, and maintained active member-ship of an action learning set. I have also sought career development-type mentoring to enable me to develop my career options and provide support for inevitably tricky transitions in the future.

Summary

In summary, a national job can be extremely rewarding learning experience, and at the same time occasionally frustrating and isolating. In my experience, there is a need proactively to build one's own support network, both for the new role and to enable career development, rather more than was the case in an institutional role.

CONCLUSION

These case studies do not, of course, exhaust the range of senior roles that are open to developers. One might, for instance, also consider a role that focuses on research into staff and educational development, or on authoring practical guides to teaching and learning. Or one might consider roles that extend beyond development activity, perhaps looking at roles in related fields or at the most senior roles in higher education. The case studies presented here, however, concern mainstream areas of development that are likely to draw increasing numbers of developers in the longer term.

A focus on moving to more senior roles, however, tends to reduce attention to the way in which the nature of development activity shifts as one becomes more experienced. It is, therefore, helpful to review the study by Kapp *et al.* (1996), which looks more specifically at the different stages of a development career. In looking at the final stage of a developer's career, typically at around 15 years of professional service, they suggest that the developer will increasingly be concerned with stretching the boundaries of development activity, as well as engaging in more specialist work. While developers with somewhat fewer years of professional service might argue that they also have a contribution to make in extending practice, this does suggest that progress in a career cannot simply be measured in terms of the roles that one takes on; other factors also come into play.

This chapter has also sought to explore ways in which developers can tailor their careers towards more senior development roles. This is true both personally for the individual developer and also for managers who take on responsibility for other developers, especially where staff are on short-term contracts. The framework that was outlined in Kahn (2003) suggested that qualifications, professional collaboration and relevant experience were all important in establishing a career in development work. This view has been borne out within this chapter.

Qualifications, perhaps, take on greater importance in the earlier stages of a career, whereas relevant experience and collaboration have been more consistently highlighted within the case studies. The emphasis here is on *relevant* experience. It is not sufficient to have been in a development role for a long period of time. One needs to use the opportunities that are afforded to engage in experience that is relevant to the next stage in one's career. Hicks (1997), for instance, notes that directors of units have significant experience of teaching – but so will many other individuals who do not reach a comparable position – something more is required than just experience of teaching for a senior development role. A willingness to collaborate with others has also emerged as critical when seeking to take on a more senior role. Indeed, collaboration was highlighted more widely in Kahn and Baume (2003) as central to staff and educational development. It should, therefore, not be surprising that it emerges as key to the development of developers themselves.

However, in addition to these elements, a range of personal qualities is also relevant for the aspiring developer. These qualities include drive, a commitment to development, a strategic sense, a concern for impact, and confidence. It is, for instance, evident from the case studies that taking on a senior role requires genuine drive; Van der Velden focuses, for instance, on the importance of seeking out a mentor and the willingness to take risks, while Wisdom looks at motivation for one's work. Part of this drive will stem from a commitment to the development of others, but concern for one's own development is also essential. It is evident that a concern for securing a personally appropriate work–life balance might well reduce the chances of achieving a more senior role. If this is recognized at an early stage, then frustration is less likely to result.

The range of activity that now occurs within staff and educational development shows the growing maturity of the field. However, in a more fully mature field, one might expect to see organized support for staff seeking to take on senior development roles. While support for newer developers is now relatively well established; for instance with the Staff and Educational Development Association (SEDA 2003) Fellowship schemes and Summer Schools for new developers; support for progression into senior roles is glaringly absent. Relevant professional associations, as well as other bodies and groupings of institutions themselves, should take the opportunity to develop support mechanisms, such as mentoring schemes, advanced Summer Schools, advanced qualifications, and so on, for developers at this stage in their careers. Indeed, we hope that this book itself represents a beginning to this task. If we are to see staff and educational developers sustain their position at the forefront of change in higher education, then the profession as a whole, perhaps even on an international basis, needs to join together in supporting its members to develop.

REFERENCES

Andresen, L. (1996) The work of academic development – occupational identity, standards of practice, and the virtues of association, *The International Journal for Academic Development*, **1**(1), pp 38–49

Blaxter, L., Hughes, C. and Tight, M. (1998) *The Academic Career Handbook*, Open University Press, Buckingham

Hicks, O. (1997) Career paths of directors of academic staff development units in Australian universities: the emergence of a species? *The International Journal for Academic Development*, **2**(2), pp 56–63

Holmes, A. (2003) Ways to make things better – one, two, three! *Staff and Educational Development: Case Studies . . .* (eds) H. Edwards, D. Baume and G. Webb, London, Kogan Page

Issacs, G. (1997) Developing the developers: some ethical dilemmas in changing times, *The International Journal for Academic Development*, **2**(2), pp 6–12

Kahn, P.E. and Baume, D. (eds) (2003) *A Guide to Staff and Educational Development*, Kogan Page, London

Kahn, P.E. (2003) Developing professional expertise in staff and educational development, in *A guide to staff and educational development*, (eds) P.E. Kahn and D. Baume, Kogan Page, London, pp 212–26

Kapp, C., Healy, M., Nellisen, C., Mihevc, B., de Winter, H.C. and Watt, H. (1996) Developing faculty developers: some issues when recruiting faculty developers and ensuring the professional growth of current faculty developers, *Journal of Staff, Program and Organisational Development*, **13**(4), pp 299–329

O'Leary (1997) Staff development in a climate of economic rationalism: a profile of the academic developer, *The International Journal for Academic Development*, **2**(2), pp 72–82

Prospects (2003) *Prospects Careers in Higher Education*, CSU Ltd., Manchester

SEDA (2003) Professional Development:The SEDA Fellowship and Associate Fellowship, SEDA *http://www.seda.ac.uk/fellowship/fellowships.htm* Accessed 8 August 2003

Taylor, P.G. (1999) *Making Sense of Academic Life*, Society for Research into Higher Education and Open University Press, Buckingham

10

Development and beyond

Graham Webb

INTRODUCTION

I hope that what follows may be useful for those working in development; for those contemplating moving beyond development; for those who manage development; and for university managers more generally.

First, this chapter looks back on my own and other developers' experiences, from the inside, seeking some further understanding of the nature of development. Second, and still under the heading 'Looking back at development', it merges into consideration of development from the outside, and more particularly from the perspective of university management. Third, it looks forward, to consider what developers have to offer an organization if or when they move on from a development role. Hence 'Development and beyond'.

That seemingly simple writing task immediately opened up for me a number of issues. Should this be an entirely personal account, or should I seek greater generality? In the event I decided to do some of both. Also, how does 'ageing' – mine – affect the account? If I remember Research Methods 101 correctly, this would translate into consideration of 'maturation as an intervening variable'! The fact is that, as I talk to people who see the end of their career in sight, even though it might be 15 years away, they tend to have different priorities and a different approach to their work than those who see only endless possibilities and an inexorably upward trajectory.

LOOKING BACK AT DEVELOPMENT

What follows is a caricature of some of my own experiences, approach and observations as an educational and staff developer, followed by a commentary 'from outside'.

Moral guardian and defender of the discourse

As a developer I saw myself as a moral guardian for what was right, true and good with regard to teaching and learning. This was based on deep convictions and values to do with treating all (including students) with respect; the personal transformative role of education (beyond learning 'the stuff'); and unease with a power hierarchy that resulted in the imposition of knowledge rather than the motivation of learning. Most developers I know share those values. However, it also needs to be said that like any group, developers are not immune from failure to translate their 'espoused theory' into their practice: their 'theory in action' (Argyris and Schön 1974).

Deep-seated values come from life experiences, and in my own case from early observation of unfairness and a lack of understanding of difference. That is fertile ground for the idea of education being transformative for the individual (and organization, and society) but it needs a body of argument to translate deep general values into a programme for action. That is where the discourse of university teaching and learning improvement comes in. By that I mean, for the most part, the core of books and journal papers that developers and others have written, and continue to quote: the body of knowledge that is familiar to knowledgeable developers. Discourse, of course, also refers to practices such as the well known methods we use, including workshops, retreats and teaching observation and to the professional paraphernalia which include professional societies, certification and awards. But here I am referring to the 'normal' body of literature developers tend to cite, and in addition, the wider body of knowledge and understanding that has informed staff development. In my own case, for example, I found more insight and guidance for my own practice in hermeneutics than I did in the main stream of 'deep' and 'surface' learning (see Webb 1997).

As an educational and staff developer I cast myself in the role of defender of the discourse, frequently using phrases like 'forty years of research on university teaching have taught us . . .'. And this is indeed an important role for developers. I am still astounded that the university, a community which honours rationality, the importance of fundamental knowledge, the testing of propositions and action being based upon evidence, still fails to learn from the discourse as it develops and delivers its core activity of teaching. The allegations against student evaluation of teaching, the defence of archaic assessment methods, the perpetuation of 'fact dumping' as a major teaching purpose and method, remain alive and healthy today, just as they were when I started my career 30 years ago. As a staff and educational developer, I therefore saw it as my duty to be moral guardian and discourse defender of the good and right in teaching and learning.

How does that position appear from outside of development? To some it is inspirational, motivating, career and life changing. To others it is arrogant, moralizing and divorced from the realities of course delivery. From outside of development (and in black moments from inside too) one sees more clearly the reasons for resistance to development. For academic staff who are pressed to gain research grants, produce papers, teach large and diverse student groups, mark piles of scripts and at the same time retain balance on the tightrope of promotion, the transformative and values base of teaching and learning is not number one on their 'to do' list come Monday morning. Neither is immersion in the discourse. It is just more work. (And why do developers give copious books, chapters, papers to read up on when staff ask a simple question? Probably to proudly display that there is a discourse and that they hold knowledge of it). There is nothing wrong with the moral guardian and defender of the discourse role of developers, but from the outside it can separate rather than unite developer and 'developee'. The major failure of development is that the developer's knowledge has not yet fully been mainstreamed into the workforce – in most of the world, the university teacher is non-credentialed, unprofessionalized and untrained in the theory and practice of higher education teaching, and ignorant of, uninterested in, or simply too busy to worry about, the discourse.

Problem with authority

This sounds like the beginning of a school report card ('Johnnie has a problem with authority'). I think that as a developer, especially earlier in my career, this was true for me. I did not trust those in authority – from V-C, through DV-Cs/PV-Cs, especially Deans, and also Heads of Schools and Departments – to safeguard and promote good teaching and learning. As a young developer I saw them as ignorant of the discourse and as being part of the problem. There remain developers who mount critiques of managerialism, the death of collegiality and so on. These may be small in number, but I suspect that 'a problem with authority' is quite widespread among developers.

Of course the problem with this kind of approach is that it tends to marginalize the developer from any chance of effecting change through the management system. True, the developer may join or even lead a groundswell of resistance, but for the most part, the management system of the organization will continue to make the crucial decisions, and do so either in ignorance of, or alienated from, the perspective of the developer. Part of growing up as a developer is learning the importance of authority in supporting change, and the importance of stakeholder and relationship management. From outside, the necessity of devoting time and effort towards this seems obvious, but it remains fascinating to see even developers who recognize the importance of authority struggling to come to terms with its consequences. That struggle is difficult for developers as the politics of effecting change necessitate compromise and bending positions that, as I have argued, may be based in deeply held beliefs. Most of us would happily sacrifice 5% of a project or proposal that we hold to be right, moral and good, in order to get 95% of it approved. But it is the days when we have to weigh up whether to support the revised proposal that has only 15% of 'good' left in it that send us home at the end of the day somewhat sullied by the political reality of change. Again, the ideals of developers are great, but unless managed, are liable to doom many a project.

My point thus far has been that developers do not always grasp the full implications for their cause of cultivating the support of authority. There is a perverse side to this however, in that when developers *do* gain political support (perhaps through an enlightened DVC, for example), it is tempting for them to imagine that authority can be enlisted in a simple and linear fashion to effect change. Again, speaking from outside of development, an interesting aspect of my own learning has been to observe how some projects with the full backing of VC and/or DVC can move effortlessly to implementation, whereas others stall and meet such resistance that, in the end, it is easier to just 'move on' to another issue. If developers need to learn to use authority channels and relationships in the organization, they also need to appreciate, counter to some opinion, that universities are still a long way from management by 'command'.

Size matters

I really did not appreciate the size and diversity of universities as organizations when I worked in an educational and staff development centre. That is not a criticism, just a statement of fact. I did have a greater appreciation of university level issues and policies than most departmentally based academics, who often struggled with the concept of School, Faculty or Division, but my university level knowledge was pretty well confined to the teaching and learning area. One of the advantages of moving out of the area is the opportunity to gain an appreciation of the size and scope of university operations more widely. This of course includes the research side of the university and the huge infrastructure implications of science, biomedical and engineering research, which in turn raise financial and campus planning issues, and issues concerning the commercialization of research and the management of university companies. Another major area is that of support services including such things as facilities, buildings, food, recreation, medical and social services, library, staff services, student administration and so on. Again, these are big budget items. Changing student administration software systems, for example, is a multi million-dollar issue. Developing service specifications, costing services and negotiating service levels and costs (including out-sourcing), are major items for university management. And the services students receive in terms of admission, enrolment, social infrastructure, care, career advice and so on are important in shaping their experience of the university. So too are the web based teaching and learning support services, the efficiency of student enquiry handling, the turn-around time and multi-modal response to course and subject enquiries. The student experience extends far beyond the classroom these days, even in terms of support for teaching and learning. Other areas include international operations, the development of international campuses, regulatory frame-works, and contract negotiation with transnational providers; local, regional and national engagement strategies of the university with govern-ments, significant lobby groups, alumni; governance and the interaction of the University Council, senior management, academic senate; the painful process of wage/enterprise bargaining, and so on.

What is the point here? The point is that educational development, from the perspective of senior managers, is a tiny and non-critical part of the operation of the enterprise. By non-critical, I mean that it does not have a risk factor attached to it; if it fails, there will be no immediate and severe consequences. The same cannot be said for the student admission software system, salaries, the failure of an international campus or a high profile commercial entity. But from within the development centre, the view of the university is very different: the university is all about the improvement of teaching and learning. What I am saying is that this latter view does not correspond with, and may be somewhat ignorant of, the view from outside. This outside view is likely to be that educational development is a tiny and single-issue item within a large and complex system that contains high-risk elements.

That all sounds terribly negative. In fact, in some universities, developers have had an enormous impact on many aspects of the organization; an impact quite disproportionate to the size of the 'development' operation and its 'single issue' (teaching and learning) focus. I think that a greater appreciation of the reality and importance of size, diversity and risk, would give developers a better grasp of how to 'sell' development ideas to senior management, and perhaps more understanding when their own priorities are not supported. In my experience, managers of very large areas within the university never act other than strategically. They link their projects and proposals to the strategic health and development of the university, countering risk and adding to the bottom line. Educational development projects are more often justified in terms of educational principles. As a senior manager, juggling priorities with limited or declining funds, which focus would you choose – principles or strategy?

On the same page: a summary

To summarize thus far, the observations I have made all concern the need for developers, and especially the leadership and management of development, to be 'on the same page' as others such as teaching staff, middle management (e.g. Heads of Department) and senior management. A more wordy and elegant explanation would quote Gadamer (1975) and the notion that we all have a horizon beyond which we find it difficult to 'see' or understand. But the 'fusion of horizons' is possible, as people authentically interact together and it is possible to test one's own limited horizon of understanding, and understand more from the perspective of the 'other'. I believe that developers can vastly enrich the university environment, not least because of their idealistic commitment to good teaching and learning, and the discourse which supports this. I also believe that to be effective, developers need wide organizational knowledge and experience, together with a degree of empathy for middle and senior managers and the difficult decisions they must make.

LOOKING FORWARD FROM DEVELOPMENT

Developers go on to do any number of things. A few become Vice-Chancellors, a few more Deputy, Pro or Assistant Vice-Chancellors. Some move from a central development role into a Faculty, sometimes as a developer, sometimes as Dean, or as a senior researcher. Others leave the university to take up a staff development role in business, government or a profession. Some go back to teaching, and so on. This next section considers what skills, attitudes and general approach developers take with them 'after development'. Of course not all developers display all of these skills, attitudes, approaches and understandings. What follows is again a caricature.

Emotional understanding

Although developers may go on to do any number of things, one thing that they never seem to do is retire. 'Retired' developers are often as busy as when they were 'working'. I think that says something about them. They tend to stay in contact with people and maintain and develop relationships over many years. So when they retire as full time developers their contacts do not suddenly disappear, and the requests for workshops, one-off projects, consultancies and so on keep coming. Being 'retired' appears to have its benefits as there is perhaps more choice concerning which offers to accept: is the work interesting, does it require travel (a positive for some and a negative for others), can it be linked with social and recreational activities (meeting up with old friends, visiting places) and so on? But is there anything in all of this that is especially revealing of developers?

I believe there is. To stereotype, good developers tend to be 'people people'. That means they like people and they enjoy seeing them do well. They get on with people and people tend to like them. People enjoy working with them and look forward to working with them again. Developers are known as understanding people. But why?

There is a little more to it than simply being a 'people' person. Developers tend to have some understanding of and tolerance for the human condition. Again, seeking illumination in hermeneutics, this means that not only do they have the ability to 'merge horizons' of understanding with others, but their understanding has a deeper side to it which is grounded in emotion. For example, I have seen many of the people I would call great developers, moved to tears. This happens when they relate to the plight of others or the beauty and magic of an experience. Sometimes it comes with laughter, and this is one of their strongest traits as a group. Developers are genuinely interested in 'the other' to the point that they quickly turn enquiries about themselves back on to the enquirer. The enquirer may be anyone from a student, junior lecturer or senior manager; great developers are interested in, mix with and talk to everyone and anyone. They engage with taxi drivers, waiters serving the conference dinner, people who happen to be in the bar. They have a desire and a talent for understanding humanity, and that is why they are in the 'people' business.

Dilthey noted how in the veins of the rational and reasoning 'knowing subject' of Enlightenment philosophers such as Locke, Hume and Kant, 'runs no real blood' (Dilthey 1958, V: 4), and how 'knowing' had become synonymous with 'thinking' and separated from feeling, willing, wanting, and the cultural and historical life experiences which shape our thoughts and actions. Because its subject comprises meanings, purposes, plans, goals and intentions as opposed to non-intentional events, the human sphere of study is different in kind to that of the physical sciences. So, where natural science may seek explanation (Erklären) of nature, human science should seek understanding (Verstehen) of human life, the kind of understanding which only one human being can show for the life experience of another. (Webb 1996, p. 42)

Developers, as a group, tend to be skilled in understanding the world of the 'other' – not just conceptually, but in terms of 'our emotional and intuitive understandings, forged in the perennial human riddles of life and death, joy and sorrow, love and hate, the value of an individual life, and its meaninglessness' (Webb, *op cit*). But what does this all mean when they leave development?

It means that developers have a special insight which, for example, many senior managers lack. Many managers rise through an organization by being ruthlessly efficient with their time and energy, by being great project managers and completers, by appearing to be immune against criticism and failure; in short, by being effective and efficient, task-oriented achievers. It is not uncommon to see the senior management of an organization dominated by this kind of person and some maintain such an approach until they retire.

However, it is also interesting to see senior managers grappling with the fact of retirement (which may still be a number of years away) – looking for more from life, and adjusting their priorities. People who have ruthlessly risen through the organization start to take an interest in protégés. They have more time to mentor and develop others within their ranks, rather than being absorbed by their own self-interest. The 'nurturing' side of people comes out, both in women and in men, as increasingly realized through the popular 'men's' literature (e.g. Sheehy 1998).

While this change comes as somewhat of a surprise for some, it is second nature to developers. What I am suggesting is that developers often fulfil this human, emotional, supportive and nurturing role throughout their careers. At various times it may be more appreciated than at others, but the need for human understanding has a habit of being recognized at all levels of an organization, over time. Essentially, the empathic emotional skills that the developer displayed working with junior lecturers in the early days of her or his career are little different from those used to support people at the very pinnacle of the organization.

The importance of emotional understanding was popularized by Carl Rogers (e.g. 1942, 1969, 1980, 1985). Rogers was astounded to find that his writings about psychotherapy found such a wide audience: 'all my writing . . . contains the realization that what is true in a relationship between therapist and client may well be true for a marriage, a family, a school, an administration, a relationship between cultures or countries' (Rogers 1980: viii). Rogers talked about 'really hearing' people, meaning 'that I hear the words, the thoughts, the feeling tones, the personal meaning, even the meaning that is below the conscious intent of the speaker' (Rogers 1980: 8). He spoke of the completeness of human understanding, the importance of empathy and authenticity, but more, that these are not party tricks or 'bolted on' to normal communication, they are the basic condition of human being. People who really listen, do so 'without judging me, diagnosing me, appraising me, evaluating me . . . without passing judgment . . . without trying to take responsibility for you, without trying to mould you' (Rogers 1980: 12). Authenticity refers to being genuine in and to one's self, and in being open towards others. Openness allows communication and others to be authentic towards you.

What does all this mean in practical terms for the developer *beyond* development? I would argue that the emotional understanding of a developer can find expression in a number of ways. For example, those with emotional insight tend intuitively to grasp the essence of problems. This is because most problems, such as difficult issues or halted negotiations, have an emotional basis. The 'ruthless project manager' type of leader will analyse the situation and suggest any number of excellent, rational solutions, each of which will be doomed to fail. The manager with 'emotional understanding' will see that a rational solution is irrelevant, in the first instance at least. Someone has been hurt, they feel that they have not been respected or listened to, they feel vulnerable, marginalized, left out, by-passed, demeaned, threatened or something else unpleasant. Until this emotional message is picked up and dealt with, the most rational of solutions is doomed to fail. Picking up on the 'real' issue, hearing and acknowledging it, may be all that is necessary for progress to be made, notwithstanding that this can take a long time. After this, however, negotiation of a rational solution may move very quickly. So, I am suggesting that, because of their 'people' person orientation and talent for emotional intuition and understanding, former developers can be effective problem solving leaders and managers.

Universities have faced hard times of late, with government funding declining or remaining static, while student numbers have dramatically increased. Rationalization has been a necessity, course costing has had to develop from vagary to efficiency, the hidden costs of research together with support service levels and costs have had to be identified, permanent staff have been replaced by short-term contract staff, performance management and promotion processes have been sharpened, Departments have been rationalized into Schools and Schools into Divisions. None of this has been particularly popular with staff, and neither has the often new layer of management that has effected this change. There is no surprise then that a 'hard-nosed' and non-emotional style of management has emerged. It seems to me, however, that management trends go in cycles, and it is interesting to note (albeit shallow) approaches to what I have been calling 'emotional understanding', increasingly finding voice. I am thinking here of things like 'emotional intelligence' and the 'psychology' of troubled organizations. For example, on the morning that I wrote this paragraph, I received a Corporate Leadership Council Briefing quoting Harvard Business School Professor Rosabeth Moss Kanter in a *Harvard Business Review* article identifying CEOs who have turned round troubled organizations. They have done this by 'promoting dialogue, engendering mutual respect among employees and managers, and restoring organisational confidence' (http://www.corporateleadershipcouncil.com). In summary, the 'emotional understanding' that is the hallmark of developers is of value in a general management sense within organizations, and may be particularly valuable as universities move through a period of severe rationalization, to a period where management values the development of relationships and the nurturing of community as necessary conditions for the organization to flourish.

Cognitive understanding

There are also some aspects of the experience of staff developers that can inform the ways in which they conceptualize and 'think' their way through the non-emotional aspects of problems and issues. For example, I made the point earlier that, although developers may not fully comprehend the size and complexity of the whole organization, they may well appreciate this more than many of their departmentally based colleagues. By working across departments, schools, disciplines, faculties and professional contexts, developers are exposed to greater complexity than those who see the world of the university entirely from within their own discipline and context.

One of the first things a developer learns is that almost every lecturer with whom they interact will start by saying something like 'of course, teaching . . . (insert an area such as mechanical engineering, maths, German, econometrics, chemical pharmacology, early Roman history) . . . is much harder than teaching anything else because . . . (insert statements such as) the students are not sufficiently prepared, the subject is just very difficult, it is impossible to make "interesting", the students won't work hard enough, I don't have the right equipment . . .'. And almost every solution that the developer advances will initially be met with 'that may work in (insert subject) but it will not work here'. (This is one of those times when advancing a perfect solution misses the point, because there is an emotional issue to confront before the person will take ownership of a rational solution.) The point is that developers have to learn to leave the comfort of their own discipline or professional area to modify and apply their knowledge to a wide range of areas and contexts. If they are to do this effectively, they must also listen carefully and pick up on the differences that are 'really' there in each situation. And in doing so they learn about the complexity of their craft as it is played out in different contexts and situations within the university. Of course, the ability to apply core concepts to many and varied situations, to acknowledge difference, modify and apply principles, and think one's way through to solutions that remain principled and conceptually valid, while fitting the 'presenting' situation, are core skills of leadership and management. I would suggest that there is much in the experience of developers to nurture this.

Working in different disciplines is but one aspect of the developer's experience with organizational complexity. Most developers 'teach' and 'research' to an extent, although often not in the quantity nor in exactly the same way as departmentally based academics. However, developers may also be far more involved in developing educational or teaching and learning policy. More than that, they may be involved in developing probation, promotion and performance management policy, as it is enacted in the area of teaching and learning. They may be involved with new technologies and their impact on teaching and learning. They may create, mould or otherwise inform leadership development initiatives. They may be involved with general staff development, with executive retreats of senior management and/or governance, with multi-campus or international operations, with institutional quality and accreditation issues, with course approval and review, course planning, instructional design, costing and financial modelling. There are opportunities in all of this for developers to find special or 'niche' interests, but the main point is that they may experience a far wider exposure to the organization than a typical departmentally based academic. Again, this offers significant opportunities for learning to think, modify and apply their knowledge and skills in many and varied situations. (The argument in the first part of the chapter was that developers need to appreciate and bring into play wider organizational experience far more than might currently be the case.)

There is one other aspect of 'thinking' that I would like to raise. It comes from the 'classic' period of hermeneutics and has important consequences for problem solving. It is an approach to thinking that I have watched good developers apply, and although it is not confined to developers, I would argue that it is perhaps seen disproportionately in their number. It is the notion of understanding gained through an appreciation of the hermeneutic circle.

Early hermeneutics was concerned with how one could 'understand' the meaning of texts, religious texts such as the Talmud, Midraschim and Bible, and secular texts such as laws, treaties, statutes, constitutions. What do the words actually mean, what were the writers trying to convey to us, and how do the words apply today? This was the realm of early hermeneutics, of translation and interpretation. In the late eighteenth and early nineteenth century, Schleiermacher conceived of two aspects to this: the psychological and the grammatical. The psychological was concerned with what I called 'emotional understanding' above, and involves appreciating the experience and horizon of understanding of 'the other', especially in terms of empathy. For grammatical understanding, he developed 44 canons, with perhaps the most important of these being that the meaning of each word from a particular piece of text must be determined with reference to the words that surround it. This leads directly to the paradox of the hermeneutic circle.

> A good example of an hermeneutic circle is found in the way we attempt to understand a sentence. We can only understand the meaning of a sentence by understanding the meaning of each individual word. This could result in the reductive (scientific) position that if we understand each small constituent part, we will understand the whole. Yet at the same time, individual words have many interpretations and functions. If we look up each word in a dictionary we are offered a number of alternative explanations and equivalents. It is argued that the meaning of a particular word in a particular context is given by its place in the sentence, and by reference to the meaning of the sentence as a whole. The paradox of the hermeneutical circle is that we cannot understand the meaning of the whole without understanding the meaning of each of the parts, and yet we will never know the meaning of a particular part without first having a grasp of the meaning of the whole.
>
> (Webb 1996: 38–9)

Staff developers experience hermeneutic circles all the time. A common example from my own experience came in a course comprising a large element of self-direction including a significant research project. Students needed to decide on something to research, and also how to research it. Most, with some help, quickly settled on a few possible areas for investigation, and some ways of going about the study. But others would ask 'how can I start researching something when I don't know what to research?' and 'how can I know how to research if I don't know all the ways that there are of doing research?' More generally, whenever a teacher brings a new problem for a class to solve, the question can be 'how can we make sense of and solve this problem when you have not shown us how to do it?' But all important problems and tasks resist formulaic solution. Important learning usually requires a leap of faith. Anything new challenges us to interpret the new 'part' (the new problem) in terms of our existing 'whole' knowledge. To do so we constantly move between the part and the whole, seeking meaning from our present very limited understanding of the part, in terms of our present 'whole' understanding. When we do find a way through, our 'whole' understanding has changed. Those students who said they could not start because they did not have the understanding to start were right, in a way. When they have solved or made progress on the new problem, they have a new and better 'whole' understanding which they did not have at the beginning. But they only achieved this new understanding by action: by wrestling with the new 'part' – the new problem. They achieved greater understanding by attempting to appreciate the part and the whole, and this resulted in a greater understanding of both. Action, leaping into the hermeneutic circle (at any point), is the only way to resolve the paradox.

Developers are not only grounded in the nature and paradoxes of education, but they also tend to have a 'meta' comprehension of theories and concepts concerning teaching and learning. Although some developers are captured by the dogma of a particular position, many appreciate the insights that can be gained from various perspectives (for example behaviouralism, phenomenography, reflective practice, humanistic approaches, action research or Habermasian knowledge-constitutive interests).

This 'meta' conceptual insight can illuminate a variety of management situations. An example from my own experience may be of interest. I vividly recall a meeting of a small group of very senior managers to plan a complex, long term and multi million-dollar project. One of the managers had an engineering background, and unfurled a rational, linear, project-management approach to the project. In terms of epistemology it was positivistic and in terms of methodology, scientific and quantitative. The approach was laid out on an electronic whiteboard as a series of boxes with an arrow carrying progress inexorably forward from one box to the next, almost in parody of the enlightenment project itself.

However, another senior manager, with a background in literature and the humanities, raised objection after objection. This person took possession of the whiteboard and noted that feedback loops were needed at each point, to the extent that once a small part of the project had been undertaken, there was need to reassess the whole concept, based on the intelligence gained from iterative communication and stakeholder feedback strategies. The first manager wanted completion of defined stages, clarity, preordained accountability, control and linear development. The second thought (and drew the project) in terms of circles, contingency, communication, feedback and uncertainty. I remember thinking that the confrontation between positivism and hermeneutics was being played out before my eyes, and how interesting it was that neither could see why each was so exercised by the approach of the other. In fact neither positivism nor hermeneutics won the day. The project was carried by the 'circular' thinker, not because of the strength of hermeneutics over positivism, but because this person was even more senior than the 'linear' ex-engineer. The time-honoured notion that 'right (justice) is the power of the stronger' (Thrasymachus' argument in Plato's *Republic*) prevailed, and critical theory took the day!

To summarize, developers have skills to bring to situations outside of development by nature of their experience of different contexts, their ability to appreciate (and if necessary transcend) 'one-eyed' ways of thinking, their experience of working the hermeneutical circle from whole to part, back and forth, and their appreciation of the 'leap of faith' necessary for progress to be made in all learning situations.

POSTSCRIPT: LIVING AND LEADING BY EXAMPLE

There is no more powerful way of leading than by modelling values and behaviour. The best developers I have known live their lives, interact with others and complete their projects modelling values and an integrity that is central to their being. I illustrate this with the story of the genesis of this chapter.

The idea for this chapter came from David Baume. David first asked me to write on theories of knowledge relating to staff and educational development, based on a book I had produced some years previously (Webb 1996). I found it difficult to motivate myself to do this, pointing out that it was hard to go back to something that I was not really dealing with any more. When I explained this to David and apologized for my failure to produce, I said something to the effect that he had every right to be angry. Rather than admonishing me (as I expected), David 'heard' the (Rogerian) message I was sending, attempted to 'merge horizons' and see the world from my perspective, and responded by challenging me to do something that would interest me – he suggested something about moving on from development. Faced with his own deadlines to meet, he nonetheless grasped that I was not motivated to do something repetitive and removed from my daily experience, and that if I did produce, it would be lifeless. He therefore reconfigured the task to get something (which is hopefully more worthwhile) out of me.

REFERENCES

Argyris, C and Schön, D.A. (1974) *Theory in Practice: Increasing Professional Effectiveness,* Jossey-Bass, San Francisco
Dilthey, W. (1958) *Gesammelte Schriften,* G. Teubner, Leipzig and Berlin
Gadamer, H.-G. (1975) *Truth and Method,* Sheed and Ward, London
Rogers, C. R. (1942) *Counseling and Psychotherapy,* Houghton Mifflin, Boston
Rogers, C. R. (1969) *Freedom to Learn,* Charles E. Merrill, Columbus, OH
Rogers, C. R. (1980) *A Way of Being,* Houghton Mifflin, Boston
Rogers, C. R. (1985) Towards a more human science of the person, *Journal of Humanistic Psychology,* **25**(4): 7–24
Sheehy, G (1998) *Passages for Men: Discovering the new map of men's lives,* Simon and Schuster, Australia
Webb, G. (1996) *Understanding Staff Development,* SRHE and Open University Press, Buckingham
Webb, G. (1997) Deconstructing deep and surface: Towards a critique of phenomenography. *Higher Education,* **33**(2): 195–212

11

How shall we enhance staff and educational development?

David Baume and Peter Kahn

This concluding chapter is constructed in two main sections.

We explore the evolution and nature of staff and educational development, all the time seeking implications for the enhancement of staff and educational development.

And then we draw some specific conclusions to answer the chapter's title question.

THE NATURE OF STAFF AND EDUCATIONAL DEVELOPMENT

Which 'we' will be enhancing staff and educational development? That will probably continue to be staff and educational developers ourselves. As a profession we mostly do a fair job of developing ourselves, certainly as established developers, through conferences and networks and qualifications and formal continuing professional development, and increasingly through writing and reading publications. We are as yet less good at supporting the induction and development of those entering the profession. Training events for developers are starting to be run, such as the SEDA Summer School for new developers, and qualifications such as SEDA's Fellowship and Associate Fellowship are increasingly being used as frameworks for development as well as for accreditation. But there is much more to be done. We give further consideration to the new developers later in this chapter.

Working still further back, and to help us see how we may enhance staff and educational development – where did staff and educational development in higher education come from? Until now, staff and educational development has mostly invented itself. This invention has been undertaken mostly in response to a perceived need rather than to an expressed demand. No one in the institution in which one of us (DB) first became a developer cried out 'Please I need some development!' – certainly not within DB's hearing. (New lecturers and teaching assistants may have felt and even expressed the need, but who listened to them?)

How, then, did development emerge? We had hoped to include a chapter on this. Characteristically, the author we invited was too busy developing to look back! Some of this history is provided in Chapter 1 of our *Guide to Staff and Educational Development* (Kahn and Baume 2003). Somehow, the full story will be told.

But we can reconstruct some of the story, some of the history of development. Part of the story began when enthusiastic teachers, proto-developers, noted that not every academic colleague shared their own enthusiasm for teaching and learning. These proto-developers found a small literature of ideas and theories and models about student learning; and also about areas such as management development and counselling; that contained ideas with clear implications for the practices of course design, teaching and assessment. They also found one or two like-minded souls, usually in other institutions. They invented; and the community of developers now continues to invent; what we do and how we do it. Since the mid-1990s, new developers have also found a small literature about the practice and theory of development itself (Brew 1995; Webb 1996). Beneath the surface of this current book and the companion *A Guide to Staff and Educational Development*, beyond the accounts that they contain of practice and explanation, you can see this invention happening. As the years pass, this invention is happening with a greater and more sophisticated attention to the many contexts in which we work, and with greater attention to theories and models of learning and development drawn from education and from a growing range of adjacent disciplines.

This continued self-invention and re-invention is of course a quality of most disciplines and professions. Two things make this process particularly exciting and important in staff and educational development.

First, the profession and discipline of staff and educational development is still young. And second, development is an odd kind of profession.

The profession is still young. It has not yet accumulated unto itself many of the barnacles and other accretions that sometimes slow down more established professions and disciplines. Nor of course has it accumulated the wisdom and expertise that makes older professions so confident, and often such powerful and effective voices – the authors are not suggesting that age and experience are all bad. But because development is young, the growing edge of practice and understanding is still fairly close to the centre. This growing edge is thus also readily accessible to those at the start of their careers in development. This, and the hopefully welcoming and open style of development and developers, mean that everyone in development can, within a year or so of starting, be contributing to the invention and reinvention and extension of development as well as simply (!) doing good development. This has certainly been the experience of one of us (PK), still early in his career as a developer, planning and conducting summer schools for new developers, running innovative development projects, conscious of the needs of new developers; and, perhaps, having a little more time and energy to devote to such activities, not yet having accumulated the range of responsibilities that fill the time and may dampen the creative energies of more experienced developers.

In a little more detail, who is this innovating new developer? They may bring into development substantial experience as a discipline specialist and/or teacher. They may be a younger entrant to development, bringing more recent experience of being taught and the good questions and new perspectives that flow from this student experience. They may be a learning technologist, a project manager or other specialist, bringing their particular expertise into the service and support and development of new approaches to learning.

Second, development is an odd kind of profession, in that is not a primary profession. It is not even a secondary profession. It is, the authors suggest, a tertiary profession. Bear with us for a moment.

Civil engineering, for example, is a primary profession. Civil engineers design and build structures and research and advance civil engineering theory and practice. Teachers of civil engineering, as well as retaining and perhaps continuing to practise their primary profession, do something else with their primary profession. They also teach it. They thus have a secondary profession. They are dual professionals. Developers work with and support those who teach their own primary discipline in higher education, those who have both a primary and a secondary profession. Hence development as a tertiary profession. (Primary, secondary and tertiary here do not represent a hierarchy of professions. We are not describing teaching and development as either superior or inferior to the academic's original discipline. We are trying to elucidate the relationships between these various professions in order to understand better the role of the developer.)

How does the nature of this youthful tertiary profession – development – relate to its continued self-invention and re-invention? It makes development work complicated, and also potentially unstable.

Complicated, because developers are working with teachers, who as suggested already have two professions. And these dual professionals themselves have to maintain each of their two professions; primary (for example civil engineer) and secondary (teacher of civil engineering).

Some teachers, of any subject at all, reject the idea of teaching as their second profession, and regard teaching as a relatively unproblematic activity that they do with, or about, their primary; indeed their only; profession or discipline. Others may already be wrestling with the issue of their dual professional identity. Their views of their professional identity or identities will in turn have implications for their views of their development needs and priorities. So any group of teachers with whom a developer works is likely to be rather more challenging than a group of people each of whom cheerfully acknowledges a particular and similar professional identity and set of development needs. Any policy for development is like to face similar contradictions and difficulties.

The developer's situation is potentially unstable. If an image helps; the teacher is riding a bicycle, the discipline. Different disciplines are themselves to various extents stable. Riding the bicycle here stands – indeed, sometimes wobbles – for the teaching of the discipline. The teacher as she or he rides is on a moving platform, representing the ever-changing University itself, in the high and gusty winds of policy and funding emanating from government and funding councils. The staff developer is the helper alongside the cyclist, helping the new teacher to ride, helping the more experienced teacher to attain additional speed or style or versatility. The educational developer is also trying to improve the platform (the University) and to plot the best course through the continuing turbulence. The developer has a partial but growing grasp of the physics and psychology of the situation, of what actions and reactions are appropriate and helpful under what conditions, and is trying to capture and codify this understating. As we said; occasional instability is to be expected.

SOME SPECIFIC WAYS IN WHICH WE CAN ENHANCE STAFF AND EDUCATIONAL DEVELOPMENT

So, against this complex and dynamic background – what can we say about how we may enhance staff and educational development? The following suggestions and proposals are drawn in part from the discussion above, in part from the preceding chapters, in part from other sources and experiences. We were tempted to impose or find a narrative in what follows, but for the most part have chosen rather to let you make your own connections, or not, as you wish. More important than making connections among these various approaches to enhancing development, we suggest, is making connections to your own situation, to your own practice, to the enhancement of your development service and the work of yourself and your colleagues.

1 We can see enhancement happening, before our eyes, in the often very sophisticated development practices described in the chapters here and in the work by the authors to understand and invent and advance development practice. We can enhance development by learning from the particulars described, adopting and adapting what we read to our own settings. We can also learn from the approaches that underpin these particulars, from the development methods as well as the development outcomes. Authors value the coherent narratives that they produce, but readers may treat chapters as quarries or stores as well as narratives.

2 A recurrent theme of many of the chapters is the vital importance of attention to the many and different contexts and environments in which development is undertaken. Within the University, these contexts include the disciplines taught and their changing natures, concerns and priorities; department and faculty policies, needs and demands (these latter two not always the same); the University itself, its formal strategies on policies on learning and teaching, human resources, C&IT, support for students with disabilities and many other policies and strategies. And the weight and priority given to these various policies at various levels. And the interactions among them, at the level of policy and of implementation. And beyond policy and strategy, the culture and style of the University. And beyond that, and perhaps above all, the people.

Outside the University, and greatly affecting it, these contexts and environments include national policy and strategy and their expression through targets and priorities and the associated funding, both core and programme or project funding. European and global issues and movements are growing in importance and effect, though more slowly than we might sometimes wish.

Individual developers (and our clients) will feel varying degrees of enthusiasm for these various institutional, governmental and other targets and priorities. But we must not adopt the ostrich position on those targets and priorities that we dislike. We will engage with the debates which inform policy. But, whatever the outcome of our attempts to inform policy, we then need to live with the resultant policy and find or (more likely) make ways to support the implementation of that policy to good ends. There is (almost) always a way.

3 Development must be a collaborative business. We see in the chapters developers seeking and forming tactical alliances, within the University and beyond it, in the region and nationally. These alliances are also important within the unit. Developers must share their evolving expertise. A development that one developer supports in one particular discipline may be translatable to development work

with a range of other departments; as long as knowledge (and also ignorance, questions, the 'How on earth can I . . .?') are shared. Collaboration requires a longer-term perspective, one which values and works to sustain long-term, strategic, relationships between all of those involved (see Jaques *et al.* 2003).

4   Unfortunately for the development of these important longer-term relationships, development work is often funded on a short-term basis. We need to make best use of these funding opportunities. At the same time we also need to find further ways to manage the tensions that arise from this short-term funding; ensuring good personnel practices, and maintaining continuity of personnel wherever appropriate, perhaps through seeking to maintain at least some continuity of funding.

5   Securing funding can allow the new developer to make their mark on the field. The youth of the field is a real advantage here, one that we sometimes find it hard to appreciate. For example, a new developer may obtain funding for a new idea, for example a collaborative staff development model to introduce enquiry-based learning, whilst a distinguished colleague with an international reputation in a more established discipline may find it difficult to get their ideas funded from the relevant research council. The gatekeepers to development funding are often much more responsive to new ideas.

6   Development work must value and make best use of the talents of each member of the development team. This further suggests that a development unit should over time form itself with a variety of developers with different enthusiasms, disciplines, backgrounds, age, experience, approaches, styles. An enthusiasm for development and a valuing of each other's expertise and approach are about the only common requirements.

7   Though not explicitly described in the preceding chapters, we can see one particularly significant change taking place in UK development. There is a shift in some Universities from a large central development unit, perhaps working directly with all staff in the University, to a smaller central unit which, along with other policy and support functions, works with and through department- or faculty-based staff, sometimes called learning and teaching coordinators. This move can be seen as an attempt to bring the disciplinary dimension more strongly into development work. It can also ensure that development work addresses local as well as institutional needs. It may also be part of a wider move to increase local accountability and responsiveness on the part of hitherto central functions. As so often in development, the motives of those who propose and implement such changes are much less important than the ways developers first try to shape, and

then do respond to, the changes. The development unit needs to ensure that the learning and teaching coordinators have space and opportunity to talk about the realities of doing development work in schools, department and faculties, and that they receive support to develop as particular kinds of developers. The central development unit also needs to learn from the coordinators about current issues and concerns at local level, and to consider their implications for University as well as local policy, practice and resourcing. These learning and teaching coordinators, well supported, bridging between development unit and academic department, are potentially very powerful and effective agents of change at local and, mediated through the central unit, also at institutional level.

There is the possibility of a larger realignment of development here, as learning and teaching coordinators, and the innovating teachers considered immediately below, can in the UK derive an increasing amount of discipline-specific teaching and development support from the national Subject Centres set up for this purpose. The central University development unit should encourage and facilitate these connections – the unit will always have a role in linking strategy, policy and development within and across the institution even if it loses one particular role, as a conduit to discipline-specific ideas and information outside the University.

8 There can be a blurred boundary between teachers who innovate in their own practice and those who help others to innovate. It can be a boundary, or it can be a zone of transition, as the innovating teacher reaches the limits of how far they can innovate without involving and enthusing their teaching colleagues. We must enhance development by ensuring that those who work in this transitional zone feel multiply supported, rather than pulled apart; by the subject department (where we can help departments to find ways to value and guide their work), by the local learning and teaching coordinator (who can work with them on development processes as well as on the particular innovation) and by the development unit (with information, resources, consultancy and networking).

9 We must offer evidence to support our views and recommendations, and we must help such evidence-based working to become a part of institutional culture and practice. Such evidence comes at at least two levels. Evidence about what works and does not work in programme design and teaching and learning and student support and assessment. And evidence about what works in development itself.

Before getting into how we offer evidence – why should we bother? How shall we sell the idea of evidence-based practice and innovation, in teaching and in development, to our colleagues and institution? There is a spectrum of reasons.

At the pragmatic end of this spectrum we find the increased pressure on institutions to do, at best, more with not as much more. We also find a general move towards greater accountability, led in the UK by the Government's Treasury, to show individual expenditures having their intended effects and more generally to show that the billions spent on higher education teaching represent best value for money.

At the other end of the spectrum of reasons we have academic and professional reasons. Surely a higher education system substantially committed to achieving a more sophisticated understanding of every discipline and profession through research will be unstoppably keen to apply its many tools for enhancing understanding to its own practices? Well, on the evidence to date, no. But the proposal that we should seek to understand our own practice and then apply this understanding to enhancing our practice is hard to argue with, though it attracts large-scale passive opposition.

Thus there are both pragmatic and principled reasons to seek evidence for the effectiveness of our work, though many difficulties and obstacles on the way.

The answers to 'How do we do this?' are contained in outline in the previous paragraphs, and in much more detail throughout this book. In summary: we use the scholarly approaches from our various disciplines, and particularly from the disciplines of higher education teaching, learning, assessment and development, to research and extend our own practice.

As we do this research, and as we help and support our teaching colleagues to do this, we will find that our various interventions have impacts which vary from negligible to transformational. The research will at times be uncomfortable, at others celebratory. But we need to know and understand the effects of at least the major elements of our work. We need to research and understand what we do, to identify why what we do has the effects that it has, to inform our individual practice and that of our development unit and University, and where appropriate more widely through scholarly publication. We are, after all, among other things, scholars.

10 We must continue to practise what we teach. If we encourage teachers to adopt appropriately interactive learning and teaching methods, then we must use such methods in our development work, and use them well. Our website must be pedagogically sound: Bobby-approved (2003) (a standard for assuring website readability for those

with sight difficulties), and not intimidatingly flash (or indeed Flash), but rather a model of attainable good practice. Our written papers must be clear; cognizant of and informing current policies, strategies and debates; scholarly, and appropriately (but not extravagantly) referenced. We will be judged for what we do and how we do it as much as for what we say. Our practice must be exemplary. And when we slip, which we will, we must acknowledge it.

11 We must continue to develop and professionalize ourselves. There were many motivators for SEDA's initial work on the accreditation of higher education teachers. One of them was a concern that higher education teaching was still in many senses an amateur business. Despite the often great subject expertise of teachers, teaching and related activities were largely uninformed by scholarship about learning and teaching. With the teacher accreditation scheme in operation and increasingly widely adopted, the development community looked into itself; realized the potential hypocrisy inherent in an unaccredited group of developers going around accrediting others; and instituted a professional qualification for developers, the SEDA Fellowship and later also Associate Fellowship.

Of course it doesn't end there. Two purposes of accreditation are development towards, and then assurance of attainment of, a standard of capability. But capability, competence, professionalism are not static qualities. Competence is time- and context-specific. It fades if not renewed, as the years pass and the world changes around us (changes in some part because of our work). SEDA Fellowships contains a requirement for an (in the authors' experience) powerful and valuable process of annual continuing professional development. Developers must continue to renew and develop ourselves.

But; accepting this chapter's focus on developers taking responsibility for our own professional definition and development; we should not allow our institutions to shuffle off their responsibilities to support our development. More experienced developers need to ensure that they and their new developers are effectively supported as appropriate at each stage of their career.

CONCLUSION – THE END OF DEVELOPMENT?

One view of development is that we developers should be seeking to do ourselves out of a job. That is, we should so develop and enthuse and empower those with whom we work, our various clients, that they no longer need us.

We should certainly be helping our colleagues and clients to become enthusiastic and scholarly researchers and improvers, of their own practice and of institutional policy and practice. We should certainly be exploring new models of development, new systems and structures and methods. We should certainly be helping everyone to become a developer. (Should we then consider development as a quaternary profession? Only if it helps.)

But, even as everyone becomes in some sense a developer, those of us who see ourselves substantially or mainly or even solely as developers continue to have roles. Three key roles are in developing policy and strategy; in developing new teachers, innovators, developers, educational processes and systems; and in developing the institution's capacity to develop itself.

REFERENCES

Bobby (2003) http://bobby.watchfire.com/bobby/html/en/index.jsp

Brew, A. (1995) *Directions in Staff Development*, SRHE and Open University Press, Buckingham

Jaques, D., Kahn, P. *et al.* (2003) *The Role of Authentic Relationships in Academic Development*, Cambridge Conference 2003 Issues of Engagement, Madingley Hall, Cambridge

Kahn, P. and Baume, D. (Eds) (2003) *A Guide to Staff and Educational Development*. The Staff and Educational Development Series, Kogan Page, London

Webb, G. (1996) *Understanding Staff Development*, SRHE/Open University Press, Buckingham

Index

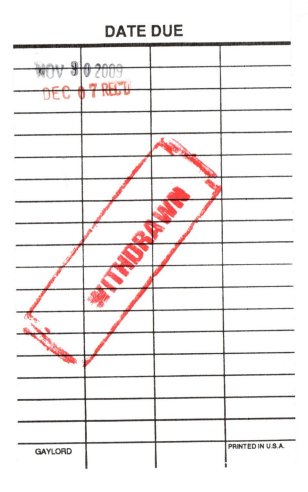